Aberdeenshire Libraries
www.aberdeenshire.gov.uk/libraries
Renewals Hotline 01224 661511
Downloads available from
www.aberdeenshirelibraries.lib.overdrive.com

23.10.13

1 1 NOV 2013
1 5 AUG 2014

- 4 APR 2015
0 5 JUN 2015

1 3 FEB 2016
HEADQUARTERS
3 1 OCT 2016

2 1 APR 2022

OUT OF THE BLUE.

27 JUL 2022

Out Of The Blue

The sometimes scary and often funny world of flying in the
Royal Air Force - as told by some of those who were there

Compiled and edited by
Ian Cowie, Dim Jones & Chris Long

Foreword by
Air Marshal Cliff Spink CB CBE FCMI FRAeS RAF R'td

ABERDEENSHIRE LIBRARIES

1937515

First published in 2011 by Halldale Media Group.
Halldale Media Ltd.
Pembroke House, 8 St. Christopher's Place, Farnborough, Hampshire, GU14 0NH, UK.
Halldale Media, Inc.
115 Timberlachen Circle, Ste 2009, Lake Mary, FL32746, USA.
www.halldale.com

Copyright © Halldale Media Group, 2011
Foreword © Cliff Spink, 2011

The moral right of the authors has been asserted.

This book is sold subject to the condition that it shall not, by way of trade or otherwise,
be lent, resold, hired out, or otherwise circulated without the publisher's prior consent in
any form of binding or cover other than that in which it is published and without a similar
condition including this condition being imposed on the subsequent publisher.

ISBN 978-0-9570928-0-8

Designed by David Malley, Halldale Media Group.

Printed and bound by The MANSON Group Ltd.,
St. Albans, Hertfordshire.
www.manson-grp.co.uk

Distributed by Flostream Ltd.,
Slough, Berkshire.
www.flostream.co.uk

**358.
4**

The Editors would like to thank all of the contributors,
Andy Smith of Halldale Media Group,
Rob Sargent, Elizabeth Wilson and John Malley.

Contributors
Kevin Atkinson, Chris Bain, Norman Bonnor, David Bywater, Dave Cockburn, Ian Cowie, Tom Eeles, John Finlayson, John Fraser, Stephen Gilbert, Joey Gough, John Hall, David Herriot, Taffy Holden, Dave Hunt, Paul Ingoe, Bob Iveson, Jake Jarron, Martin Johnson, Dim Jones, Patrick King, Terry Kingsley, Peter Kingwill, David Kitching, Chris Long, Peter Long, Ken MacKenzie, Bob Marston, Alan Martin, Grant Mcleod, Andrew Neal, Alick Nicholson, David Noon, George Perrin, Vic Pheasant, James Phillips, Al Pollock, Rod Sargeant, Rob Sargent, Sir John Severne, Pete Spofforth, Art Stacey, Dr Alan Stevenson, Nigel Sudborough, Pete Taylor, David Thomas, Graham Thomas, Tim Thorn, John Trueman, Nigel Walpole, John Wilson, Chris Wren, Ed Wyer.

The publisher would like to thank the Photographic Archive Department at BAE Systems Heritage Centre, Warton. Unless otherwise stated, all images are courtesy of BAE Systems.

The Editors would also like to acknowledge the crucial support of their sponsors:

BAE Systems
Warwick House, Farnborough Aerospace Centre, Farnborough, Hampshire, GU14 6YU, UK.
www.baesystems.com

CAE
8585 Cote de Liesse, Montreal, Quebec, Canada H4T 1G6.
www.cae.com

Foreword

Air Marshal Cliff Spink CB CBE FCMI FRAeS RAF Rtd

Fact is always stranger – and more amusing - than fiction and this can be never truer than in this collection of stories from those who have had the privilege to fly in the Royal Air Force. The Aircrew who have contributed their stories to this book have thousands of professional flying hours to their credit, very often gained in the most demanding circumstances. However, routine aviation does not make for a good story, it is always the incident or unusual happening that makes the tale that will be told and retold in the bar. The air has always been an unforgiving environment that has provided many a close call, which has either called for sheepish reflection... or placed you victim to the razor wit of squadron chums. In sharing these stories more than a few souls have been laid bare, and the result is a unique insight into the character – and courage – of those who chose to fly in the Royal Air Force.

A few of my friends from those heady days at The Royal Air Force College, Cranwell have orchestrated the production of this book on behalf of the most worthy of charities. I congratulate them and commend this book to you.

Cliff Spink
Keyston, November 2011

Contents

Featured Aircraft

[1] Andover   [2] Argosy   [3] Balliol   [4] Beaufighter   [5] Britannia   [6] Buccaneer
[7] Canberra   [8] Chipmunk   [9] Dominie   [10] Harrier   [11] Hercules   [12] HS125
[13] Hunter   [14] Hurricane   [15] Jaguar   [16] Lightning   [17] Magister   [18] Meteor
[19] Navajo   [20] Nimrod   [21] Phantom   [22] Provost   [23] Sedbergh   [24] Shackleton
[25] Shooting Star   [26] Starfighter   [27] Swift   [28] Tiger Moth   [29] Tornado
[30] Varsity   [31] Vega Gull   [32] Venom   [33] Victor   [34] Voodoo   [35] Vulcan

---

Featured Aircraft

[1] Andover   [2] Argosy   [3] Balliol   [4] Beaufighter   [5] Britannia   [6] Buccaneer
[7] Canberra   [8] Chipmunk   [9] Dominie   [10] Harrier   [11] Hercules   [12] HS125
[13] Hunter   [14] Hurricane   [15] Jaguar   [16] Lightning   [17] Magister   [18] Meteor
[19] Navajo   [20] Nimrod   [21] Phantom   [22] Provost   [23] Sedbergh   [24] Shackleton
[25] Shooting Star   [26] Starfighter   [27] Swift   [28] Tiger Moth   [29] Tornado
[30] Varsity   [31] Vega Gull   [32] Venom   [33] Victor   [34] Voodoo   [35] Vulcan

Nice View From Up Here

It was the beginning of December 1976. "Just one month to go before the squadron reforms with F4s at Wildenrath, so we will all have to fly at least one more night trip to keep current for Battle Flight" said the Boss. This was it - the reign of 19(F)Sqn's Lightning F2As at the sharp end of NATO's air defence forces was coming to an end. Battle Flight, as QRA[1] at RAF Gutersloh was known, required 2 aircraft with their pilots to be airborne within 5 minutes of an alert – we were based just 70 miles from the East German border, and felt very vulnerable. No longer would we sleep fully clothed and booted (apart from Trevor Beadle who used to put his flying boots at the bottom of the cockpit ladder!) to be airborne as soon as possible at any time of day or night.

Night currency: no problems, we all thought; it's dark by 1700, so a couple of pairs each night for the next 2 weeks and that should do it. A few nights later, my name appeared on the programme as No 2 to John Brady for a 1930 take-off. As 1800 approached, I changed into flying kit and then found John in the Ops Room. "Right," said John, "we brief in half an hour".

The brief was very straightforward. Two aircraft were soon to land; the excellent 19(F)Sqn ground-crew, under Chief Tech Dave Branchett, would refuel and service them as quickly as possible, probably within 20 minutes. The first aircraft to be ready would launch immediately, fly to the top of the designated supersonic area, some 200 miles north near Hamburg, and then head south as high and as fast as it could go - Mach1.7 (some 1400 mph) and 56,000 feet. The second would maintain a ground alert state, and then be scrambled by our fighter control site (callsign Backwash) to meet the threat.

For good or ill, John's aircraft was the first to be ready. True to his word, 30 minutes later he was near Hamburg, turning south, accelerating from Mach 0.9 and climbing from 36,000ft. Meanwhile, Backwash came on the alert frequency and gave me the order to scramble "HH13 scramble, vector 360 degrees, climb Angels 350, call Backwash on tactical". Off I went, with a good idea of my task. I was to simulate shooting down an aircraft flying as high and as fast as it would go, in an aircraft which would not go higher or faster - or at least was not

---

[1] QRA – Quick Reaction Alert

supposed to! I also had to do a stern attack, as the F2A did not have a head-on engagement capability.

Once on tactical frequency, Backwash confirmed that John was indeed very high and pretty fast. The Lightning radar was basic, but Backwash was invariably accurate with target information, and my radar should pick up John by 25 miles. And sure enough there he was. Backwash had given me ideal displacement to allow for my 180 degree turn, and I had already accelerated to Mach1.3, the optimum supersonic turn speed and the speed on which the attack geometry was based. But the geometry was based on either a high or a fast target, not both.

I did some quick mental calculations (that looks about right), and started the turn, but it was pretty obvious that, unless I squeezed every last knot out of my jet, then John was going to get away. I rolled out within a mile of John, but lower and slower. Both engines were in full reheat and had been for a few minutes, fuel was disappearing rapidly – it always did in a Lightning – but, after dropping out of missile range, I gradually started to edge closer and to climb. I checked my speed; it was near to maximum and still increasing. I was focussed purely on simulating missile launch, and was not aware of my geographical position.

Fortunately, John and Backwash were. The call to slow down, as we approached the southern boundary of the supersonic area, coincided with John cancelling his reheat and decelerating. Needless to say, his deceleration meant that I almost immediately got the shot. But now I was in a quandary; I was at 56,000 feet at close to Mach 1.7, and I too had to slow down. Like John, I cancelled reheat but, in the heat of triumphalism, decided to convert speed to height, although I was already at the Lightning's maximum approved height. I pulled the nose up to about 15 degrees of pitch, and up she went, higher and higher. At about 65,000 feet, I checked the speed; I was still supersonic, but thought that, if I rolled inverted and pulled gently to the horizon, by the time I was descending, I would be just subsonic, but still with plenty of control effectiveness to flutter earthwards and land with a reasonable amount of fuel.

At over 70,000 feet, the view of northern Germany was magnificent. It was a crisp and clear winter's night. Off to the left (I was upside down), I could see the lights of the Ruhr stretching away towards the Rhine valley and the Ardennes beyond. To the front and the right there were far fewer lights; the

Sauerland Plateau and Weser valley were identifiable, but further east was 'the East' and south was towards Frankfurt. I then noticed a few more lights, but these were in the cockpit on the auxiliary warning system; a split second later, and whilst the caution lights stayed on, all my main cockpit lighting went out.

"This might be serious" I thought, and it was. It soon became apparent that both engines had flamed out, but were wind-milling at high rpm. Now that was a good thing because they would provide me with pressurisation, which I needed to stay reasonably conscious, and hydraulic power from the engine-driven hydraulic pumps to give me some control over the aircraft's flight path. The rest was a bad thing, and there were several seconds of reflection (panic, to the layman) before I turned off the fuel.

Without power, the aircraft was in a comfortable, if speedy descent; I had lots of height to lose, and that conferred plenty of thinking time. At some stage in the descent, I pressed the engine relight buttons, which gave continuous ignition (jets are normally self-sustaining), and turned the fuel back on. Wonder of wonders, both engines relit, even though I was well outside the normal relighting zone (I seem to remember seeing Mach1.3 and 43,000 feet). Not only that, but they and the aircraft showed no ill-effects from their recent excursion to the lower stratosphere.

I checked my position (still mortal), and started talking again to a slightly perturbed Backwash who, a minute before, had been told, in a higher pitch than my usual manly baritone, to "Standby: minor problem: call you back". Now, still high-pitched, it was, "Problem solved, ready for recovery".

Ten minutes later I landed, and 10 minutes after that was in the Ops Room, resolved to keep mum about my abortive attempt to join the space race. Both John and Al Martin, who was duty ops officer, asked after my trip, and John and I did debrief the operational aspects of the sortie. John wondered why I landed so much after him, and Al was intrigued that I had snagged the main altimeter for reading 25,000 feet too high. Apparently, he said, that only happened if your engines flamed out above 50,000 feet! I offered no explanation to either but did buy them a couple of Warsteiners later that night.

Callout Binned

This goes back to the days of Victor Mk 1 tankers, based at RAF Marham during the summer of 1970, when I was on 55 Squadron.

The station was being subjected to a no-notice exercise, and the three tanker squadrons had been on an hour's standby since the early hours. We were all dressed in uncomfortable immersion suits[1], ready to get airborne and waiting for the next increase in readiness to '15 minutes', which would require us to strap into our aircraft. With nowhere else to go, people were wandering about the squadron, and passing the time by catching up with paperwork, drinking coffee or just chatting. Such exercises always followed a predictable pattern and, as the day dragged on, we waited for something, anything, to be announced over the Tannoy.

A standard-issue metal waste paper bin was located in most rooms around the squadron, and there was also one in the hall. Some days earlier, we had discovered that, by speaking forcibly into it, you could produce a very convincing impression of the station Tannoy system; but, by now, just about everyone had forgotten about this. In my aimless wanderings around the squadron, I came across one of these bins in a corridor and, out of sheer boredom, bellowed into it "This is the bomber controller, Readiness 15 minutes is now in force". I put the bin down, feeling quite pleased with how convincing I thought I had sounded, and was nearly trampled underfoot by the tide of aircrew heading towards me. It never occurred to me that this could be in response to my 'announcement', so I joined the rush in the belief that it was genuine.

Outside the squadron buildings, people piled into any form of transport that happened to be around. One of the crews had a very rusty Mini, and a large individual put his foot through the floor as he got in, and another stressed the door hinge and broke off the window winding handle. By whatever means available, we rushed out to the parked Victors, climbed up the steps and strapped in. Inside our aircraft, everything was duly switched on (apart from the engines), and we felt quite proud that we had made it in such a short time. It was a warm and sticky summer's day as we sat there, catching our breath and sweating gently

---

[1] The immersion suit was worn by aircrew to provide additional protection in the event of having to bail out and ending up in the sea.

inside our immersion suits. The Air Electronics Operator duly called up Station Operations to pass our 'crew ready' message, and there was a discernible pause before we were asked exactly why we were sitting in our aircraft. I can't quite remember the answer we gave, and neither am I sure who was more surprised!

Anyway, we were all stood down, along with the rest of the squadron crews who had also charged out to their aircraft after seeing us running. Strangely enough, they never figured out the source of the bogus Tannoy. Well, probably not until now!

Victor Mk 1 (Credit: Adrian Pingstone)

A Winter's Tale

I spent most of my formative flying years in the Lightning, which went so fast and stayed airborne for such a short time that icing was never a problem and, in the fullness of time, I was lucky enough to get an exchange tour with the Royal Canadian Air Force on the CF-101 Voodoo, which had a comparable performance. At our Canadian base, we also had access to half a dozen Lockheed T-33 Shooting Stars, an American-built basic jet trainer, which we used for communications, target profile flights and similar purposes. It was in the T-33 that I learned about icing.

I had flown to Toronto to attend the Exchange Officers' conference, and planned to return on the Friday evening, in time for a dinner party that my Boss was hosting. The function was due to commence at 1930, but the forecast showed freezing drizzle until 1800. With the benefit of hindsight, I should have made the decision right there and then to repair to the hotel and fly home the following morning. However, my planning showed that I would not arrive back at base until 1830, so all would be well, wouldn't it? Diversion airfields were few and far between, with most of them showing RED[1] or AMBER but, undeterred, I started up and took off into a very black night.

At height the weather was actually quite nice, so on I pressed, and all went well until I contacted base with 50 miles to run. Air Traffic told me that the cloud base was 200 feet (very low), with half a mile visibility (very poor) in freezing drizzle (very bad), and the one decent diversion airfield was GREEN. I should have cut my losses and diverted, but I was a steely-eyed fighter pilot who could easily cope with the conditions, and there was the Boss's dinner party to consider. Down I went through thick cloud, levelled at 1500 feet and started my radar-guided approach. All seemed well until, at about 1000 feet, I glanced up from the instruments to look for any sign of the approach lights, and realised that my windscreen was covered in ice - thick ice! The quarter-lights on each side of the windscreen were also about 90% covered, with only a small strip about an inch wide around the edges still clear. I looked to my left and right,

---

[1] NATO airbases used a colour coding system to indicate the prevailing meteorological conditions in relation to cloud base and visibility. Starting with the best they were BLUE, WHITE, GREEN, YELLOW, AMBER and RED.

and was alarmed to see that the wing tip fuel tanks had become very large ice lollies, so goodness knows what the engine air intakes looked like! They probably resembled small, ice-filled tubes. Air Traffic interrupted my growing consternation by asking me what my intentions were if I couldn't land. "Overshoot and go to Greenwood (the diversion airfield)", I replied confidently, although secretly I was concerned that the engine might not take kindly to me opening the throttle and asking it to suck in more air.

At 200 feet, I popped out of the base of the clouds and could just make out the runway approach lights on both sides through the clear portions of the quarter-lights. The windscreen was a mass of brightly coloured ice but, using peripheral visual cues, I managed an ungainly landing, and being on solid ground never felt so good. The runway had been treated, so the surface was fine but, as soon as I turned off it and tried to taxi, I realised how treacherous freezing rain can be. With great care, I manoeuvred the aircraft before shutting down and walking gingerly into the Operations Centre.

The dinner party? Oh, that was cancelled because conditions were too bad for driving!

Ejection From A Harrier

Casting my mind back to the early 1970s, the Harrier had only recently been introduced into the RAF. In 1971, the Wildenrath Wing in RAF Germany had been formed with Nos. 3, 4 and 20 Sqns, and I was posted to 4 Sqn as a Flight Commander. The early Harrier was a tremendous aeroplane, albeit a bit of a handful. I think most of us had great respect for her, and simply couldn't get airborne often enough. However, a combination of a novel aircraft, demanding operational flying and a general lack of experience, resulted in occasional accidents and incidents. We had our share at Wildenrath, and the Station Commander would 'encourage' us to the effect that, while we could and should press on operationally, we should do so with care!

In May 1972, the Squadron was detached to RDAF Skrydstrup, Denmark, for a 10-day exchange visit. On the morning of 4 May, I was tasked to lead a 4-ship attack mission on several targets in the Flensburg area of Northern Germany. The formation was also to be attacked by 2 other Sqn Harriers, which were acting as enemy defensive fighters, armed with simulated air-to-air missiles and guns. The planning and briefing for this type of sortie was lengthy and very thorough, and I remember filling at least two blackboards with administrative and operational detail.

At the appointed hour, 6 aircraft were allocated to us, and the 4 attack pilots and their 2 defensive counterparts gathered for the briefing. This lasted about an hour, by which time there was just one aircraft still available: mine! There was no alternative but to go on the sortie by myself, converting the profile to a solo attack/recce mission. So much for planning!

At about midday, I got airborne in XV794, turned south and headed for my first target, flying at 420 knots and 250 feet AGL[1]. All went well until I was preparing to attack my second target. I had just looked into the cockpit to re-arrange my map when, looking up, I saw a formation of three large (they have got much larger over the years!) birds flying straight at me. Instinctively, I pushed forward and missed two, but the third went straight into the engine intake. There followed an almighty BANG, followed by some rather worrying mechanical noises

---

[1] AGL – Above Ground Level

from the normally robust Pegasus 100 engine. Clearly, it did not like what was going on. I noticed that the RPM was just below idle, the JPT[2] in the middle of its range, height 200 feet and speed about 400 knots, although rapidly declining.

Generally, I was in open country, which was fairly flat with a few houses in my path. I opened and shut the throttle, but nothing much seemed to happen. I broadcast a quick 'MAYDAY' but, because I was quite low, I had no great expectations that anyone would hear me. Since I had already decided that the engine had suffered what sounded like catastrophic damage, I turned my mind to what to do next (in reality, I said to myself "I'd better jump out quite soon or I'm going in with the aeroplane!"). Then, exactly as you read it in books and newspapers, I saw that I was still close to houses, and steered the aircraft away from them towards open ground as best I could. Time was now getting short and, as I reached open ground, I saw a small hill ahead with trees at the summit. I pointed the aircraft at the hill, took one last look at the height and speed (100 feet and 200 knots respectively), trimmed the aircraft straight and level, tightened my straps and pulled the handle.

I remember everything working perfectly on my Martin-Baker Mk9 seat. I was quickly in my parachute and heading for a field full of cows. Also in the field were some quite large concrete blocks and, remembering a parachuting technique I had learned some 17 years previously, I steered myself away from the blocks, and executed a hard, but perfectly serviceable, 'side-right' landing.

The whole event had taken less than 60 seconds.

To my astonishment, I saw the aircraft continuing to fly beautifully in a slight climb away from me to the north. I cannot tell you the feelings I had as I watched what now seemed to be a perfectly serviceable aircraft leaving the scene of my ejection. Indeed, the aircraft eventually flew into cloud at about 7000 feet and disappeared from sight! Except for the cows, I was now completely alone in a field in Northern Germany, with no means of communication, a used parachute, the remains of an ejection seat and no method of transport. I had also forgotten in the heat of the moment that, on ejection, a radio signal was initiated on the emergency broadcast frequency, so that the emergency services were becoming aware that there was an aircraft in distress.

---

[2] JPT – Jet Pipe Temperature

I gathered myself together, and began to walk across fields in search of a road. After about 20 minutes I found one, absolutely deserted, and eventually came upon a farm. My German wasn't too good at the best of times, and my attempts to explain to the farmer's wife what had happened to me took some time. Eventually, and mainly through a combination of sign language and the sight of my parachute, I managed to explain my predicament and persuade her to let me use her telephone to contact the Sqn at Skrydstrup. The resulting conversation with 4 Sqn Ops, about an hour after my ejection, was surreal. The phone was answered by Flying Officer Andy Bloxam and the conversation went something like this:

"4 Sqn Ops, Fg Off Bloxam speaking." "Hello Andy, Pete Taylor here." "Oh! OK, aren't you still airborne? Anyway I'll get Roger Austin."

That was it. No questions, no 'How are you?', 'What's happened to the aircraft?', or 'Where are you?'. Andy just put the phone down and took about 5 minutes to find Roger. After that, things moved fast. Roger Austin established what had happened, and the rescue process was put into action. Apparently XV794 had climbed to over 20,000 ft, and continued to broadcast on the emergency frequency. Because the aircraft was close to a Warsaw pact border, a German F-104 was sent to intercept and was, I understand, mildly surprised to find a Harrier flying very nicely but with no one on board! Shortly after that, the aircraft ran out of fuel and glided into Southern Denmark, where it crashed in an open field, narrowly missing a farmhouse.

The Harrier stayed airborne for 38 minutes after my ejection. Apparently, the reason for XV794's 38-minute solo trip was that the bird which I hit had spread itself quite thinly across the engine's compressor. The flames and gases from the Martin-Baker ejection seat dislodged the bird as I left the aircraft, whereupon the engine heaved a sigh of relief, drew a deep breath and started working normally again. As it happens, I had trimmed the aircraft rather well and XV794 flew until she ran out of fuel! For my part, having given Roger an idea of where I was, the German Air Force sent an S-65 helicopter to pick me up. However, as I was apparently difficult to find, I had to use my SARBE[3] beacon and flares to direct the S-65 to me. As far as I know, I was at that time the

---

[3] SARBE – Search And Rescue Beacon Equipment

only person to have used my SARBE beacon on land, and the Company very kindly presented me with a silver pot.

At Skrydstrup, I met up with the rest of the Sqn, was given a brief but thorough examination by a lady doctor, and went back to the Officers' Mess. Life was never dull at Wildenrath in those days! I have a SARBE silver mug, membership of the Caterpillar and Martin-Baker clubs, an ejection seat handle and my log book to prove it all.

Harrier GR1 (Credit: John Malley)

Discretion

One Friday morning, shortly after getting airborne from our base on what had been planned as a 4 hour radar training flight, the port wing fire warning light illuminated. Unfortunately, the Victor SR2 had no fire suppression equipment fitted for such an eventuality (in fact it was an almost unheard-of occurrence), so the drill was to land as soon as possible. In our case, that meant reducing weight first, so we duly climbed to the appropriate height and started to jettison fuel. Some 30 minutes later, we were back on the ground and, with no possibility of any more flying, our crew was stood-down for the weekend.

I had already made plans to take the train down to London, in continued pursuit of a nurse from St Mary's, Paddington whom I had recently met (LD – where are you now?), so after lunch I cadged a lift to Huntingdon station and boarded the first available train. Two middle-aged ladies also got on, and sat opposite me in the carriage. Not long after the train had pulled out of the station, one of them said, "I nearly didn't make it today, you know".

"Why was that?" her friend enquired.

"Well", she said, "I went out into the garden to see if the washing was dry, and for some reason it absolutely stank of paraffin so I had to do it all again".

"Who on earth would spray someone's washing with paraffin?" asked her friend.

"God knows, but if I ever get my hands on them they'll live to regret it".

For a second I was tempted to explain, but the expression on the lady's face made it clear that, on this particular occasion, discretion was most definitely the better part of valour.

From Russia With Love

I was a pilot on an F-4 Phantom squadron during the late 70s, and remember us all being detached to Cyprus for weapons training on an Armament Practice Camp (APC). This was an annual event and, during the third week, there were two evening flying programmes to ensure that everyone was 'night current' before we returned to the UK. A few of our aircraft had been fitted with half-decent Radar Warning Receivers (RWR) as part of an upgrade programme and, on this particular evening, my back-seater was a qualified Electronic Warfare Officer (EWO), so he was delighted when we were assigned one of the modified jets.

The other participant in the tale was moored out in the Mediterranean, at a location known as the South Cyprus Buoy, and was a large piece of ironmongery owned by the Soviet Navy, which was causing quite a stir. There was often a Soviet vessel deployed there, gathering electronic intelligence on NATO forces and, although never officially sanctioned, it was common practice to 'pay them a visit', at high speed and low level. However, on this particular occasion, the visitor was not the usual disguised trawler, but a modern warship seldom seen in those parts.

Just before we started briefing for our sortie, the EWO took me to one side and said, "I'm sure that boat has got SAN 6 (a naval surface-to-air missile system) stuff on board. I got a 'sniff' on the RWR yesterday, and I'd like to check it out. How about we go and annoy them a bit, and see if they turn their radar on?" His interest had been sparked because this particular type of vessel was not supposed to carry such weaponry and, like many things seen in retrospect, it seemed a good idea at the time. "OK, we'll send our number two (the other aircraft programmed to fly with us) home after the intercept practice, and go have a look!"

A couple of hours later, we'd had enough of practice intercepts, and I sent our number two back to Akrotiri before we set off for the Buoy. It was a black night, with a solid overcast at 2000 feet but very good visibility below, so even the few lights showing on the Soviet ship were visible from some distance. Our plan was to overfly very fast, and as low as I wanted to go on such a night, and then continue for around ten miles, before turning back to see what reaction we had provoked. I'd made sure we had plenty of spare fuel and, with the luck of flying an aircraft without gun pod or drop tanks to slow us down, there was no problem with achieving an impressive speed as we hurtled noisily over the ship at about 500 feet. So far so good, we continued in the general direction of Israel for about a minute, and then turned back towards the Buoy.

"I was right!" the EWO exclaimed on the intercom, "He's got SAN 6, listen to that!" I turned up my RWR receiver volume, and listened to 'that', the sound of a surface-to-air missile radar searching for us. "I'll tell them at Episkopi (the Intelligence Centre) about this tomorrow," he added, "they didn't believe me yesterday!" I pressed on towards the ship, more slowly this time, as we had clearly succeeded in getting their attention.

Around three miles from the ship, the RWR audio changed. "Ah," said the voice from the back, "I think he's locked on to us."

Shortly after this the audio changed again. "I think that's launch!!"

I was about to say something extremely caustic, when my attention was grabbed by the fiery trail leaving the ship and heading in our direction. "Holy ****, they've fired at us," I yelled and, after a pause to kick-start my heart again, pulled the Phantom into a missile break. I remember thinking briefly that we were definitely within the missile's range, but then all my concentration was taken up with throwing the aircraft about, in the inky blackness above an unlit and unforgiving surface that wasn't far away.

After what seemed like an eternity, several things dawned on me. Firstly, if we were going to be hit it would have already happened; secondly, the flame trail was a bit puny for the large motor on a missile; and, thirdly, even the most gung-ho Soviet Naval Captain would probably stop short of starting a major diplomatic incident over a Phantom crew that had spoiled his after-dinner snooze.

I stopped acting like something out of Top Gun (still some time in the future at that stage, but you catch my drift), and set course for Akrotiri. "What the hell happened?" asked a slightly unsteady voice from the back. "I'm not sure," I replied, and then it dawned on me. "I think they went through radar search, lock and all that stuff, and then fired a signal rocket at us." There was a pause before we both started laughing, mainly from relief, but also in admiration. "Sneaky buggers," said the EWO. "Yes," I agreed, "Ivan one, us nil I think." We flew on in silence towards Akrotiri, and the prospect of a most welcome beer.

Just before landing, the EWO said, "I'll let them know tomorrow at Episkopi about what we found out, but let's not tell anyone about what happened, shall we?" It sounded like a good plan to me; in fact, it sounded like the best plan we'd come up with all night. "Good idea, let's not," I responded and, until now, I've kept my promise.

F-4 Phantom

An Unusual Forced Landing

The following story is taken from SILVERED WINGS, by kind permission of the author, Sir John Severne.

Towards the end of 1950, CFS took possession of a Balliol Mk1 for some trials; I was selected as the project officer to fly the aircraft, and this proved to be a most interesting experience. The Balliol was intended to replace the Harvard for advanced instruction, and the Mk1 was fitted with an Armstrong Siddeley Mamba gas-turbine turbo-prop engine. There were some development problems with the Mk1, so the Mk2 was produced with a Rolls Royce Merlin engine. In the event, the Mk2 was ready for production first, and that was the one that finally went into RAF service.

A Mamba had been fitted into the nose of a Dakota for in-flight trials, and I experienced some engine handling instruction on this unique aircraft, before being given a ten-minute familiarization flight in the Mamba-powered Balliol MkI by one of the test pilots. Gas turbines have a high idling speed, and it is therefore necessary to have a variable pitch propeller, preferably one that can change pitch very quickly. If I remember correctly, this propeller changed pitch at 60° a second and consequently, if you flew along slowly with the engine throttled back and then slammed – literally – the throttle open, fuel would immediately be pumped into the engine and the rapid pitch change would take up the power, resulting in a dramatic acceleration. I remember flying on one occasion when a Harvard drew up alongside for a little formation flying. I thought I would show this chap what the Balliol could do, so I slammed the throttle open and the aircraft shot forward to the amazement of the Harvard pilot. Many years later, I read that this Balliol, VL892, was the world's first single-engine turbo-prop aircraft.

The Mamba-powered Balliol had one disconcerting habit. If the propeller detected an engine failure, it would automatically feather, thus offering the least possible wind resistance whilst the pilot attempted a forced landing. Three months later, I was delivering this aircraft to RAF Strubby. As I approached the airfield, I was informed that no-one else was in the circuit, so I accelerated to high speed and did a very tight turn over the top when the engine decided to quit. I was immediately confronted with a stationary propeller in front of me, but I was over the airfield and it was just a question of selecting the most convenient runway to land on, which was not, as it happened, the runway in use. As I came to a halt, a car drew up and the Wing Commander Flying got out and said 'Do you usually land those things like that?' What I had not realized was that, in concentrating on doing a safe landing, I had forgotten to turn off the fuel. Consequently, kerosene had entered the hot engine and had produced a most impressive trail of white smoke. I suppose if I had watched a single-engine aircraft land on the wrong runway, with a stationary propeller and trailing white smoke, I too would have been a bit surprised.

Boulton Paul Balliol T.Mk2 (Credit: RuthAS)

Evasion In The Falklands

I took off from HMS Hermes, as the leader of a pair of Harrier aircraft, for my second mission of the day, in support of the attack being carried out by 2 Para against Goose Green in East Falkland. We were working under the direction of the Air Liaison Officer, as contact had been lost with the Forward Air Controller, and we were directed to attack a number of enemy troop positions. These were extremely difficult to see in time to attack, so it took several passes before we had both dropped our cluster bombs. Throughout these attacks, both aircraft were subject to a considerable barrage of both small arms and medium calibre anti-aircraft fire; so, thinking that our own forces were in trouble, I decided to press home our attack with guns. However, on the next pass my aircraft was hit and caught fire. I was initially able to maintain some control using the nozzle lever and rudder, as I flew west to distance myself from enemy held ground, but was finally forced to eject at about 50 feet and 480 knots, as fire entered the cockpit some five miles from Goose Green.

During the ejection I suffered cuts and lacerations to my face, and my parachute landing was a typically uncontrolled toes, knees and face affair. After landing, with my vision still very blurred from the blast, I thought I saw Argentine troops approaching my position, and therefore legged it as fast as I could in the opposite direction. However the blurred dots were later thought to be sheep although, by the time I tell the story to my two grandsons, I am sure it will be an entire battalion of Argentine paratroopers!

Sometime later, I came across an apparently deserted farmhouse but, to be sure, I did not enter it until just before dark, when I discovered it was indeed devoid of life but well stocked with food and bedding. After gratefully eating my fill, I took blankets and a map and, still fearing capture, spent the night under the heather some distance from the house. The next day, I returned for another meal and to shelter from the strong winds and wintry conditions, but again decided not to risk staying there permanently, despite the comfort it provided. Once away from the house, I activated my personal locator beacon and transmitted on the distress frequency but, having made my call, I decided that further transmissions might attract Argentine attention. Although I didn't know it at the time, my call was heard both by Sea Harriers on a combat air patrol and by Harrier GR3 aircraft en route to the Islands. In the interim, attempts to rescue me had been vetoed by the Navy, on the grounds that I might already be in enemy hands.

By this time, I had decided that the battle for Goose Green was probably over and, perhaps optimistically, thought that we had won, so I spent the next 24 hours living in the farmhouse. I was eventually picked up by a Gazelle helicopter of No 3 Commando Brigade, but not before I had at last managed to light the peat-fired Rayburn range, and cook myself a huge fry-up of sausages, bacon, corned beef and baked beans. I was later honoured to be awarded the RAF Escaping Society Trophy for 1982, and was probably one of very few evaders who actually gained weight during the experience!

Sea Harrier FRS1

I Can't Believe I Did That!

One of the most interesting tours I ever did was on exchange with the French Air Force, as a Basic Jet Instructor at Cognac (yes, where they make the stuff). It was the first time that post had been set up, and it attracted a certain amount of interest from both air forces. At my very short interview with the then Defence Attaché in Paris, an Air Commodore, he confined his comments to, "They send back the ones they don't like". So, no pressure there then!

After a quick instructor course at the French equivalent of CFS, I started in my role on a squadron at the base at Cognac. The aircraft was a little twin jet Fouga Magister, with a butterfly tail. It was somewhat underpowered, and the engines made a particularly piercing noise, most evident on start up, but it was noisy in the cockpit at most power settings. At that time, the French hard flying helmet had quite poor sound suppression, and the aircraft radios were of an earlier generation and were subject to a lot of crackling and distortion. All of this the more obvious after years of operating with pretty good RAF equipment of the era, but normally this noise was manageable. However, there were situations when it became more than ordinarily difficult.

In the early 80s, a common form of equipment to guide pilots to land was the Precision Approach Radar (PAR). This was situated on an airfield, close to the runway, and measured very accurately the aircraft's position, relative both to the centreline of the runway and ideal glidepath, to fly to the touchdown point. A well-trained radar controller then broadcast instructions to the pilot, to help him keep the aircraft on both centreline and glidepath. These PAR approaches typically allowed you to descend to 250 feet above the touchdown point, at which point you had to decide to land if you could see the runway, or put the power on and climb away if you could not. This was the standard way of making a bad weather approach at Cognac.

All that was very good in theory, but essentially depended on good communications between the pilot and the radar controller and, as you can imagine, it was critical that both could hear the other clearly. My problem, however, was the noisy cockpit environment and this, coupled with my less-than-expert French, led to me adopting a novel way of flying the PARs until my linguistic skills finally improved. Let me explain: keeping on the centreline was fairly straightforward – not only were the words right and left ("droit" and "gauche") distinctly different, but you were also given a heading in degrees (212 degrees, or whatever). However, the same was not true of information for the glidepath. After holding a level attitude at a specific altitude (e.g. 1500 feet), you were instructed to start the descent, and it was at this stage that things became difficult. The French for "above the glidepath" was "au-dessus", and "below the glidepath" was "en dessous". Not easy at the best of times, but particularly difficult with the excessive background noise in the cockpit. However, I was determined not to get sent back to the UK before the official end of my tour!

This is how I solved the problem. I was confident that I could stay on the centreline and, with a quick bit of mental arithmetic, it was possible to take the wind velocity on the surface, estimate the wind at 1000 feet, and thus work out the strength of the headwind component. That, together with the planned airspeed indicated in the aircraft, gave a groundspeed which would then guide me as to the required rate of descent. So, in practice, I would set my calculated rate of descent, carefully make the heading corrections given by the controller and, for additional guidance on the glidepath, I simply listened to the tone of his voice. If it stayed at an even pitch, I knew that I was there or thereabouts. If his voice became slightly higher, I listened more carefully and, if he was obviously becoming worried, I levelled off for a bit until he calmed down. Thereafter, I set a slightly reduced rate of descent than before, and continued down the slope. Believe it or not, the system worked well enough to give me time to attune my ear to the aural conditions in the aircraft but, as I look back at it now, I can't believe that I did that!

Making Your Mark

It was a warm summer's evening as the Shackleton took off from RAF Kinloss, to cross the Scottish Highlands and carry out an exercise to the west of Arran. Climbing high to avoid the hills, the crew were just settling down for the transit to Arran when No 4 engine fire light illuminated. The crew carried out the fire drill, but the extinguisher failed to douse the growing flames, so the captain pointed the aircraft's nose at the ground, and used most of the available 10,000 feet of altitude to try and blow the fire out, but to no avail. He therefore called the crew to their brace positions and, by the light of the now blazing engine, performed an immaculate crash landing on the northern side of Culloden Moor.

The Shackleton's fuselage offered a number of escape routes, including a hatch above each pilot's seat, so the normal procedure was that the captain went through the left one, followed by the radio operator, and the co-pilot used the right, followed by the flight engineer. The rest of the crew piled out of the hatch nearest to them, and they all gathered in a group upwind of the flames.

The first thing to do was a head count. One, two.....eight, nine. NINE? Hang on a minute, let's do this again. One, two.....eight, nine. DEFINITELY NINE! Ok, let's do it by a process of elimination – two pilots, two navigators, one air electronics operator, four signallers.....where's the flight engineer? The captain asked the co-pilot if the 'eng' had followed him through the hatch, but the co-pilot couldn't recall, as he had other things on his mind at the time.

By this time, the aircraft was well alight and, if the flight engineer was still on board, there was nothing that the rest of the crew could do to help him. With heavy hearts, they set off across the moor in the direction of the nearest lights.

As they approached the village, the unmistakeable sounds of a Ceilidh came floating on the breeze and, as they entered the bar, an elderly gentleman approached them smiling broadly. "Come in, come in", he said. "We've been expecting you, your friend's been here for some time".

FRIEND?? Across the bar sat the flight engineer, busily putting himself outside a bottle of whisky. The rest of the crew turned to the dumbfounded co-pilot who, in the light now available, clearly bore the imprint of a large boot on each shoulder of his flying suit.

How To Cheat – Akrotiri Style

It wasn't difficult really; you could see it coming a mile off. The Akrotiri Officers' Mess bar had been the pivot point for similar "My Dad's bigger than your Dad" discussions for many an evening previously, so why should this night have been any different? During the day, the Phantom mob was there to ensure that the bar always opened on time, and we were there because we hadn't had a kebab for a while and there was a rumour going around that the Tombs of the Kings at Paphos were worth a look. In reality, and although it never seemed to stop the Luftwaffe from having a go 40 years before, the weather in the UK in November had been predictably appalling. Thus it was, for a training unit tasked with 'maintaining the line' on hours flown, that alternative plans were made to provide clear blue skies, and ensure that we stayed at least 'on the line'. God knows why the air defence Phantom mob was really there. I have always discovered that, once the grey mist and 8/8^{ths} cloud cover have been breached, there is always ample blue above to have a bit of a punch up!

This was 237 Operational Conversion Unit's annual Exercise WINTER WATCHER. We were getting back to the line, at the request of a very considerate staff at HQ1 Group, by taking two weeks in Cyprus with few students, as I recall, and a bunch of instructors who were not in the habit of routinely getting many overseas perks. We were led by a spirited Boss, with a number of irrepressible and renowned members of the Buccaneer brotherhood in our midst, while the crews of 56 (Fighter) Squadron, our near neighbours from RAF Wattisham, were there to practice air-to-air gunnery and protect the Sovereign Base Areas (SBA) if the bad guys (you decide who!), in the littoral states at the eastern end of the Mediterranean, cooked off.

The Keo (local beer) had been flowing for nearly 2 weeks, and the Brandy Sour Lake had been drained on more than one occasion. Banter levels were high in the bar and, with that rather annoying air of arrogance that a group of Flashhearts bring to any party, the schoolies[1] had fallen for the rather doubtful and outspoken 'charms' of the 56 Squadron aircrew! We, of course, were not

[1] Overseas bases often had their own British schools, staffed predominantly by young, single, female teachers who lived in the Officers Mess. These ladies were known (affectionately) as 'schoolies'.

troubled by the air of superiority that pervaded the atmosphere because, as mud movers, we had a natural understanding of our own value. We also knew that revenge would be ours!

So it flowed across the bar. "My Dad's bigger than your Dad!" "No he's not!" "Yes he is!" You know the sort of mature conversation that aircrew have, when they are happily sitting outside the contents of a rather large brewery. We were past masters of both, and confident that a few misguided words from a bunch of prima donnas would reap their own reward in due course.

"You guys do airfield attacks, don't you?"

"Might!"

"Nah!" in an inebriated slang, "You do, don't you!?" "Bet, you can't get through to this one while we defend it!"

"Oh yeah!" "How much?"

"One Brandy Sour Lake (BSL)!"

"Yer on!"

"Right, we'll set up a Combat Air Patrol (CAP), and you attack Akrotiri!"

"OK!"

"When then?"

"Whaddya mean, when? You guard it, we'll attack it; winner takes all, or one BSL for internal consumption as appropriate!"

"No! We need to know when, we can't guard it forever!"

"What? Thought you were fighters! Isn't that what you're supposed to do? Defend the SBA?"

"Yeh, but! We've got the banner[2] as well you know! We need to know when?"

"OK! Thursday!"

"What time on, Thursday?"

"Give us a break! You're Air Defenders, use your mates at Olympus Radar and defend the SBA on Thursday!"

"OK! But we need to know the time!"

"No way! You said you'd defend Akrotiri, so get on with it! See you Thursday!"

---

[2] Air-to-air gunnery is practiced against a 27 foot long flag known as a 'banner' that is towed behind an aircraft – usually by a different squadron. If the fighter crews are not doing very well, it's not unheard of for the ground-crew to paint BARN DOOR on the banner.

So the scene was set. There were 24 hours in Thursday the 20th of November 1980, so we had the upper hand already and, needless to say, there were not many Phantom guys in the bar the evening beforehand. They were evidently keen to win, as Quick Reaction Alert (QRA) had been mounted by midnight, for the first time at Akrotiri since the Turks had invaded Cyprus 6 years before.

The Dissimilar Air Combat Training rules of the day stated that any such activity should, at the very least, be preceded by a telephone briefing. Accordingly, our Senior Navigator Instructor had been despatched earlier in the week to thrash out the Rules of Engagement for the mission, but with strict instructions to give nothing away. Thus, everybody would play by the rules, and injury to anything other than pride would be kept to an absolute minimum. He returned, pleased as punch that he had "secured a good deal" by agreeing an attack corridor "anywhere north of the 270° radial", and fixed that we would squawk (airborne identification) the required code, when under radar control from Olympus Radar. However, a quick look at the map, and knowledge of the local 'no over-flight of Cyprus' rule, made it obvious that this was a huge constraint for any attacking force. He had failed, and the poor chap lost any goodwill previously acquired, and was pilloried mercilessly for days. In fact, he had just handed all the advantage back to the enemy! Undeterred, and with the Boss's blessing, we vowed to cheat, but remain within the rules set, if only in principle, whilst at the same time ensuring that we regained the advantage.

Not a Phantom wheel turned that morning, as the Flashhearts wrestled with the tricky problem of identifying when they might be required to defend the hallowed Akrotiri soil. They were at the Eastern end of the airfield, and we occupied the Western sunspots, so they couldn't easily see what we were up to, and had to rely on scouts to do their spotting for them. Without any warning to our brethren in QRA, we slipped our mooring at about 1130 hrs, and managed to get airborne on a westerly heading with little or no fuss - but with a positive identification from the 'enemy'. Departure was uneventful as we climbed to high altitude, squawking as required and under radar control from Olympus. They clearly thought that, with us held tightly in their grasp, their Flashheart mates were up for a 'Turkey Shoot'. Not if we had anything to do with it, they weren't!

At top of climb, around 35,000 feet, we levelled off, and proceeded as

planned through West Point and onwards towards the Maros and Toska Reporting Points, making like airliners whilst the 'enemy' gathered themselves and
their mighty weapon systems into the air. The incessant height and heading
confidence-boosting chatter from Olympus began to wear us down but, like
the true professionals that we were, we responded, and assisted them in their
preparations to provide a top-notch Ground Controlled Intercept service to 56
Squadron. We were, of course, lulling them into a false sense of security, as we
had no intention of playing absolutely by the rules. Beyond Maros, we turned
starboard as if to intercept the 270° radial from Akrotiri and, once established
inbound, formed loose arrow, throttled back, rolled, opened the airbrakes and
switched off the squawk - we were about to cheat! We would soon be below
Olympus radar cover and out of radar control, so there was little point in providing them with height updates during our visual descent. The Buccaneer Flight
Reference Cards quote 16000 feet per minute for a maximum rate descent at
0.85Mach/400knots. However, my memory tells me that it seemed much less
than 2 minutes, on that day in 1980, before we were at low level over the Med,
where the Buccaneer was happiest, at 100 feet (give or take) above the Oggin!
Echoing in the ether behind us were the plaintive cries of Olympus, asking us
politely to check our squawk and altitude, so we changed radio channel to our
squadron discrete frequency as, quite frankly, their pathetic wailings were beginning to get on our nerves.

Meanwhile, our temporarily grounded students at Akrotiri were noting the
antics of our adversaries, in preparation for reporting them later to the attacking force. The valiant 4-ship from 56 had got airborne in reasonably short order
after our departure, and 3 CAPS were soon established; one Phantom on the
270° radial South of Paphos; one orbiting in Episkopi Bay; and 2 capping over
the airfield itself, all at about 10,000 feet. They really must have believed that we
would be easy meat, and that we lacked cunning or any intent to deceive – little
did they know! Upon reaching our new 'cruising' height, we selected maximum
thrust and turned south-southeast to follow the route of the airways that cir-
cumnavigate Cyprus to the south, but far below them and any possibility of radar contact. Our intent was to confuse Olympus and our foe, before they could
establish any Mental Air Picture (MAP) or catch a glimpse of us at low level, but
we needn't have worried, as reports subsequently revealed that the volume and

confusion of the calls on GCI were proof enough that any Radar Air Picture or MAP had gone out the window!

When we ran out of Cypriot airspace at the Egyptian Flight Information Region (FIR) boundary, we turned northeast and flew parallel to it, still at low level, aiming for an Initial Point (IP) 70 nm southeast of Akrotiri, and on an attack heading of approximately 310° - some 140° different to that briefed to our adversaries. OK, we were cheating now, but we satisfied ourselves that the Russians would have done the same, and anyway the fighter jocks clearly needed the practice! The noise and accusations on GCI were evidently something to be heard, as both Olympus and the 56 formation scoured the skies for our 4-ship to the west of Akrotiri.

Once at the IP, we pushed up to 580 IAS and pushed down to an 'appropriate' attack height. As we ran from Israel towards Akrotiri, the Approach Controller rumbled us, but only when we called for attack clearance. She had no reason to show allegiance to either us or 56, but there was absolutely no need to tell the chap at Olympus where we were; at best, she could only have been seeing him at the weekends, when we were in the bar every night! So the game was up, but far too late for the defending force to gather itself in time to repel our attack from the southeast. Our spies on the ground later reported that, once the confusion of where we were had been resolved, and the overhead CAP despatched for the intercept, they were disturbed by a thunderous roar. The Episkopi Bay CAP passed through the overhead at about 10,000 feet, heading in our direction, followed in short order by the blue haze shadow of the Phantom from Paphos Bay at close to Mach 1.

It was all too little too late. Yes, they saw us heading directly towards them, but we were far too low and they were far too disorganised (subsequent confession) to get a reasonable head-on shot off, and by then our front pair were over the beach. My pilot and I were about 40 seconds behind and, just as we were crossing the beach, I looked out and reported a Phantom turning in our 4 o'clock in an attempt to gain a shot on us. My man took immediate straight line evasive action, by slamming the throttles shut and popping the airbrakes fully out. XT274 stopped on a tanner, causing the Phantom to overshoot and (by his own, later admission) failing to get his shot off. We, on the other hand, were now ideally placed for a 'kill'. However the Buccaneer never had guns, and back in 1980 it had yet to be fitted with AIM-9G Sidewinder air-to-air missiles.

The 'team' assembled at bar opening time, with a buoyant Boss and his mob of staff and students gathered to receive their prize. The boys of 56 were, of course, noble in defeat, as they ate rather generous helpings of humble pie. The lake was declared open, and a bloody good night was had by all! My pilot had got his kill, and I am sure to this day that the back-seater of that Phantom has still got the imprint of his radar screen firmly embossed on his face, from the deceleration as his pilot realised that his firing solution would never come and the game was up – he had been about to "die"!

"Hey, have you guys ever done gunnery against the banner?" (My Dad's STILL bigger than your Dad).

Pass me another Brandy Sour, there's a good chap!

237OCU Buccaneer S2 (Credit: John Malley)

On The Ball

On the morning of 28th October 1953, I awoke from a strange dream that I soon forgot when I looked out of the window, and saw that it was a beautiful autumn day. After arriving at work at Hawarden, my first task, as one of the test pilots, was to undertake the initial flight of De Havilland Venom Mk1 No 458. The normal flight profile consisted of a climb to 45,000 feet, a dive at M0.86 to check trim and stability at high speed, a further descent to 10,000 feet to check low speed handling, and a return to base.

After take-off, I was cleared to climb in a northerly direction and, as I passed 40,000 feet, all was well with the world. Visibility was superb, and I had a terrific view of the Great Orme to my right and Anglesey straight ahead. Then, without any warning, the engine stopped.

I tried calling Hawarden, but the radio was dead, in fact the whole cockpit was dead with no warning lights showing anywhere. By this time, I had already turned back towards base and started a descent, but repeated attempts to relight the engine met with no success. It was now clear that I had suffered a total electrical failure, and my only option was to carry out a glide approach.

I arrived in the circuit at about 4000 feet, positioned myself downwind, and lowered undercarriage and flap. Luckily, the circuit appeared to be clear, so I continued round finals and landed in total silence. There was plenty of air in the brake system, so I was able to turn off at the runway intersection with sufficient momentum to continue all the way to the flight line where, with the over-confidence of youth, I brought the Venom to a halt, in line with the other aircraft waiting to be flown.

I got out of the Venom, and it was immediately obvious that there had been a serious fire in the engine bay, which had melted away most of the under-belly cowlings exposing flying control cables that had overheated and were hanging from their pulleys.

I walked back to the pilots' office, and called air traffic control to report what had happened but, out of interest, first asked if they were in touch with "Tibbet 38" which had been my call-sign. The response was, "No, he's still airborne but he should be back soon!"

Post Script: In my dream, I had been flying an aircraft that caught fire.

My Personal 9/11

During the late eighties and early nineties, I served as a staff weapons instructor on 56 Squadron, the Tornado F3 Operational Conversion Unit and, in my spare time, was privileged to fly the Hurricanes and Spitfires of the Battle of Britain Memorial Flight (BBMF).

On 11th September 1991, BBMF deployed to the Channel Islands for a series of fly-pasts and displays, and we were scheduled to take-off at 1400. Consequently, I was committed to a morning of lectures beforehand, followed by a staff critique, which resulted in me missing lunch and having to grab a Mars bar instead. I arrived at BBMF, just in time for briefing, and was allocated Hurricane IIc LF363 to fly which, at that time, was one of only three airworthy anywhere in the World.

I took off just behind a Spitfire MkXIX, with the Lancaster following me. Normally, both fighters would have completed an orbit, and then joined up with the Lancaster for the transit but, on this occasion, the Spitfire pilot was required to do a practice display before departing. However with a 37 litre, 2000bhp Rolls Royce Griffon, it would not be long before he caught us up. I therefore joined on the wing of the Lancaster, and we gradually climbed, before being handed over to Wittering Radar and levelling at 3000 feet. I cursed at this because when, you're flying a 46-year-old aircraft, you really want to be as high as possible in case the engine fails, but I consoled myself with the prospect of getting clearance to climb once we had passed RAF Wittering.

We had been airborne for about 10 minutes, and were just north of Stamford, when there was an almighty BANG, and light grey smoke started pouring out of both sets of exhaust stubs. The engine began to run very roughly, giving intermittent bursts of power but not enough to maintain altitude, so I converted speed into height, slowed to the best gliding speed of 90 knots, and transmitted a "Mayday" call. I knew that RAF Cottesmore was on my right side and slightly astern, but Wittering was almost directly ahead, so I decided to aim for there, and attempted to restore some power. The throttle was fully forward at maximum boost, but I still had the propeller lever to play with, and discovered that 2400 rpm gave the smoothest running, although I was still losing height.

Time to make a decision! Could I reach the runway at Wittering or, if not, was a forced landing in open country possible? To my left was Burghley Park, where preparations were well under way for the Three Day Event with people, horses and marquees everywhere while, to my right, was undulating land with small fields. That was it then, I had to make the airfield.

In the cockpit, I made preparations for a crash landing on the airfield, by sliding back the canopy, locking it into position, and tightening my straps as I had never done before. The engine was still giving bursts of power as I changed radio channel to call Wittering Tower, but I was concentrating on flying at exactly the right speed to maximize my distance, and initially misdialled one of the numbers. When finally on frequency, I learned that I would have a slight tailwind and, as I started the 60 degree turn onto the runway centreline, I was becoming increasingly optimistic that a normal, wheels-down landing was possible. In common with the Spitfire, the Hurricane's undercarriage selector is on the right-hand side of the cockpit, which necessitates changing hands on the control column, and I had just done this when the right wing dropped without any warning. I had accidentally stalled the aircraft.

I had a definite impression that I was still 50-100 feet above the runway, and therefore decided that I was a dead man, and how sad it was that my life should end in this way. So, under the circumstances, I simply relaxed and thought of my wife and children. I suddenly realised that I had crashed. I felt a crack on my head, and was aware that the aircraft was sliding along the runway, as I could see sparks through a transparent panel in the floor that was normally used to see if the undercarriage had locked down.

As the Hurricane came to a halt, the main fuel pipe that ran through the cockpit fractured and caught fire. The open cockpit acted like a chimney and, in no time at all, there were flames filling the whole void. Those who know me will confirm that I never swear but, faced with the prospect of being burned alive, I made up for it in spades as I struggled out of my harness. Fortunately for me, Sydney Camm, the designer of the Hurricane, knew all about the problems of exiting burning aircraft, and had provided a large escape panel on the right hand side of the cockpit, which had fallen off on impact. I stepped through the hole onto the wing, which was already melting as the fire spread, and jumped onto the runway. My left leg gave way but, anxious to distance myself from the fire, I managed to struggle a few more steps before collapsing. I then noticed that the kneeboard of my flying suit had somehow slipped down to cover my ankle, so I removed it, only to discover that my left foot was at a very odd angle.

Unable to move further, I had a front row view as LF363 was transformed into a smouldering skeleton, despite the speedy attention of the Airfield Fire Service. The medical team also arrived, and set about treating my injuries. The Doctor asked what my pain threshold was like and, when I replied that I hadn't a clue, he set about pulling my foot back into alignment and immobilizing it. Unfortunately I had also sustained burns to the back of both legs, and the metal mesh splint he used stuck to the back of my left thigh, which was the first time I felt any real pain – what a wonderful thing adrenalin is!

I was duly carted off to Peterborough Hospital and, after what I saw as an unacceptable delay, was finally admitted to Accident and Emergency for treatment. However, my situation was put firmly into perspective, when I realized that the reason for the delay was a young man who had suffered the most appalling injuries inflicted by some piece of agricultural machinery. No matter how bad your day is, you can always guarantee that someone else's is far worse.

Post Script: I had an operation to fix two broken ankles which, due to my snack lunch of a Mars bar, was able to go ahead without delay. Later, while sitting up in bed waiting to be questioned by the Board of Inquiry, I became aware of a persistent foul smell that I finally discovered were my eyebrows that had been singed by the flames.

The cause of the engine failure was a broken camshaft, which had not been modified in accordance with instructions issued in 1948! LF363 was subsequently rebuilt by Historic Flying Limited and flew again, some seven years after the crash.

My 9/11 – Revisited

I returned to flying in December 1991, just 13 weeks after the Hurricane crash, and started my work-up for the following season at the beginning of April. This time I was flying Spitfires and, after 10 sorties on various Marks (derivatives), I completed my formal AOC's approval on the 22nd of April. My first display was to be at the old RAF airfield at North Weald on 16th May and, as more than 10 days had elapsed since my formal approval, I was required to complete a practice display first. The Lancaster and a Spitfire were scheduled for other events, prior to participating at North Weald, so we agreed a rendezvous point (RV) and time to join up beforehand.

At the appointed time, I strapped into Hurricane IIc PZ865, which was now the only one left at BBMF and, coincidentally, the last one ever built! This was the first time I had flown a Hurricane since the crash at Wittering but, after completing the practice display, I felt completely at home again, and duly set course for North Weald. The RV was straightforward, and we ran in for a three-aircraft close formation entrance to the sequence. I did my display, and handed over to the Spitfire without any problems, before standing off until the Lancaster had finished, at which point I had to lead the rejoin. The last pass by the Lancaster was a run along the crowd line from right to left, before turning away 40 degrees. This meant that I had to fly a diving path to join up on the inside of the Lancaster's subsequent left turn, ahead of our final flypast in close formation. All was going well as I approached the left wing of the Lancaster but, before taking up a close formation position, I did a quick check of my engine instruments, and was puzzled to see that the boost gauge was reading +12 psi, when I had expected to see zero. This was confusing, as the engine had shown no sign of stress.

A mighty BANG BANG made me realise that I was in serious trouble. I converted what little speed I had to height, and transmitted a "Mayday" call on the display frequency, stating that I had engine problems. Our final run was from the southwest, where the runway is hidden by rising ground and tall trees; so, with the advice of my Air Officer Commanding ringing in my ears about how options diminish as you lose height, I looked around for a suitable field to carry out a forced landing. Fortunately, there were plenty of them but, on the other hand, the engine was now running smoothly, and producing just enough power to maintain height.

I could not bear the thought of being responsible for the loss of a second Hurricane, and made the decision to land on the runway, even thought it was still obscured. With careful nursing, I cleared the trees, and a beautiful stretch of runway appeared under the nose. Very aware of how quickly things might go wrong if I changed the engine setting, I waited until there was runway directly underneath me before closing the throttle. North Weald Air Traffic Control reminded me that the aircraft was still "clean", and I confirmed I was aware before gently lowering the nose, selecting undercarriage and flap, and executing a perfect three-point landing at the mid-point of the crowd line.

The whole incident had only lasted a couple of minutes and, as I taxied clear of the runway, I wondered if it had all been a ghastly figment of my imagination. After shutting down the aircraft, I climbed on to the wing of the Spitfire that had landed behind me, and told the pilot that I really wasn't sure if I hadn't imagined the whole episode. All I knew was that my mouth felt like the bottom of a parrot's cage, and my legs were trembling uncontrollably. As it transpired, the incident was real enough, and had been caused by (yes, you guessed it) another camshaft failure - only this time the drive had failed so, fortunately, the camshaft just stopped rotating. This had the effect of turning my V12 engine into a straight 6, with the working side rotating the failed side as well as the propeller to keep me airborne!

Post Script: Despite only three months between the first flights of the prototype Spitfire and Hurricane, they were very different beasts. The Hurricane was part of a logical progression of designs by Sydney Camm, who had earlier been responsible for the Fury and Hart bi-planes, and latterly the Typhoon, Tempest, Hunter and Harrier. It was very hot and noisy for display work, but had a certain solid charm. Its handling was strange, in that it was quite sluggish in roll but neutrally stable in pitch, and was very highly regarded as a gun platform by those who flew it in combat. In fact, the Hurricane accounted for 60% of German aircraft destroyed during the Battle of Britain.

By contrast, R J Mitchell's Spitfire represented a huge leap in technology, with minimal frontal area and a narrow track undercarriage, to accommodate the wheels in the very thin elliptical wing. Its construction necessitated the introduction of new building techniques, and it was therefore available in much smaller numbers in 1940. On the same power, the Spitfire was about 30mph faster than its contemporary and, although both types remained in frontline service throughout the war, the Hurricane's development was limited to only two main Marks. By contrast, the Spitfire was continuously developed, starting with an 1175bhp Rolls Royce Merlin in the 1939 Mark 1 which, by 1945, when the Mark 24 came into service, had been replaced by a 2375bhp Rolls Royce Griffon, offering greatly improved performance over the original.

Hurricane IIc PZ865 (Credit: John Malley)

Let There Be Light

It had been a very long day and night. We'd been held on standby before getting airborne and now, 6 hours into the sortie, it was time to go home. When I say home, I mean Jorge Chavez International, the main airport for Lima, Peru that had been our operating base for some weeks. The flying had been challenging and interesting but now, some 700 miles off the west coast of South America at 4am, we could relax a bit on the inbound leg. Up at the front, it was agreed that we would take an hour on in turn, as was normal practice in such circumstances. With routine checks completed and the aircraft cruising leisurely at 40+ thousand feet, I made myself as comfortable as it's possible to be when you're strapped into a bang seat, and closed my eyes.

I was startled into consciousness by a blinding light. It was now broad daylight, the sun was coming up over the Andes, and it was shining straight into my eyes. For a few seconds I drank in the magnificent view, and then I looked across the cockpit. The other pilot was slumped forward in his harness, head down and clearly fast asleep. I, on the other hand, was now very awake! I quickly scanned the instruments; everything seemed to be working as advertised, the fuel was still flowing, and we were obviously heading eastwards. I turned up my intercom volume and quietly asked "How are things in the back?" No reply. Let's try that again. "HOW ARE THINGS IN THE BACK?" After a brief pause, there was the click of microphones being switched on, followed by a lot of mumbling. Across the cockpit there were also signs of life, and a hastily scribbled note was handed over that said, simply, "Sorry".

A few minutes later, the navigators came up with a Top of Descent time, contact was established with the Ops Room, and we trundled down from high level for an uneventful recovery and landing. We never spoke about the incident, and I'm not even sure that the rear crew members were aware of what had happened. I could offer excuses about how stressful and debilitating the previous twelve hours had been, but we were a fully Combat Ready crew, trained for the task, and we should have been more aware of the risk.

The following day, a group of us took a taxi to a street market on the outskirts of Lima and, on one of the stalls, there was a number of cheap guitars for sale. "Let's buy a detachment guitar," someone said, looking at me, "And you can play it in the hotel bar when we next have a sing-song."

Later that evening, around twenty of us ended up in the bar, and I was despatched by the Boss to collect the detachment guitar. When I returned, the Boss, in a vain attempt to avoid the usual mix of aviation and rugby songs, exclaimed, "Let's sing some Beatles stuff for a change".

"Ok," I said. "Let's start with Here comes the Sun".

A Bridge Too Far...?

The erosion of the RAF, as a result of The Defence White Papers of the 50s and early 60s, and the scrapping of the TSR2, had led to a decline in morale. For one experienced aviator, the decision that the RAF's 50th Anniversary would not be marked by flypasts was the final straw. This is the story of his very personal response.

As we accelerated, rolling down Tangmere's runway in two pairs and a singleton, with a five second stream spacing, my main pre-occupation was how best to break away from the rest of the section without attracting anyone's attention. I was aware that a pair of eyes were looking down my jet-pipe as we took off to the east. Immediately after take-off, and the reassuring, quiet rumble and clonk had signalled the wheels locked up, I watched as the Hunter behind me turned belly on to me to beat up the airfield, as a farewell fighter tribute to such a legendary airfield, symbol of fighter excellence - what a splendidly good and indiscretionary Boss! I knew that I would not now be seen by him!

I eased my throttle back, reverse rolled, and slipped gently away from the others towards the north, descending rapidly to low level to melt my Hunter's camouflage droptank deep into the dense eiderdown of the Sussex countryside. After an intentional one-and-a-half minute delay, I then told the formation leader, with speechless code on my R/T button, that I had "lost" visual contact and pretended my radio had failed, using speechless transmissions to avoid any further embarrassing conversations on the R/T. With things to do, I certainly didn't need a dialogue on the cancellation of TSR2, or the rights and wrongs of initiative! Before taking off on my way north, I had realised my route would take me close to Dunsfold's idyllic, rural aerodrome, the airfield home of Hawkers, where such a small team had assembled and tested so many fine and famous aircraft for the RAF, including my own much loved Hunter FGA9. Aware my flight would have certain consequences, I had decided to pay them a brief Anniversary visit and, after a careful check for other air traffic, I streaked low over Dunsfold.

Two brief minutes later, I was at my "initial point" over the lakes, three miles south of London Airport. As I banked to the right, turning clear and safely below London Airport's approach lane, I saw a stately Boeing 707 glide-sloping its studied, final approach onto Heathrow's westerly runway. Crossing the green area of Richmond Park, I joined the silvered brown Thames, following its sharp, sinuous bends down river in a melody of delightful Fairey and Dowty banked reversals. Over London, the weather was still one of those rare perfect, 8/8 Gordon's, crystal, gin clear days, when all the colours shout out brightly. Definitely cerulean, not just azure. There was not a breath of wind; the blue sky too shone cloudlessly.

For obvious reasons, at this stage my crumpled quarter inch map of the route became useless. I had no 50,000 or 100,000 target map on this particular sortie! With bursts of flap and power, I now concentrated all my attention on flying down the centre of the stream, startled by the varied beauty in the arches of each bridge, just seconds apart. I swept round over Wandsworth, Battersea and Chelsea bridges, keeping a special eye open for any helicopters. Straightening up after the next bend, I crossed Vauxhall Bridge and there, a mile or so ahead, was that familiar and splendid silhouette of the Houses of Parliament, viewed within a special sense of Triplex privacy. This was my main target area.

As I banked over, climbing slightly to circle Whitehall and the historic seat of British government, I had to open my throttle fully to maintain a good tight orbit. I realised this would put the noise level up considerably, which up to now I had been careful to keep as low as possible, to avoid offence or complaint. As I put the Rolls-Royce power on, I decided that this was perhaps what was really necessary at this juncture, to wake up our MPs and remind other august figures, sitting chair-bound at their ministerial desks below, that we still had a fighting Air Force, one small unit of which was celebrating its anniversary, despite the dead hand of government policy and the sickening cut-backs of previous years. The message to Westminster was received. A debate was interrupted. Later, a four MP cross party inter-service motion of support for the tribute was ruled, retrospectively, out of order. Quashed, it was reportedly deleted from Hansard!

Three times I circled, fascinated like any Gulliver looking down at Lilliput by the scene below, and with not dissimilar motives to its author either, exactly as Big Ben struck 12 noon. Having been abroad for some years, I was now conscious of the high Vickers Millbank tower block, which came as a surprise to one who had not been in Central London for some long time. Its bulk spoiled the even radius of my turns. Quite suddenly I felt a little tired, rather annoyed that, for once without a target map, I could not readily pick out No.10. With care, I kept well clear of Buckingham Palace, which was plainly visible outside my orbit. Surprisingly there was time idly to wonder in the final turn exactly how many regulations I was breaking at this rather exclusive and delicious moment.

After my final orbit, I levelled out again over the Thames, dipping my wings past the RAF Memorial and, coincidentally, the statue of Viscount Trenchard, who had helped to found the RAF in 1918, exactly 50 years earlier, despite tremendous opposition. With a quick glance at my fuel, I decided that, rather than cross the heavily populated area to the north, or climb through the airspace used by inbound airliners, the safest plan for all concerned was for me to follow the Thames eastward at low level, out into a less populated area, and then turn north for home. At one minute past noon, I turned happily down river. Over Waterloo Bridge, I could see the architecturally pleasing Post Office Tower away over to the left, then suddenly ahead a fine view of St. Paul's Cathedral, at this time with its lattice work curtain of scaffolding. Despite thousands of sorties in Europe, Africa, Asia and the Middle East, I felt now like some voyeur or landscape artist, so intoxicated with the various views to the left and right of me that it was literally just before my wings crossed London Bridge when I looked ahead, and suddenly saw Tower Bridge. There, standing like some proud, strong sentinel across the Thames, this famous matronly structure blocked my low level path to the east.

Until this very instant, I'd had absolutely no idea that, of course, Tower Bridge would be there. It was easy enough to fly over it, but the idea of flying through the spans suddenly struck me. I had just ten seconds to grapple with the seductive proposition, which few ground attack pilots of any nationality could have resisted. My brain started racing to reach a decision. Years of fast low level strike flying made the decision simple. From a trained low level pilot's point of view, it provided an interesting penetration problem. To give added decision time, I jinked hastily to line myself up directionally, and pre-position down low over the river, with my eager fighter well beneath the tall cranes standing like silent, puzzled spectators on the banks. This manoeuvre would give me a full extra three seconds of decision time to study defloration further.

There was considerable road traffic, I could now see, including a red double-decker bus, slowly lumbering across the famous, double-basculed bridge from north to south. With less than half a mile or so to run, I realised that it would be easy enough to fly through, but what would be the best and safest way? Swiftly I concluded Sydney Camm's favourite fighter would have to fly as close to the top structure as possible. Rather like a reverse skip bombing run with target cues above! At the last split second before I crossed underneath, the steel girders suddenly seemed to explode all about my cockpit, above, below and about my ears, totally engulfing canopy and one's traditional sense of flying fun! That microsecond my mind felt quite certain I had overcooked it, and the top span would certainly take my fin off the next millisecond.

Something then happened which had only occurred once before to me, when I had mushed after pull-out from an FAC attack, with over-sufficient aircraft weight and "g" and insufficient speed, power and thought! Thinking I had hit the ground, but missing Cloud Ninety Nine by a whisker, my heart actually had missed a couple of beats with the shock of expected imminent disaster. After that, there was the acute, physical reaction as the heart fires up to full stroke again, just like a fighter's fuel pump, trying hard to catch up again.

My Hunter flew on, rather unexpectedly finding itself still completely functional, and not a finless wonder, and I headed out over Greenwich and Hornchurch, heading towards Clacton. With not overmuch to hide now, I opened up a separate Anniversary sortie call-sign on the R/T, Romeo Alfa Foxtrot 01 (rather lost on the controllers). Then, with R/T permission from the ground, ceremonially I beat up RAF Wattisham, home of some of the Lightning force, and whose Station Commander was decidedly an accessory before this particular crime!

Lakenheath was next on my list, and Mach .93 dive-brake sonic boom-letting where No 1 's fellow squadron, with their parked USAF F- 100's, were based. I recalled an earlier incident when, with three other instructors in brand new Jet Provost Mk4's in February 1962, as leader I had called up another US base: "Four basic trainers at 10 miles, permission for slow flyby". Then we steamed over right on the deck at almost 400kts, to remind our transatlantic cousins how we trained our UK basic pilots at that time! Only the other three were reported as seen by the tower! Lastly, without really the fuel to do it justice, and only after a very careful R/T check on the position of a Victor on its extended final approach lane, I flew across RAF Marham. Thus the flight had correctly covered both halves of the former Bomber and Fighter elements, which were just now combining as the new "Strike Command". Sic transit gloria.

With less than 400 lbs of fuel now remaining, I carried out a rather hurried, inadequate, inverted run over the squadron hangars at RAF West Raynham, before breaking downwind, punching down the gear and landing, with the brake parachute bobbing about contentedly behind my precious fin. Somewhat pensively I taxied slowly in, expecting, like most other privileged fighter drivers in their time, that a formal reception committee might already be there, as on one or three previous occasions in my flying career.

Only the normally cheerful airman was there to greet me on to my chock. Cutting the HP cock, the Hunter's Avon shut down, with that unique intermittent cacophony of cooling blades and tolerances like some giant desyncopated lawnmower. Feeling rather pleased that I had a few more minutes before the thunder of the gods was unleashed, I asked the lad if he'd mind getting my overnight bag out of the radio bay, something I invariably did for myself. While he proceeded with this task, I had the opportunity of doing what I wanted to, but thought I might not get any chance to. Professionally, I felt thoroughly ashamed of the scribbled marks and tatty appearance of the quarter-million map on which I had navigated up from Tangmere without problem. Certainly I did not want this dog-eared relic produced as an exhibit before some bleary Group Captain at my, or should I say Tangmere's, Court Martial. So, I casually walked in to Wing Ops, borrowed some matches and burnt the map, outside, out of sight.

Next, I went to ground in the MT section, to chat up the switchboard girl and put through private calls to my wife, my wife's mother and my parents. I told them what had happened, and why my Anniversary sortie was flown, that I would be under close arrest for at least a couple of days, and on no account were they to say anything to the Press if badgered by them. The station telephone operator, somewhat apologetically, said there was a small delay as they'd just had two "Lightning" priority calls, quite outside her long experience. "The balloon's possibly gone up" I said drily, without too much revelation to her. Then I went back to the squadron, climbing upstairs to tell first Boss Jones, who was with our OC Flying, Wg Cdr Ron Wood, and later the Station Commander, Gp Capt Basil Lock, what they knew already. By nature used to fast moving situations, they took it all coolly in their stride. Spike Jones seemed strangely relieved that Whitehall wasn't littered with leaflets!

At the end, it was left to me to suggest that perhaps I ought to be placed under arrest!

Hunter FGA9 (Credit: John Malley)

South Pacific

It's 0930 on an overcast morning in late October 1988, on an island in the South Pacific. I am sitting in the front seat of a Tornado, watching the palm trees swaying in the breeze and the surf breaking 200 yards away, waiting to takeoff on Runway 05 at Pago Pago, Western Samoa. We are number four in a trail of Tornados, Tristars and C130s, recovering from Australia to the UK via Pago Pago, Hawaii, Travis Air Force Base and Harrisburg. The first Tristar and two Tornados took off 30 minutes ago, and now our Tristar is rolling down the runway. As it takes off, we are cleared to follow in turn. Our departure instructions are to climb on runway heading to 1500 feet, turn left on to a heading of 360°, and continue climb to FL250. Both the radar and Tacan in our aircraft are unserviceable (Number 4 always gets the broken jet!), but I don't want to be left behind on my own, the Lame Duck plan from here would be rather challenging! No matter, the cloud is forecast to be only a couple of thousand feet thick. We line up for take-off, as a pair in echelon for a 30 second stream departure. All as per Standard Operating Procedures so far! As the leader rolls, I start the clock and look into the Head Up Display. It's then that I notice that the heading is indicating 150°, although we are lined up on Runway 05, so I question my navigator as to the state of the navigation kit. The answer is an unprintable expletive, followed by some nonsense about an Inertial Navigation System (INS) Heading Align which has gone wrong. The Tristar is now about 8 miles ahead and going away, and my leader has just got airborne. What do we do? The choice is recall them (most embarrassing), or press on. Yes, you've guessed it!

Airborne, clean up, 1500 feet, turn left onto 360° using the standby compass. At 4000ft, we break through the top of the cloud, and expect to see the leader 2 to 3 miles ahead. Nothing. I must be blind, look again, still nothing. On the auxiliary radio, I call the lead to confirm that he is heading 360°, but he has missed the left turn in the departure instructions and is still heading 050°. All of a sudden, the Pacific Ocean becomes very big and very empty. No matter, the 'Big White Bird' is only 12 miles ahead, and it's the only airliner in this part of the Ocean – I think how embarrassing it would be to follow a 747 inbound to New Zealand. After scanning the horizon, I think I see a glint of a Tristar in our one o'clock, and turn to join.

Once we join the tanker, there is a sigh of relief and, after a couple of minutes, my leader comes barrelling in from the East, as though nothing has happened. My navigator and I now start trying to remember Tornado ground school, and recall those boring lessons about the compass system, the Main Computer and the INS. He is insistent that I can select Direct Gyro, and we can slew the main compass to match the heading on the standby compass to give us a reasonably reliable direction indicator. However we have two problems. The standby compass was last calibrated with the gun camera dummy magazine (which is located near to it in the cockpit) in position, and the engineers have not fitted one. Therefore, the compass readings could be up to 40° out. The other problem is that, despite my navigator's protestations, I keep telling him that the Tornado does not have a Direct Gyro Mode in the compass system. He has come from Bucaneers and me from Phantoms, both of which did have Direct Gyro Mode.

Without a reliable compass, radar or Air to Air Tacan, it very quickly becomes blindingly obvious that we don't want to lose visual on the tanker at any cost. The weather is forecast to be OK for the first thousand miles, but then we will have to fly through a frontal system with embedded cumulo-nimbus. Also, at the mid-point of the route, the closest diversion is Fanning Island which is hundreds of miles to the east and, in our state, there is no way we would find it on our own.

Sure enough, after we have been airborne for about 2 hours, the cloud starts to thicken, and we move into close formation on the tanker's right wing. No problem, I have previously flown for hours in formation in Instrument Meteorological Conditions, and at least the Tornado is a lot easier to fly than the Phantom was. As we progress, the cloud thickens until I can hardly see the fuselage of the tanker. With the massive dihedral on the wings of the Tristar, the normal formation position becomes increasingly uncomfortable to hold and, as the fuselage disappears completely in cloud, I decide to drop low and under the Tristar's wing. Now I can easily formate on the engine and, with the Rolls Royce motif staring me in the face, the engine is about the size of a fighter aircraft, and it's quite a comfortable position for me to hold. It is, however, about this time that my navigator starts to complain that he doesn't really like being this close to such a large aircraft. I have yet to do the Cockpit Resource Management Foundation Course (which is all about getting the best from the people you're flying with), so my response is rather terse and lacking in any understanding - definitely not acceptable behaviour in today's Royal Air Force!

After 40 minutes, we get through the weather front without losing contact with the tanker, take on our last load of fuel, and continue towards Hickam AFB for an eventful arrival; but that's another story! After just over 5½ hours of flying, we taxi the 2½ miles across Hawaii Airport to the adjoining Hickam AFB, and shut down our aircraft. An hour later, while downing the first beer, I reflect on how a number of minor and unconnected incidents conspired to generate a few anxious moments.

I'll let you draw your own conclusions as to what you might have done in the same situation!

Tornado

Right Up Your Street

As a newly qualified C-130 Hercules captain in the early 1970s, I proudly (and somewhat smugly) headed off to the Middle East, in charge of my own crew for the very first time. I had picked a route that I knew well from my years as a co-pilot, which included Akrotiri in Cyprus, and Sharjah on the Arabian Gulf coast, so there was no problem getting the trip authorised. However I was, essentially, on probation, and not permitted to carry passengers until I had a few more command hours under my belt.

We duly staged through Cyprus without mishap and, the following day, approached Sharjah from the northwest, just as it was getting dark. The Australian air traffic controller on duty indicated that runway 35 was in use and, with no other aircraft airborne, offered us any type of approach that we cared to make. While the rest of the crew were quick to point out to me that a left-hand join downwind for a visual approach would minimise the time delay before a wind-down beer and dinner, I decided on another course of action. Back in the '70s, training hours were hard to come by and the 'steam driven' simulators we used bore little resemblance to the real thing. Consequently, each flying sector was supposed to be concluded with some sort of instrument approach as a means of keeping skill levels as high as possible. Mindful of this, and wanting to demonstrate my undoubted ability to my new crew, I elected to carry out a VOR[1] approach, and briefed the navigator to supply me with periodic drift and ground-speed readouts. I advised my Australian friend in the tower, who indicated that we should call again when on finals to land with undercarriage down, and set course for the beacon. The crew somewhat reluctantly joined in my attempt to over-fly the VOR and head south-ish outbound, but not without pointed comments from the loadmaster and flight engineer about bar closing times.

From my perspective, things appeared to be going well as I turned inbound, skilfully(?) interpreted the VOR needle to acquire the runway centreline, descended to minimum altitude, and searched the highly illuminated town of

[1] VOR - VHF Omni-directional Radio ranging is a type of radio navigation system for aircraft. A ground-based radio beacon transmits a signal which is picked up by the aircraft and the display in the cockpit allows the pilot to determine his angular position relative to the beacon.

Sharjah for the runway approach lights. After a while, my co-pilot broke his uncharacteristic silence by asking air traffic control to turn up the runway lighting, to which the Australian sarcastically responded that they were already on maximum, and that the runway was about 45 degrees to our right!

I had never been more grateful for the C-130's manoeuvrability in the landing configuration, as I 'hoiked' it onto something resembling finals, or for the darkness inside the cockpit that hid my blushes. We touched down slightly nearer the mid-point of the (fortunately rather long) runway than I would have liked, and taxied into dispersal in silence.

The post-flight debrief was short and to the point. Unsurprisingly, no-one bought my excuse that the illumination on the main street in Sharjah looked rather like runway lights and, when we finally made the bar, a very chastened new captain found himself somewhat out of pocket.

C-130 (Credit: John Malley)

The Currie Wot

The following story is taken from SILVERED WINGS, by kind permission of the author, Sir John Severne.

Each type had its own story to tell, but perhaps one of the most intriguing began in 1959, when Viv Bellamy, the Chief Flying Instructor at the Hampshire Aero Club at Eastleigh, invited me down to fly his Currie Wot. This little 22ft wingspan, single-seat, ultra-light biplane had been designed by Joe Currie in 1937, for engineering students to build as an exercise. Whilst Joe Currie was building the first aircraft, he got fed up with people asking what he was going to call it. 'Call it Wot you blooming well like,' he said and the name stuck. He built two aircraft, which he offered at a price of £250, but unfortunately they were both destroyed during an air raid in 1940 at Lympne.

In 1958, Viv persuaded Joe Currie to let him use the original drawings to build a third Wot at Eastleigh. Like the first aircraft, it was fitted with a 36 hp JAP J-99 horizontally opposed twin cylinder engine. After a short briefing from Viv, I flew this aircraft, but I can't say I particularly liked the engine, which appeared to have the odd 'flat spot'. However, the overall impression was one of sheer elation, as I climbed away from the airfield. I had been airborne for only a few minutes when I realized, to my horror, that I had failed to do up my straps – worse still, I must have forgotten to do the entire pre-take-off checks. There is no possible excuse for this, but my explanation at the time was that I must have been so overcome by the excitement of the occasion that I simply forgot. This dangerous omission was a salutary lesson, and I certainly learnt about flying from that.

This third Wot was subsequently fitted with a 62 hp Czechoslovakian Walter Mikron engine, and it then became known as the 'Hot Wot.' It was later fitted with floats, to become the 'Wet Wot', but this version was not successful, and the floats were soon removed. The original JAP engine was re-installed, and the aircraft sold to Harald Penrose, the Chief Test Pilot of the Westland Aircraft Company. He christened the aircraft 'Airymouse', and wrote an enchanting book with the same title about the joys of flying this delightful little aircraft.

Viv Bellamy then built a fourth Wot, with a Walter Mikron engine. This was subsequently fitted with a 60 hp Rover TP60/1 industrial gas-turbine engine, a similar engine to the one that powered the world's first gas-turbine-driven car. This aircraft was the world's first gas turbine powered biplane. The story goes that he had a problem finding a suitable propeller, because the first one he fitted had too coarse a pitch and taxying became somewhat interesting, due to the high idling speed of the engine, and the fact that the Wot had no brakes. He told me that he was discussing this in the club bar when he noticed a propeller hanging on the wall, and thought the fine pitch looked about right, so he took it down, found that it was out of balance, took a bit off the heavy end and – hey presto – it worked beautifully! He called this version the 'Wizz Wot.' I flew this remarkable aeroplane, and am proud of the fact that I have flown the world's first single-engined gas-turbine powered biplane, and also the Balliol Mk1 which was the world's first gas turbine single-engined aircraft. I flew the Wot, the Hot Wot and the Wizz Wot, but not the Wet Wot!

Currie Wot (Credit: Adrian Pingstone)

Kitten's Jump

RAF Tengah, in Singapore, had an airway running roughly East-West, a few miles to the South of the airfield. This meant that aircraft departing to the South would climb to an altitude below the base of the airway, level out, and then resume the climb once they had left the airway behind them. The only exception to this were the Lightning F6's of 74 Squadron, which had so much power with reheat engaged that they were able to climb above the top of the airway before they reached its lateral limit. Because 74's squadron badge featured a tiger, this was officially referred to as the 'Tiger's Leap Departure'.

The Victor SR2 was also an awesomely powerful aircraft in its own right; with similar engines to a VC10, but much less weight, its rate of climb was remarkable for such a large machine. Fed up with droning along for miles on a southerly departure until we were clear of the airway, we looked in the ODM (Operating Data Manual) to see if we could reach the ceiling of the airway before we approached its lateral limits. Imagine our delight when we discovered that, even at the very high ambient temperature of Singapore, and with 8 hours' fuel on board, we could do it!

Well, <u>we</u> were satisfied, but the Tengah Flying Order Book clearly stated that only Lightnings were permitted to carry out a Tiger's Leap Departure. So, armed with the Victor SR2 ODM, we went to see OC Operations Wing, and asked if we might be allowed to carry out the procedure. An experienced Qualified Flying Instructor, he studied the graphs, examined the limitations, and decided that he would allow us to attempt the departure, albeit with certain caveats that we were happy to accept. Before we left, he telephoned air traffic control to advise them of our special dispensation but, for some reason, he didn't seem to think that 74 needed to know.

The next morning, we were on the taxiway behind a pair of 74's F6s, with another pair behind us in turn – were they not allowed out on their own? The first pair requested a Tiger's Leap, were duly cleared, and disappeared impressively into a clear blue sky. We then requested line-up for a Tiger's Leap departure, and you could almost hear the clunk of jaws dropping in the F6s behind us when it was granted without question!

We got to Flight Level 290, before the two Lightnings that had taken off just after us went past as if we were going backwards; but we still made it over the top of the airway with several miles to spare. In so doing, we became, as far as I know, the only aircraft without reheat to successfully carry out a Tiger's Leap Departure.

That evening, after completing a 7-hour photo reconnaissance sortie, we went into the downstairs bar in the Tengah Officers' Mess, where 74 Squadron pilots were holding court in their tiger skin patterned shirts. We strolled up to the bar, ordered 5 bottles of Tiger beer, and asked what all the fuss was about this 'Kitten's Jump' rubbish.

Well, they threw us out of the window but, after we had dusted ourselves down and gone back in again, they bought us beer all night – a great bunch of blokes really!

Lightning F6

PC? What's That Then?

At the beginning of the Seventies, 'PC' still stood for 'Police Constable'. Add to that a bucketful of immaturity and there lies the basis for an embarrassing tale – or two actually!

<u>Bloop 1</u>
At that time, amongst garrulous junior aircrew, the word 'spastic' was simply a derisory term applied to anyone who did not come up to some expectation or other; it was never considered as a potential insult to the disabled.

In my second year as a first-tour Jet Provost QFI[1] at RAF Leeming, I applied for, and got, the job of commentator for the Gemini aerobatic pair. There was a full season of shows, and sometimes I would fly the spare and sometimes I'd fly with the Team 'Boss', who flew a solo display and was also the official Team Manager.

On a particular occasion, at an air show in the West Country, I was flying with aforementioned 'Boss', who had completed his display and vanished somewhere into the crowd. I headed for Air Traffic Control to do my stuff for Gemini. The day was sunny, with a clear blue sky and about 20 knots of wind down the runway. On such occasions, I would explain to the assembled crowd that the supposedly synchronised manoeuvres at opposite ends of the runway had to be intentionally slightly <u>out</u> of 'sync', so that the subsequent opposition manoeuvres remained at crowd-centre, and the whole show did not slowly disappear downwind.

I'm sure that I'm not the only person who has occasional mental blockages, but some times are worse than others. So it was here! As the boys pulled up for their (nearly) synchronised stall-turns, the scripted words vanished from my pea-like brain, and what came out over the Tannoy system was "Blah blah blah.....you'll notice that the stall-turns are not quite together, this is not because J*** and D*** are (pause/struggle) <u>spastic</u> but because blah blah blah....".

Aaaarghh!

Even in those days, I could recognise when things weren't going too well.

---

[1] QFI – Qualified Flying Instructor

The immediate solution was obviously to vanish from the local area (preferably forever), and I contemplated this as I passed through the 'Special Enclosure for the Disabled' on my high-speed-straight-line route to the display aircraft park, where I crawled into the trusty Jet Provost Mk5 and crouched low, in the hope of finding sanctuary. I mention the 'Mk5' bit to make the point that it was the one with the large clear canopy. Did I also mention that it was a very hot day?

About two sweltering, sweat-soaked hours later, the aforementioned canopy motored open and 'Sir' appeared.

"Ah, Peter" he said, "People have been looking for you".

Strangely there were no repercussions from that one. I wish I could say the same for its successor.

<u>Bloop 2</u>

Towards the end of the season came the 23 Group (Training Command) Air Show, at RAF Topcliffe on a Saturday. By that time, I had become sufficiently proficient at the commentary not to have fouled up again, but I never really enjoyed doing it.

All at once, an old 'mate' appeared. He had done the Gemini commentary two years before me, prior to actually joining the Team for the season before the current pair of intrepid aviators. Aforementioned 'mate' asked if the show was more-or-less the same, and offered to do the commentary for me. Stupidly, I accepted.

During his old commentary, and only at air shows well away from any RAF 'Heavies', he used a line which he thought amusing. To my horror, he used it again here, at Topcliffe - in front of everybody who was anybody in the RAF Training organisation!

He said:

"Gemini is named after the Heavenly Twins, Castor and Pollux. They fly in yellow flying suits, and are known as Golden Castor and Golden Pollux".

Time to flee again!! This time by car, back to RAF Leeming where I knew <u>plenty</u> of places to hide.

By late afternoon on the following Monday, there had still been no retribution. Fortunately, I had already flown three trips by that time, and so had been largely out of the line of fire. It was another warm evening, and I was sitting in the flowerbed (one did in those days) waiting to brief trip no. 4, when I espied the familiar figure of OC Ops detach itself from the base of ATC and set off in my direction. Having scrambled out from amongst the rose bushes, and established sufficient decorum to form a reception committee, I threw a very smart salute at him and tried, unsuccessfully, to smile.

"Peter" he said "You have incurred my displeasure. I have a signal here from AOC 23 Group. It is very short, I will read it to you. It says, The expression 'Golden Pollux' is to be removed from the Gemini commentary ".

He turned and left, and never mentioned it again, although neither did he speak to me for several weeks - just looked.

I still break out in a cold sweat.

Jet Provost Mk5

Venom Fires

The following story is taken from SILVERED WINGS, by kind permission of the author, Sir John Severne.

We enjoyed flying the Venom on 98 Squadron at Fassberg, but it did have its problems when it first came into service in 1953, and these are well documented in David Watkins' excellent book Venom. He tells of how Sam D'Arcy of 14 Squadron ejected in March 1954, when a wing broke off as he was pulling out of a practice dive-bombing attack on the Fassberg range. He was so low when he ejected that his parachute had only just deployed as he hit the ground. I met him in the bar very shortly after the incident – his face was cut and bruised, because there was no time for him to jettison the canopy before ejection. He therefore had to eject through it – hence the battering on his face. Luckily his injuries were superficial, and he was enjoying his well-deserved drink. There had been several previous accidents when the wings failed and, until the aircraft were modified, they had red bands painted on the wings, to remind pilots to limit the g forces. We also had a number of inexplicable fires in the air, and several pilots were killed when attempting forced landings, because the fires had burnt through the elevator control cables. Pilots were therefore given strict orders to eject if they had a fire, and not to attempt a forced landing, even if the fire appeared to be out.

In October 1954, one of the pilots on my flight, George Schofield, was killed when he attempted to land after a fire. Four days later, on 1 November, in beautiful weather, I was at the top of a loop at 10,000ft directly over Fassberg, when I decided to hold the aircraft inverted for a few moments before rolling level. Whilst still inverted, there was a bang, the fire warning light came on and the cockpit filled with smoke. After completing the fire drill, which obviously included shutting down the engine, I prepared myself for a forced landing on the airfield, which I could see clearly beneath me. I knew I was under orders to eject, but I was very conscious of George's accident, and I was overcome by a conviction that this had happened to me, his flight commander, so that the riddle of the fires could be solved. I decided to land wheels up, on the grass by the side of the runway, so that I would be able to get out of the aircraft quickly if needs be. We had all regularly practised forced landings and, with height to spare and perfect weather, I had no difficulty in positioning myself to land alongside the runway in use. I had never landed wheels up before, and was surprised how gentle it was. The moment I came to a halt the fire engines were alongside and, since there was no obvious sign of the fire still burning, I prevented the fire crews from smothering the engine in foam, in case this destroyed valuable evidence.

The first thing I did when I got back to our hangar was to brief the other pilots in the crew room what had happened, and to emphasize that under no circumstances were they to attempt to land after a fire – they <u>must</u> eject. Shortly after that, the Wing Commander Flying entered the crew room, and gave me a severe ticking off, and then added, 'But well done!' It appeared that he had also been airborne at the time, and heard what was happening over the R/T. He knew he should have ordered me to eject, but I gather he sensed what I was trying to do and kept quiet. The Board of Inquiry thought the fact that the fire started whilst I was inverted might be significant, so they rigged up a complete Venom fuel system upside down in a hangar, and they did indeed solve the problem. I have to admit that, for the first few sorties after that incident, my eyes tended to concentrate on the fire warning light, and it took me a month or so before I was able to relax in the cockpit. For this incident, I was subsequently awarded the Air Force Cross.

Venoms were not the only aircraft that tended to catch fire. The Americans were flying F84 Thunderstreaks in their zone to the south, and the story was around that, if these aircraft caught fire, you had only four seconds in which to eject before the whole lot exploded. One of the aircraft in a formation caught fire, and one of the other pilots shouted on the R/T, 'Hank, you're on fire', whereupon four Hanks throughout the zone ejected! I don't know how true the story was, but it was often used as an example of why strict R/T discipline is essential. If the pilot's callsign had been used rather than his first name, three aircraft would have been saved.

Stuck For Words

It was in 1973, during my second tour as a Qualified Flying Instructor on the Vulcan Operational Conversion Unit at RAF Scampton. I had been around long enough to see most of the mistakes that students made when handling the Vulcan with asymmetric power applied, and managed to survive the not infrequent attacks made on my physical well-being. This incident occurred when conducting the introduction to asymmetric flying for a 'fighter pilot' who was joining the Vulcan force. The sortie profile was to depart Scampton on a navigation exercise which would terminate at Flamborough Head, at which point I would start to pass on my expertise in flying the Vulcan under asymmetric power.

Well clear of the land at Flamborough Head I started the patter; 150knots at 2,000feet, pitch up to 13° as full power is selected on Numbers 1 and 2 engines with Numbers 3 and 4 at idle. Observe that, as the speed slowly reduces, the rudder must be increased to stop the aircraft yawing. As full rudder is reached, the student is directed to look outside and asked to advise you when he sees the nose start to yaw to the right. As the aircraft starts to yaw, I draw his attention to the speed and then, without pause for breath, continue with teaching the recovery drill of lowering the nose (so it is just below the horizon) and slightly reducing power on the two live engines, in one synchronised movement. Then, with the combination of a slightly nose low attitude and power set somewhere close to 90% RPM, the aircraft starts to accelerate and full rudder control is restored. The student then takes the controls to note the stick and rudder deflection, and to feel the stick force required to hold the aircraft in that position. Exercise completed, we lower the nose a little more to accelerate slowly to 150 knots, as the aircraft sinks back down towards 2,000 feet.

"Your turn Bloggs (generic name for all student pilots!)" and, with a little reminder here and there, he began to repeat this complex handling exercise; 150 knots, two engines to full power, nose up, speed slowly reducing towards our minimum asymmetric control speed. I started to relax slightly, this boy obviously had everything under control. Just as the aircraft started to yaw the student initiated a recovery procedure - unfortunately, not the one previously demonstrated. Stick back (wrong!!).......in a flash I seized the controls but it was too late.

The Vulcan rapidly lost speed, yawed instantly to the right through 90° and then flipped upside down. I do not know why, but I did notice that our maximum height was 3,200 feet above the water, she was yawing uncontrollably in an inverted position, and I also noted that I was discussing the student's heritage in an ancient language with which I was only vaguely familiar. I aligned all throttles at a low setting, to reduce the yawing due to asymmetric power and, now going vertically down, I fought to stop the aircraft oscillating rapidly from side to side. Time appeared to stand still as I did, and then the reason for my difficulty came to me. The rudder motor took 1¾ seconds to move the rudder from fully left to fully right. By the time this had happened, the aircraft's natural stability had already started to have a righting effect, but this was suddenly being given a destabilising shove by the rudder, and consequently we were mimicking the pendulum of an old clock. The solution was to select a small rudder deflection to stabilise the yaw, and directional control was recovered rapidly. However we were still going vertically downwards!

The sea seemed awfully close, but I remember thinking that I did have enough height to recover to level flight before hitting the water. During the pull out, I regained the capacity to check around the cockpit to make sure every aircraft system was still functioning correctly, and noticed the student. His eyes were like saucers, his hands were grasped firmly on the ejection seat handle between his legs, and his mouth was so wide open that his chin was resting on top of his hands. I remember my comforting statement, "You ******* idiot, you've got four guys down the back." Note: Rear crew members in V-bombers did not have ejection seats.

We eased out of the dive, and I noticed my minimum height during recovery was 1500 feet. I looked at the student, white-faced and, for the first time in his life, completely speechless.

Meeting in the bar, later that evening after the formal sortie debrief, the staff navigator, who had been in the rear-crew compartment during the sortie, took me to one side, chastised me for being hard on the student and remarked that he had never heard me use such language. He insisted that my tone would have destroyed the student's confidence, and that I apologise to him immediately or he would report me to the Boss. I duly summoned the miscreant from a gathering of other students on the course, and explained to him the concerns of the staff navigator. I then added, curtly, that I meant every word and that he should get out of my sight! The staff navigator looked somewhat perplexed until I explained the full implications of what had happened, whereupon there followed a further one-sided debrief between him and the luckless student!

In the end, at least some good came out of it - we witnessed a fighter pilot stuck for words twice in the same day!

Vulcan

Some People Never Learn

Variety is the spice of life, it is said, and certainly this was true for those Jaguar pilots who got to swop the grey and dank UK winter, normally spent schnee-bling from letterbox[1] to letterbox in the UK low flying system, for a week or two in Gibraltar. OK, Gib in January ain't tropical, but it was pleasant enough. The 2 or 3 aircraft stationed down there were ostensibly the Commander's recce as-set. However, being an aircraft which relies heavily on the curvature of the earth to get airborne, the Gib runway is a bit of a challenge for a Jag, so we had to fly without external tanks. This meant that, when recce tasking was not required, we were neatly positioned for a spot of doggers[2].

On this particular morning, however, we were tasked for recce, and not just any recce. Word had it that Kirov, the newest, vastest and nastiest thing in the Soviet naval inventory was headed for the Straits, en route to the Black Sea, her first foray away from the Northern Fleet. She was accompanied by Udaloy, a new anti-submarine destroyer. The wacky scheme hatched up by me and my trusty wingy – I'll call him Tom, mostly because that was his name - was to fly at high level outbound, posing as innocent airliners, and then drop down to low level to the west of the ships. This was approved by the Gib staff, all went to plan, and we acquired the ships visually, in long line astern, Kirov leading.

The crew of Udaloy must have been on a day off, because there was no indication that they had seen us as we sneaked in behind them in a fairly tight formation. However, when we split to go either side of Udaloy, and became vis-ible to Kirov, everything changed. Every light on the Radar Warning Receiver illuminated, it emitted some whirring and fizzing sounds, and appeared to be on the verge of melting. We had briefed to be at slow speed for some piccies, and this approach was going swimmingly until my aircraft flew through the lee

---

[1] Schneebling is the time-honoured art of wandering more or less down a planned low-level route in marginal – or, let's face it, somewhat below marginal - weather, hoping not to have to pull up. A letterbox - or potential barrier to effective schneebling - is a small gap between a ridge and the cloud-base, which always looks big enough until one is committed to it, and almost invariably turns out not to be.

[2] Air Combat

of the Kirov's massive superstructure, and all the Bernouillis[3] that had, until that point, been keeping my wing working deserted me en masse, to be replaced by some nasty turbulence with a severe absence of lift. As my little jet sogged closer to the wave-tops, it occurred to me that ditching Her Majesty's aircraft alongside the pride of the Soviet fleet was probably going to get my name up in lights, whether I survived the experience or not. Judicious use of burner at that point was probably a waste of time, but it made me feel better, and I slowly clawed back some airspeed and climbed away. Nobody shot at us – they were probably curled up laughing.

Anyway, I was nothing if not thick-skinned and, on the return to base, we had arranged to give a small send-off to the departing Gib guard-ship – HMS Zulu, my logbook informs me – which was outbound for Blighty. We didn't have much fuel, so it would have to be a straight pass, low and fast down either side, front to back. Normally I would have been wary of birds off the back of a boat, but the RN did not sling 'gash' over the rail, unlike a trawler. One large and clearly ignorant gull, however, had not read the script and, in a heartbeat, had impacted just forward of the canopy and spread itself, thinly but effectively, in a sort of gull soup, over the entire front part of the canopy, reducing the forward visibility to nil.

A quick check of the engine instruments satisfied me that I didn't have any problem in that area. Tom had seen the impact and my pull-up, so joined without being asked. Tangier was the diversion, it was closer than Gibraltar, and that's where I should have gone. By the time my few remaining brain cells had evaluated the pros and cons, however, we were closer to the Rock, and I had persuaded myself that this was the best option. Unsurprisingly, yet again on this particular sortie, I had failed to think it through properly. Aficionados of Gibraltar will know that a stiff, south-westerly breeze creates a lot of turbulence off the Rock on the approach to the westerly runway; add to that the sensitivities at that time over Spanish airspace, which required a tight final turn, and the lack of forward visibility which required a pairs approach, and it can readily be deduced – with more clarity than I was able to summon until the die was cast – that this

---

[1] Daniel Bernouilli was the eminent scientist whose principle of fluid dynamics governs the pressure differential between the lower and upper surfaces of an aerofoil section and, therefore, results in 'lift' - a good thing.

was going to be an entertaining landing. Ultimately, thanks to an outstanding piece of leading by Tom, it proved less heart-stopping than it might have been. Not only did he dump me at the right spot, on the centreline and on landing speed but, having overshot as my wheels hit the deck, he was even able to offer me some advice during the landing roll as to where the centreline might be.

In sum then, by dint of some eye-watering folly, I had managed to inject into this relatively short sortie some spectacular lapses of airmanship, with the result that it had contained more excitement than I would normally like to pack into an entire tour. My trusty jet survived, battered but uncowed, more in spite of me than because of me; my trusty wingy survived to consume copious 'green bottles' by way of thanks. Little did I suspect at the time that that particular year was going to get even more exciting for me; but that, as they say, is another story.

Jaguar

Contact Breakers

In October 1966, I was the Signaller in an RAF Britannia crew sent to the United States Peterson Air Force Base, near Colorado Springs in the middle of the State of Colorado, to collect an Army detachment for return to the UK. As much of the State of Colorado is desert, I would guess that they had been on exercise there. We were told that there would be a ceremonial send-off, so we arrived early at the aircraft for the departure. Having loaded all of the kitbags, we were in our seats waiting when we heard the sounds of a military band; shortly afterwards the band hove into view. With flags and standard flying, the band looked resplendent in their enhanced uniforms and wearing shiny chromed helmets. They were followed by the British Army contingent, in columns of three in their not so flamboyant uniforms, and they in turn were followed by a US Army contingent in uniforms not quite as gaudy as the band. But they were all very smart, and in step – an impressive sight.

As the band passed by the left (door) side of our aircraft, the parade came to a halt. The band then about turned; the British Army contingent turned to the left to face away from us, with their officer marching to be in the centre front, and the US Army contingent performed a smart marching manoeuvre to end up two lines deep, facing the British Army contingent, and evenly spaced either side of a dais, which was mounted by a US Army officer. Speeches were made, gifts presented, salutes exchanged, hands shaken, and then the band started up again as the British Army contingent turned to peel off smartly in columns, climbed the entrance steps and entered the aircraft.

When they were all aboard, seated and doors closed, and with the band still playing and the US Army contingent remaining in place, we went through the pre-start checks. `Start No 1 Engine' intoned the Navigator, reading the check list; the Captain checked around, looked up and pressed the overhead master start button – and nothing happened. A repeat gave the same result. "Must be the contact breaker", said the Flight Engineer, "it's on the roof of the rear freight compartment, would you like me to try and fix it?" "OK" said the Captain. So the doors were opened, the troops disgorged into their three ranks (but at ease), and throughout the band continued to play. The rear freight bay door was opened and kit bags removed, so that the Flight Engineer could get to the offending contact breaker. He crawled in and disappeared into the rear freight bay, and did whatever engineers would do to try and fix an errant contact breaker (a few hefty belts I would imagine). Kit bags were replaced, more salutes, the Brits re-boarded the aircraft to the strains of the band as before, all seated and doors closed, pre-start checks again, button pressed – and again nothing happened.

At this point, the Officer in Charge of the British team came into the cockpit with a worried look on his face (he had been watching proceedings through the door). With an imploring tone in his voice he pleaded, "Captain, you must do something, we just can't go through that again." The Captain sort of shrugged his shoulders and raised an eyebrow, looking at the Flight Engineer. "What do you think Eng?" The Eng reached across to select one of his manuals from the rack behind the pilots seat, thumbed through to an appropriate page which gave distances and layout of aircraft components, studied it for a while, then left his seat and paced down the centre aisle of the aircraft until he came abeam an unsuspecting and very large soldier; all passenger seats in RAF aircraft faced aft, so none of the soldier passengers had seen what had been going on.

Having estimated that the offending contact breaker was directly under this seat position, the Eng tapped the soldier on the shoulder and told him to stand up and to face forwards so that he could see the Engineer through the cockpit entrance door; when he saw the Engineer give a smart wave down with his hand, he was to jump as hard as he could. Now I could see all of this, looking aft through the cockpit door, as my Signaller's position alongside the door also faced aft. The soldier looked rather nonplussed, not sure whether he was being `had on'. As the Engineer came forward again, there was a little jeering from his mates, and he did look rather sheepish, but he had been given an instruction by an officer, and soldiers, above all else, are trained to do whatever an officer instructs them to do, so he waited. Pre-start checks again from the Navigator; "Start No 1 Engine"; the Captain looked up, the Engineer turned and waved his arm down, the soldier jumped, the Captain pressed the button – and No 1 engine burst into life. Watching the soldier, I am sure his height visibly increased and his shoulders went back a little. The same start procedure was followed for the remaining three engines, the soldier's chest expanding a little more each time, and his jump increasingly violent. And so, with engines running and checks complete, we taxied away for take-off, with the band still playing and much waving from the Americans.

I am sure that somewhere, today, there is an ex-soldier who takes great pride in telling his grandchildren how he was responsible, many years ago, for starting the engines of one of the RAF's Britannia aircraft.

Bristol Britannia (Credit: Adrian Pingstone)

A Blob Of Grease

On 6 July 1979, a Royal Air Force Hawker Hunter aircraft crashed on the town of Tintagel in Cornwall. I was the pilot of that aircraft, and this is my account of what happened.

In 1979, I was on 79 Squadron, as an instructor in the Tactical Weapons Unit at RAF Brawdy in south-west Wales, flying both the Hunter and the Hawk. The Hawk had only recently entered service and, while it was a nice enough aircraft, it came nowhere near the Hunter in terms of firepower and the sheer joy of flying. However, all the pilots were aware that it put the Hunter well into the shade in terms of reliability and safety.

In my opinion, the Hunter remains one of the greatest aircraft ever built - a sensory aircraft, full of emotive sounds and vibrations (you could hear and feel the engine) and haunting smells, especially when firing the guns. The handling was both unusual and magical, an interesting balance between a short stroke aileron and long stroke elevator that gave superb lateral responsiveness, coupled with stable and very progressive pitch control. Quirky systems, a fuel system that had a 'sense of humour', flaps that almost spoke to you in combat, and an elevator control system that could kill you at high Mach number. There were four magnificent, internally mounted, 30mm Aden cannons that were always available to you, no matter what other weapons load was carried, and they were supported by a gyro gunsight based firmly on a World War 2 design. A gunsight, it has to be said, that required very high levels of imagination, skill and respect to determine how to get good air-to-ground results from a device designed for air-to-air use. The aircraft was also a potent force, being fast and electronically silent because the gun-sight radar had long since been removed, and there was no radar altimeter or any other equipment on board that could be electronically detected. Finally, the maximum speed of 610 knots in level flight at sea level was not matched by many other aircraft at the time.

And so it was that I came to be flying airframe number XG 197, a Hunter Mark 6a, on 6 July 1979. The aircraft had flown less than four hours since an engine change, and I had done all those hours, including the engine air test and some aggressive low level flying in Scotland, the latter in company with some of my students, who were coming to the end of their Weapons Instructor course, so the engine had been operated at full stretch without any problems. Oh, and the night before its final flight, the ejection seat was replaced because the one installed was time expired; the newness of the seat harness was to have significant consequences a few hours later.

I was assigned the lead of a four aircraft formation (call-sign Bronze) for a low level sortie, mainly in Devon and involving simulated attacks on various targets. Fighter opposition was to be provided by Hawk aircraft, also from Brawdy. A key part of the exercise was the preparation of the aircraft in a state of operational readiness, and this involved loading two guns with live (high explosive) ammunition, and the other two with practice (inert) rounds. Each gun was primed with a round in its breech, as was normal, and the electrical firing circuit was disconnected to ensure that the guns were incapable of being fired.

The sortie did not start well when two of my aircraft went unserviceable before take-off, though one was fixed and joined up later, when we were already in Devon. On the run in to the second target, we were intercepted by a pair of Hawks, which we countered before attacking the target and then re-engaging them. Turning in behind one of the Hawks at a range of about a mile, I coasted out about 5 miles north of Tintagel and began to set myself up for an easy burst of well -tracked gunsight film. Once over the sea, I descended to very low level and accelerated to around 600 knots to close on the Hawk, which was maintaining about 450 knots.

As I closed to 800 yards range, I gently closed the throttle, aiming to run through an ideal firing bracket between 400 and 300 yards. With speed dropping towards 525 knots, I reapplied power to stabilize my closure rate, and immediately the engine surged with three very loud thuds that shook the whole aircraft. I had experienced engine surges before, but this was different, and a glance at the engine instruments showed a serious mismatch between RPM, temperature and throttle position. The target was now perfectly positioned in the gunsight, so I recorded a short burst on the gun-sight film for posterity's sake, jettisoned the external 230 gallon fuel tanks using the Emergency Jettison, started a gentle climbing turn towards RAF St Mawgan, and switched the radio to emergency. With the throttle left fully open, the engine RPM continued to reduce as I converted excess speed to height and topped out at 3500 feet and 180 knots, which is the best glide speed for the Hunter. A clean Hunter at 180 knots will glide 2 nautical miles per 1000 feet, so I had a range of 7 miles and a remaining flight time of a little over 2 minutes. I knew that St Mawgan was my nearest suitable airfield; however, it was at least 20 miles away!

At exactly the same time as my initial engine problem occurred, Bronze 3 of my formation transmitted a PAN (aircraft with urgent problem) call on 243.0 MHz, the International Distress Frequency, after suffering a failure of both his fuel booster pumps. He elected to divert to St Mawgan, under the control of Drayton Centre, the agency that handles aircraft in distress. I was about 3 miles northeast of Bronze 3 when I made a MAYDAY (aircraft in distress) call to announce my engine failure, and confusion then reigned, because two aircraft in the same piece of sky with almost identical callsigns wanted to go to St Mawgan. To Drayton, it was obvious that the pilot who had made the PAN call had upgraded his emergency to MAYDAY, and consequently I simply didn't exist! Taking into account the likely link between fuel and engine, the confusion was very understandable. However, back in my cockpit there was little time or enthusiasm to sort out the confusion; I still had my problem with the engine.

By this time, the engine RPM had decayed to 6100, and I knew I could maintain level flight with 6000, so getting to St Mawgan seemed like a real possibility. The coast was just visible to my left through the haze as I headed south, but the RPM slowly continued to reduce, and moving the throttle made no difference. It was peaceful in the cockpit with the engine running at low speed, and I still had full hydraulic and electrical services, so what had caused the problem? Why had the engine surged? What had caused the loss of throttle control? What options did I have for increasing power, even by a small amount? There was clearly nothing wrong with the Rolls Royce Avon engine or the airframe, so it had to be the low pressure side of the fuel system, didn't it? I deselected the Top Temperature Control (which governed the engine), but that had no effect, and then I remembered that the relight system gave a separate 20 second burst of fuel, even if the engine was already running, so I tried that. Hitting the relight button immediately increased the RPM from 5950 to 6050, so that was the answer - I would limp home using the relight system to periodically boost the engine!

Unfortunately, my theory failed as it quickly became apparent that my first burst of power was also to be my last, and the engine RPM continued its gradual reduction towards 5000. I was now down to flight idle RPM, and my rate of descent was increasing as I passed 1500 feet with land coming up on my port side. I was already below the prudent minimum ejection height for the ancient seat fitted to the Hunter, but as I passed 1250 feet Drayton finally worked out that they were dealing with two aircraft! By this time, the emergency radio was getting busy, thanks to a number of interested parties joining in, so I elected to keep quiet. However, as I passed 1000 feet, I heard the RAF Chivenor rescue helicopter come on frequency as it was getting airborne, which was comforting as I was fast running out of options.

800 feet – The surface of the sea is now very clear but land is too close. I gently roll into a right turn, with Tintagel Head in front of me. I know I should have ejected by now.

600 feet – I continue my turn until Tintagel Head is about 40 degrees left of the nose.

400 feet – I am very conscious that I have stupidly allowed myself to run out of height. I confess that I have probably been caught out by the rapid increase in my rate of descent as the engine RPM reduced, and I am most reluctant to admit that such a fine aircraft is giving up on me.

300 feet – I stretch the glide to 160 knots to briefly kill the descent rate, trim a little nose up so that I can release the controls without any risk of a sudden nose down movement, fix myself squarely in the seat, grasp the bottom ejection handle with both hands, and pull as hard as I can.

The canopy jettison gun fires instantaneously, the canopy is gone, followed by my map, and all the muck and dust of ages is sucked into the cockpit space. I know the seat will fire one second after the canopy goes… but it doesn't, and there is a loud ticking in my left ear from the time delay unit on the seat. I instinctively start to turn my head towards it, just as a sickening, crushing explosion strikes pain into the middle of my back, followed by an even louder crack as my neck is whipped like a rope, throwing my head into my knees. The seat has fired after what seemed an interminable second.

Suddenly, every tumbling and rotating sense is saturated, before I am aware of a comforting airblast. The stabilising drogue has fired, and the seat is separating, leaving me in total peace and silence, apart from the flapping of my flying suit. I am flying feet first over the sea, with my aircraft just a little in front and about 100 feet below me. It seems to be maintaining height and turning very slightly left.

I am abruptly jolted back to reality by the parachute snapping open. Time to do the pre-landing drills; get rid of the oxygen mask to avoid breathing in sea water, inflate my life jacket, lower the dinghy pack by releasing the side clips, and rotate the harness release box in preparation for squeezing it as I impact the water. Every action practiced and rehearsed countless times, but never with only one arm functioning – for some reason my right shoulder is immobile. My height is now too low to do much apart from dump the mask and inflate the jacket just before touchdown. I can't reach the dinghy clips, and the harness release box refuses to rotate.

A sudden rush of sea water full of bubbles, and I am aware of rising back to the surface, but seem unable to break through into fresh air. I'm floating on my back, with my life jacket inflated, but my head is down because the dinghy pack is still firmly attached to my backside. No matter how hard I try, I simply cannot operate the harness release box with one hand, and the straps on the recently installed ejection seat assembly are so tight and so inflexible that nothing will move. There is a growing pain in my back and a lack of response from my legs, so I let go of the release box, relax… and float free of the harness to break the surface just in time. I believe that Houdini used this escape trick by design, but mine was purely involuntary!

I quickly inflate the life raft, haul myself on board and deploy the Search And Rescue Beacon Equipment (SARBE), which will allow the helicopter to locate me. My aircraft has disappeared, and I regret not seeing it hit the sea. I feel heavy, cold, immobile and in pain but, within a few minutes, I'm looking up at a row of faces peering down at me. It 's The Lady Jane from Boscastle, and expert hands quickly lift me carefully onto the deck. The thud of rotors overhead announces the arrival of the helicopter, and I am soon winched on board and en route to the Royal Naval Hospital at Plymouth, via St Mawgan to collect a doctor. When we arrive, there are journalists waiting to greet us; what's going on?

It was in the examination room that I heard the shocking news that my aircraft had crashed on Tintagel and, to make it worse, there were rumours of casualties but no other details. Suddenly my own problems seemed much less important. So began a long recovery period for me, with expert attention at various military hospitals, but the effects of multiple and serious crush fractures to vertebrae, and whiplash injuries to the neck, do not ever go away. One adapts to a new degree of facility, and unexpected opportunities and challenges open up.

So what made my aircraft turn away from the open area of sea that I had so carefully selected, and why was it able to make landfall at all? Firstly, I confess that I was closer to the coast than I had intended; I was trying to get to St Mawgan, and I knew that every mile counted, so initially the shortest route was more important than the location. Also, I was stuck in a layer of haze above 1000 feet and, with my attention on other things, I had not taken early enough action to steer away from the coast. However, the real problem was the aircraft. XG197 was simply one of the best airframes we had, because it was still straight! Most Hunters had become bananas in their old age, and would generally roll or yaw at low speed and high angles of attack. XG197 did not and, as a result, it was a delight to fly in air combat, because it could be controlled at very low speeds.

Prior to ejection, I had trimmed the aircraft slightly nose up and, when I ejected, the reduction in weight as the seat and I left would have caused the nose to rise further still. It is also possible that the engine RPM increased slightly. In addition, I had jettisoned all the wing stores, and so the airframe was clean and the aircraft was light. Very little good performance data existed for a Hunter in that state, but everyone knew that it flew exceptionally well when clean. I believe that, as the nose came up and the speed bled away, the aircraft gracefully slipped into a gently climbing left turn, probably at about 140 knots, turned left through 60 to 70 degrees, dropped its nose as the speed fell away below about 125 knots, slowly re-gained some speed, and rolled back to nearly wings level. By contrast a 'normal' bent Hunter would have departed from steady flight during that slow speed turn, and almost certainly have ended up in the sea.

XG197 hit the ground from a shallow descent, in a gentle left turn with the engine still running, and the subsequent investigation proved that the RPM at impact was less than 6100. The airbrake and outer section of the left wing were torn off on impact, but there was sufficient energy left for the rest of the aircraft to bounce and tear its way a little over 100 yards up to the houses, shedding other parts as it went. The fuselage came to rest between two houses, and the nose section, including the cockpit and gun-pack, broke away and ended up in the main street.

So what caused this event that touched several other people and totally changed my way of life? Now for the technical bit…..

Attached to the side of a jet engine is the Fuel Control Unit (FCU), which controls the flow of fuel to the engine at a rate that is mainly dependent on throttle position, height and speed. Two of the vital parameters that are used to control the FCU are engine intake pressure (known as P1), and engine compressor pressure (known as P2). These two values are taken from small air bleeds on the engine casing, and are fed to the Acceleration Control Unit (ACU) section of the FCU via small diameter pipes. The two bleed pipes cross in a P1/P2 metering orifice, and the highest pressure determines which side of a diaphragm is pressurized which, in turn, controls the initial position of the FCU. More importantly, with reference to this incident, the pipes need to be leak free and clean, and consequently, where joints are required, dry paper gaskets are used.

The engine was a newly reconditioned unit and, when it had been ground run at the manufacturer's factory, the P2 bleed had leaked where it attached to the engine casing. This necessitated a gasket change on a joint with restricted access, and this was further compounded by the engine being mounted in a cradle for ground running. A tried and trusted technique was to use a small blob of grease to hold a paper gasket in place while the bolts were positioned, but this was specifically forbidden on P1 and P2 pipes! In the event, the fault was rectified and the engine re-issued to the RAF. After 3 hours and 40 minutes of subsequent flight time, a small blob of grease no bigger than a match head, and now hardened by heat, broke free from the P2 gasket when I applied power at 525 knots. It lodged in the P1/P2 metering orifice of the ACU, reduced the P2 pressure to zero, and caused the engine to surge when the fuel flow became unstable. I was right to think that it was an unusual surge, because the FCU now believed that the aircraft was parked on the ground with the engine shut down, rather than proceeding at 500 knots. It also meant that the engine would no longer respond to throttle inputs.

The FCU was one of the few parts that were still undamaged by the crash. It was removed from the wreckage, bench tested, and gave exactly the fuel flow rate I had reported. It was then stripped down, and the type of grease that had been found blocking the orifice was also discovered on the P2 paper gasket - the very same gasket that had been replaced before the engine was returned from the manufacturer. Needless to say, once the blob of grease had been removed and the FCU tested again, it was fully serviceable. However, no explanation was ever offered for its presence, and nobody ever admitted any involvement.

Post Script

Finally, my heartfelt apologies to the people of Tintagel for when I inadvertently came your way. It remains a great blessing that the wreckage did not burn, as I believe it possible that the guns could have cooked off live rounds if they had been sufficiently heated, and the Aden's gas return system could have cycled further live rounds into the breech. This was undoubtedly a bigger danger than the petrol tanker that was close to the crash site, and the inhabitants of Tintagel were much luckier than they might have realised.

Deci Diary 1

When I started flying with XV Squadron at Laarbruch in January 1972, the squadron was in the throes of converting to the Buccaneer. Not all of the requisite crews had arrived from 237 Operational Conversion Unit (OCU), and the squadron was very much Day Fighter Ground Attack (DFGA)-minded. Indeed, to my delight (but probably not his), I had been crewed with an ex-208 Squadron (Bahrain) DFGA Hunter pilot for the OCU course. He and I were posted as a crew to join the nascent XV Buccaneer Squadron in October 1971, from the first first-tourist course to be held on 237 OCU. DFGA was the only way to go and, after a "Long OCU" course with him, I was fully inculcated as a DFGA navigator! It was just as well because, on our arrival, the ethos and training on XV Squadron were very much DFGA! OK, SACEUR[1] did want us to have the capability to deliver "buckets of sunshine" as well, but in 1972 what was wrong with delivering them visually – we all knew that the Buccaneer's Blue Parrot radar was not designed for, or capable in, the overland role! The soon-to-be-famous epithet "Blind Tom" had not even been dreamt of, and the young pretender to the squadron radar leadership was known only by his christened name in those early days. Laydown, MDSL, SNEB rockets, 5° Dive Retard at Nordhorn Range were routine weapon tasks for the crews working up on XV, and all were delivered visually. Initial concentration was on passing the Limited Combat Ready work-up, to get you "Strike Qualified" and onto QRA[2], and then the Combat Ready work up so that you could go to war but, even better than going to war, you were qualified to go on detachment!

It was here, in the bar at Happy Hour, that the first germs of the XV Squadron songbook were written. Songs like, "When XV came to Laarbruch what a happy day, Rocketry and Stripro visual all the way." (to the tune of Lily Marlene), and "2's little boys fly 2's little toys, they call it the Phantom jet" (to the tune of Rolf Harris's Two Little Boys) positively flowed from the musical talent

---

[1] SACEUR - Supreme Allied Commander Europe is the title of the most senior commander within NATO

[2] QRA – Quick Reaction Alert, refers to aircraft and crews that are held at a high state of preparedness

of our irrepressible song writing duo. We all worked tirelessly to hone our skills in the air and improve our singing voices in the bar. We were, we knew, the ultimate DFGA professionals, above average aircrew, exceptional party animals and competent consumers of alcohol who, with further training on detachment, could become well above average in this latter discipline also. We were invincible, or so we thought! It was with this in mind that XV Squadron deployed to Decimomannu (universally known in the RAF as 'Deci') for its initial detachment on 3 July 1972. Exactly 2 years to the day since an RAF presence had first been established on Sardinia, and a destination that I was bound to return to many more times during my career.

For those who flew the Buccaneer in the 70's, Deci conjures up images to most of rowdy weekends in Sardinia; intoxicated soirees at Fortes Hotel Village, where golf carts floated mysteriously in swimming pools; gastronomic extravaganzas of barbecued king prawns, and consumption of the local wine, commonly known as Deci Red which, in 1972, cost ridiculously large sums of Italian Lire but, on conversion, was dirt-cheap; death-defying journeys in a J2 van to get to Capo Carbonara for sand-infested (but compulsory) beach barbecues, and luxury golfing at Is Molas, which for most was, and still is, beyond the pocket of the average punter. Not to forget the regular funfair in the local towns that, unfortunately for the showmen, was a strong magnet for Buccaneer aircrew, and yours truly in particular. I once knew an F4 Phantom navigator who used to brag that, over time, he had spent one whole year of his life (365 accumulative days) at Deci - he loved the place, poor sod. On second thoughts, I suppose it was in the Mediterranean, it had sun, sea, sand and Italian ladies – well I was a bachelor! But the base was spartan to say the least, no closer than an hour to the nearest beach, and the RAF accommodation lacked the comforts of modern living, even by 1970s standards. The only decent establishment on base was the Italian Officers Mess, known as Spaghetti Palace (pronounced 'palachi' by the Brits) and the only "place to be" was the Brit pub – The Pig and Tapeworm.

Anyway, Deci was much more than an overseas Butlin's. At the height of the Cold War, and with the Italian Air Force as its hosts, NATO had secured territory and airspace in south west Sardinia for United States Air Force and Royal Canadian Air Force aircrews, deployed from their bases in Germany, to conduct air-to-ground weapon training on Capo Frasca Range. The German Air Force, as guests of the Italians, and Italian Air Force aircrews also performed weapons training sorties there, and thus was born the first multinational air base within NATO. Its sole purpose was to permit the conduct of intensive weapon training for strike/attack aircraft, but the RAF, unfortunately, failed to gain access to the quadripartite agreement until the Canadians withdrew in 1970. However, not long afterwards, Buccaneers from XV were among the first RAF assets to take up position on the flight line.

For our NATO allies, the Buccaneer was a weird and wonderful aircraft. Predominantly, the Italians and Germans were flying Starfighters, and the USAF deployed to Deci in 1972 with Phantoms, A10 Warthogs, and F-111s. All those aircraft were instantly recognisable in the NATO catalogue, but the Buccaneer was new to theatre, and unique in more ways than one. Consequently, as carousing Buccaneer crews, we drew some lively attention in the Spaghetti Palachi from our inquisitive foreign brethren, and The Pig and Tapeworm was always the place that USAF crews seemed to discover after the Palachi bar shut, or sometimes before it even opened. The prospect of strong English Beer was too much for them to refuse, and sufficient to soon have them joining in with the XV Squadron songbook lyrics. Of course, it was all cloaked in the mystery of "tactical discussions", but it undoubtedly ensured that there was always a strong bond between the visiting squadrons at Deci. Of all the nationalities the Italians were perhaps the most reticent, and not renowned for being particularly wild partygoers. However, the Base Commander was an Italian, with the obvious implications that this could have for an Italian officer's career! Nevertheless, on one very memorable occasion, and after a particularly enervating day on Frasca Range, two Italian G-91 pilots approached us in the bar, after a particularly pleasant meal of spaghetti washed down by copious quantities of Deci Red. They explained that they had been at Frasca Range on RSO duties that day, and were intrigued to learn how the Buccaneers carried out "pairs dive" bombing. Well, of course, in the early 70's there was no such thing as a Qualified Weapons Instructor, the term Buccaneer Attack Instructor was only just being thought of, and the closest Air Weapons Instructor to the Spaghetti Palachi was at HMS Fulmar (Lossiemouth). Anyway, we were all experts and, for the price of another Flaming Sambuca, were all happy to brief the Gino pilots. Picture the scene: hands flew, phrases like "synergistic effect" and "No 2 pickles on leader's release" fell to the carpet and, before you knew it ,the Italians had picked them all up, were fully briefed and off to their beds.

The next morning, I was in a 4-ship taxiing for take-off and bound for one of the early slots on Frasca; not the earliest slot, of course, from which we tried to shy away! Just as we left dispersal, the Local Controller announced, "London, your mission she ees cancel". "Roger, reason why?" asked London lead. "The range, she isa clos-edd" came the reply. So with no low-level booked, and an embargo on take-offs, we taxied back and shut down, despondent that our range sortie had been cancelled for some yet-to-be-established reason. We did not have to wait long to find out, however, as the range had not been closed for those early birds who were prepared to get up at about 0530hrs which, on this day, had included our 2 intrepid Gino pilots. Eager to emulate their Buccaneer brethren, the two G-91 pilots failed to follow the bar-room briefing exactly, "clapped hands" overhead the Dive Circle and crashed! One onto the target area and the other into the sea. Thankfully both pilots had survived their ejections, and were back in the bar that evening for a bit of remedial instruction.

Deci Diary 2

In those early days, the Boss of XV Squadron was a particularly capable pilot who had flown Sabres during the Korean War. Indeed, one notable story in circulation at the time was that, as a Flying Officer, he had led over 40 Sabres on a particular mission. I was too polite to ask the storyteller if this was for real but, in all my 39 years in the RAF, I don't think I've ever known a Flying Officer being trusted with himself, let alone 40 plus aircraft! Things were clearly much different in the early post-war years but, true or not, his experiences certainly did ensure that he was one of the original 'seat of the pants' pilots. On one memorable occasion at Frasca Range, he and his navigator were leading (by example) a 4-ship which was conducting SNEB[1] rocket attacks on the Dive Circle. Direct Hit (DH) followed DH until, after about his 5th pass without a miss, the Boss declared to the Range Safety Officer that he was "Off Dry". When challenged by his surprised navigator that the parameters had been perfect, the Boss replied "Sorry, I've just realised that I haven't selected the sight glass up (in other words he had been using the Mk1 Eyeball as his only firing reference) and the BAIs[2] will bollock me rigid at the debrief."

The trouble with Frasca Range, when related to the Buccaneer, was that the targets were not at sea level. It's all very well having a range on the top of a 100 foot cliff, but if the poor back-seater has only a "strip TAS" (airspeed) and a "strip Altimeter" (fixed to 1013mb), then placing the targets on top of a cliff is going to do nothing for the accuracy of the weapons. Moreover, when the peninsula is less than 3 km wide in the target area on the attack heading it is not really giving him much of a chance to "zero" his altimeter directly over the targets either. Furthermore, the rear seat of the Buccaneer was offset and provided a clear view forward to the right of the pilot's head only. Consequently, looking out, whilst at the same time trying to etch a "zero" line on the "strip Altimeter" (located in your low, left 9 o'clock, range 3 feet) with a blunt chinagraph pencil, was less than conducive to bombing accuracy. Finally when the range was split,

---

[1] SNEB (French: Societe Nouvelle des Etablissements Edgar Brandt): A forward-firing ground attack rocket system fired from pods carried on wing pylons.

[2] BAI – Buccaneer Attack Instructor: A weapons specialist position on the squadron

on the attack heading, into "Left" and "Right" Range with either Left or Right Traffic (at the Italian Range Safety Officer's discretion), and your pilot was also employing you as local interpreter, then it was clearly acceptable that you missed your mark, and that you would be eternally grateful if we could do it all again please. Well, of course it was!

Now, add to that the fact that Frasca could be as little as 10 minutes flying time from Deci, there ain't a lot of time to settle to the task before you find yourself hurtling earthwards in a 20° dive. However, as already stated, my man and I had been crewed together through the OCU, and for all of the workup on the squadron, so we were a team. He understood me and I understood him. On this day in history, we were bound for Frasca as No 4 to conduct MDSL[3]. For those who have never had the delight of doing MDSL (or any other DSL for that matter), MDSL was conducted from a pattern height of 4000 feet, and release was initiated by the Navigator's "NOW" call as the Bucc passed through 2150 feet on its way to the ground. Highly accurate over a flat calm sea.....but on Frasca Range, see above!! Following a very short hold, we descended towards the coast to be low-level over the sea as we turned onto the attack heading. During the routine 4G turn in arrow formation, my bang seat dropped unexpectedly by about 2 inches with a quite solid and noticeable "CLUNK". Time waits for no man and, by the time I had panicked, fiddled and failed to ascertain what the problem with the ejection seat was, the four aircraft had joined the range, broken into the circuit, and my height mark had been, to all intents and purposes, non-existent. Now was the time to call it a day! We were now downwind at 4000 feet for MDSL and I was unable to rectify the problem. However, what I had discovered whilst joining the range was that I could not talk on the intercom or radio, and the first panic breath only resulted in my oxygen mask clamping itself firmly to my face. Undeterred, I released the mask and, now breathing cabin air, I wrote on a scrap of paper Bang seat dropped 2 inches; can't breathe, can't speak and signed it, just in case there was any doubt! Then, having stamped my feet to gain his attention, I passed it forward through a gap where the roller map used to be. By now, we were established in the 20° dive and my poor pilot was struggling to assess

---

[3] MDSL – Manual Depressed Sight Line: A type of dive attack using bombs or rockets

his dive angle without the usual calls from the rear seat, so he pulled off dry[4].

Without the use of dialogue, it is very difficult to translate ones emotions and a sense of urgency on a scrap of paper, and I had clearly failed. Once downwind, the paper came back with the message Never mind, we'll stay dry. Anxious that my bang seat was about to do what it was designed for, I was not so keen on this course of action and, in curt terminology, advised my friend (in writing) that I was less than happy with this proposal! Of course, the flying of the aircraft and the passing of notes took time, and now 2 more patterns had passed and my straps were tightened to breaking point in preparation for the inevitable. However our sense of airmanship prevailed, and we soon departed the range for Deci where, unbeknown to me, Air Traffic had been alerted to our predicament. An uneventful straight in approach (with my straps getting ever tighter) and landing followed, apart from being chased down the runway by a stream of bright yellow Italian 'blood wagons'. Upon reaching the northern ORP[5], the canopy motored backwards and my now frantically gesticulating pilot indicated that it was time for me to depart the aircraft by conventional means - sliding down the starboard under-wing tank. No sooner was I safely on the ground than my Buccaneer disappeared back to dispersal leaving me stranded. That was until, and here's where it pays to socialise in the bar, a familiar Luftwaffe F-104 pilot beamed from his cockpit and gesticulated that I should jump on to his wing and sit astride the drop tank. Five minutes later, back on X-Ray Dispersal, I was deposited amongst my fellows and that evening, back in the Palachi, I regaled all who would listen to me with my tale of adventure.

Oh, the bang seat? Yes, it had dropped 2 inches and in the process had managed to disconnect the lower seat portion of the PEC[6] which was beyond my sight. Nothing really and, with 20/20 hindsight, easily identifiable, had I investigated the problem thoroughly. But hey, why spoil a good story when it can keep you in beer for a good 24 hours!

---

[4] Dry – In this context it means that switches were left on "safe" so that no ordnance could be dropped

[5] ORP – Operational Readiness Platform: An area that allows aircraft immediate access to the runway

[6] PEC – Personal Equipment Connector: Provides connection of communication and oxygen systems

Finally

When I later joined a Tornado squadron, all the ex V-Force guys bragged about the times they had spent at Goose Bay, Labrador. What a marvellous place it was, and how there was nowhere like it on earth! Well I thought about this but, after my first visit to Goose Bay, I concluded that Deci wasn't so bad. I suppose the Ultra Low Level flying at Goose Bay was fantastic, and the scenery and wildlife utterly amazing, but the local town of Happy Valley (what's in a name?) offered little alternative to getting completely 'blootered' every night. There was no beach, sun or sand, but there were Canadian ladies (Lumberjills) who tended to leave you alone if you couldn't stand up. However, if they couldn't stand up either, you were in serious trouble. I was once there in October; on the 13th there was no snow but, by first light the following day, the whole base was covered with a good two feet of fine, powdery stuff. This added considerable credibility to a local road sign that stated - Snow chains are required during the Winter (Winter commences on 14 October). It must have been a breeze being a weather man at Goose.

Gummidge It Wasn't

I was a victim of the then Labour government's austerity campaign, and was posted out from a northern Hunter squadron to Maintenance Command, as a pilot on the Communications Squadron. Having no twin time, or much piston-engine for that matter, I was restricted by Command regulations until I had 500 hours on the Anson/Devon. However, the Squadron also used Chipmunks for various jobs, which entertained me for most of my time there: glider tows, plus an hour's aeros in the morning and another hour in the adjacent low flying area.

Local farmers used to build mounds (clamps), to store their winter root crops, and usually covered them with plastic. This was a time consuming job, but the result made an excellent ground attack target. I would try and sneak up "nap of the earth", and pop up for a shallow dive attack. I guess you get fed up with this noise after a while, and one exasperated farmer stabbed a large root vegetable and levered it in my direction. I saw it coming, but had almost no room to manoeuvre and avoid.

I felt the hit way back on the aircraft, and prayed that it was somehow deniable. Andover was a triangular grass field, and I thought I should check the tail before my difficult Boss saw it. So, I reported 'brake problems' in the farthest corner of the field, and got out to survey the damage. The muddy mark on the fin was clearly visible, and my attempt to rub it off, I think, made it worse.

On reaching the Squadron, the Boss came out and walked around the aircraft. He asked what had happened in the far corner, and clearly doubted my mumbled excuses, but what could he say? I think it was a glancing blow, mostly mud, with the faintest suggestion of an impact.

A two pound wurzel could have had life-altering significance!

Bright Spark

One evening, while I was on duty in the Air Traffic Control tower, we received a message that a no-notice security exercise had been called. This meant that the base would be sealed off, and staff sent to guard various key installations and points of access. We were also told that members of the RAF Regiment would be acting as 'enemy', and attempting to infiltrate the base.

It was a cold evening and, from our warm vantage point, we watched in comfort as guards were deployed around the various radio and radar buildings adjacent to the tower. Time passed, and all was quiet, when suddenly the area was illuminated by a bright flash. The consensus of opinion was that one of the guards had got bored and decided to light up a cigarette but, having drawn attention to himself, he would probably get 'clobbered' if any of the RAF Regiment were nearby.

A couple of minutes later, we received a phone call from the Medical Centre requesting permission for the station ambulance to cross the airfield and attend an incident nearby. We exchanged knowing glances; yes, the airman had received retribution for his indiscretion, but if he needed an ambulance then things had probably gone too far.

It later transpired that our interpretation of events was rather wide of the mark. The airman in question had decided to relieve himself against the wall of the radar building, but hadn't reckoned on the static charge that proceeded to find its way to earth by the path of least electrical resistance. Fortunately, he survived intact and without any permanent damage, although it was rumoured that he subsequently developed an aversion to thunderstorms.

The Last Buccaneer Fatigue Failure

It was 1992, and the Buccaneer was well established in its twilight years. The Buccaneer Training Flight, formed in 1991 (post-237 OCU) as an enclaved unit within 208 Sqn, was closing. I was due to take over as OC B Flight on 208, and my right-hand man had been posted to an A6 exchange at Whidbey Island, USA. Naturally(!), we had to have a farewell ranger for Steve, and an exercise debrief at RNlAF Soesterburg seemed to be the obvious choice. After the debrief, we had an excellent night in Amsterdam, and a routine return to Lossiemouth – until the arrival break into the circuit!

It was a Friday afternoon, and there was no station flying as we approached from the east and 'overflew' the 208 HAS[1] site, where the team were waiting to greet us with suitable refreshments. Of course, we also took the opportunity to 'overfly' the 12 Sqn site, on our way out to initials for the break to land. As we passed overhead 12, we noticed several buses unloading passengers who, as we suddenly remembered, were arriving for the 12 Sqn disbandment celebrations that weekend. With our focus on the Amsterdam night-stop, we had completely forgotten about it. After a brief discussion, we decided that the assembled company would definitely enjoy one last no-notice demonstration of the tactical capabilities of the mighty Bucc, so I left the handle next to the boiler fully open, as we positioned at initials for runway 23.

I selected a suitable tactical speed (somewhere around Vne[2]) and height (somewhere around two-foot six) that I felt would guarantee the enjoyment of the assembled company, and we ran right over the middle of the site. As we exited the Sqn area I closed both throttles, selected full airbrake and applied about 5G to join the circuit to land. I didn't have a chance to say 'I'm sure they'll enjoy that' (or something similar) before there was a very audible 'clunk' from the airframe, and all hell broke loose.

The aircraft started vibrating and shaking so violently that I was unable to read the engine instruments. Our initial instinct was to believe that we had had some sort of massive bird strike (it must have been a pterodactyl!), but there was

---

[1] HAS - Hardened Aircraft Shelter

[2] Vne - The "Never Exceed" speed for the aircraft

no sign of blood on the windscreen, or distinctive smell of roast chicken through the air conditioning. We had also heard only one thump, which added to our confusion. Anyway, we weren't landing off this one, so I added some power and selected airbrake in to one-half, and the vibration reduced noticeably as we continued to slow down, which was encouraging. An inspection of the engine instruments also indicated that all was normal there; another relief.

I declared a Pan on tower frequency, and turned downwind, requesting a visual inspection from anyone in the local area. As previously stated, it was a Friday afternoon and station flying had finished for the day. However, at the moment critique, a Hawk, with 2 visiting pilots on board who had, coincidentally, a total of about 6000 Buccaneer hours between them, arrived and offered to look us over. After a good close look from every conceivable angle, they declared that all looked OK and we elected to land, unblown[3] with the airbrake in its present position. The landing was uneventful; however, once safely on the ground, I selected full airbrake to aid deceleration but, when turning off the runway, discovered that the rudder was jammed in the neutral position. We taxied in to the 208 Sqn site, where our welcome committee (who had just about finished the refreshments by this stage) greeted us with incredulous looks, and a series of flat palms being chopped across throats.

What our erstwhile Buccaneer friends had failed to notice was that the box section on which the airbrake assembly was mounted had completely failed, and the entire airbrake had broken off below the rudder, and was dangling at an angle of about 25 degrees, attached to the airframe only by the stainless steel pin at the end of the hydraulic jack! Reducing speed and selecting ½ airbrake had, of course, reduced its exposure to the airflow, hence the reduction in vibration. However, when I re-selected full airbrake on the runway after landing, the effect was to ram the hydraulic jack up into the rudder mechanism, jamming it solid.

So what happened? Well, of course, the incident prompted an inspection of all remaining airframes, and it was found that (as best as I can recall), about two thirds of them had significant cracking in their airbrake mounts. Following consultation with the manufacturer, a speed and G limit for the selection

---

[3] The Buccaneer had a system that blew air, tapped from the engines, over the flaps to improve low-speed performance

of full airbrake was instituted, which was generous enough to allow the aircraft to continue to serve, without significant effect on its operational role, until its eventual retirement in March 1994. There were a few more significant incidents before the aircraft reached the end of its days, but I believe that this was the last instance of drama directly attributable to a fatigue failure – thankfully with an uneventful ending.

208 Sqn Buccaneer (Credit: John Malley)

... And Relax

My first flying tour in the RAF was dominated by events in Central America. I had been posted to 1(F), Squadron flying the Harrier, and had just arrived on the squadron when we were ordered to deploy at short notice to Belize – a country few of us had heard of – due to the threat of invasion from neighbouring Guatemala. Tension rose ahead of our departure, because we were not permitted to tell anyone, including our families, where we were going, in the hope of arriving undetected. The plan was for the whole squadron to deploy, with the exception of the USAF Exchange Officer, because the USA was being friendly towards Guatemala, as it was seen as a potential block to Communist encroachment into the Americas.

In the rush, I was relegated to the position of Operations Officer (a non-flying role), and dispatched on the first support Hercules, to prepare for the arrival of our jets. They duly arrived, provided the necessary deterrent and, after a few weeks, I was allowed to resume flying. In the true spirit of expediency, this led to my first Operational Category – Combat Ready (Central America Only). A few months later, the job was deemed to be done and we all returned to the UK, where we were able to resume the normal round of training... and relax.

The signs that we might have to deploy again to Belize were there the following year, when we deployed to Denmark on Taceval[1] and were told to take our tropical kit with us... so time to tense up once more. However, we had seen it all before and nothing had come of it, so we were not unduly concerned. Sure enough, the exercise in Denmark was curtailed and off we went again, leaving our bonded stock of duty-free items locked in a hardened shelter. Once again, the plan was to arrive as unheralded as possible, and we were to take six aircraft, flying as 3 pairs, with tanker support via a night stop in Goose Bay, Canada. Due to American diplomatic ties with Guatemala, we also planned to fly the second leg to Belize outside US airspace, via the Cuban region to reach Belize. In order to cover these long distances, the Harriers were prepared in a rather ungainly configuration, with 330-gallon drop tanks and air-to-air refuelling probes, but the guns were loaded, just in case no other armament was available

---

[1] Taceval : Tactical evaluation of NATO declared units by NATO staff.

when we finally arrived. As a mid-tour Flying Officer, I was to lead the second pair of Harrier GR3s.

Before flying across the Atlantic, I took advice on long ferry flights from a more experienced (ex-Lightning, Middle East Air Force) pilot, and duly equipped myself with a plastic cup of orange juice, with handy snap-on lid and drinking spout, and a box of bite-size sandwiches, again with snap-on lid. These were designed to enable quick refreshment, while avoiding oxygen deprivation at altitude when the mask was removed; but, due to the lack of space in the GR3 cockpit, the drink had to go between the right windscreen and the instrument coaming, and the sandwich box down the left side of the ejection seat. Eventually we were ready to go and, as I accelerated down the runway and took off, tension mounted when the drink began to vibrate backwards towards me. I reached up and pushed it back, only for the snap-on lid to snap-off, and deposit half a pint of orange juice onto my transponder control box. I mopped it up as best I could, set off for the tanker and, as everything seemed to be working, we left the spare Harrier behind for the third pair, and headed west. About halfway across the Atlantic, I felt relaxed enough to try the food. Error! I reached down the side of the ejection seat, and out came the box, minus the lid and the sandwiches. As they were now deposited somewhere among the rocket pack and the various seat sears, I thought that it was best to leave them until after arrival in Canada.

The next morning, we dressed to suit the low temperatures of the air and sea in northern latitudes, and I declined the offer of in-flight rations, prior to taking off into a solid overcast that topped out above 30,000 feet. Before departure, we had been made aware that the US-mediated talks with Guatemala were not going well, so the plan was for our side to announce the reinforcement when the first pair of Harriers landed in Belize, with the subsequent pairs following at 30 minute intervals. That announcement, when it came, triggered a rapidly-moving chain of events. The Guatemalan side phoned home, and told their forces to prepare and the US advisers to leave. The US advisers told the Brits to prepare for trouble, so the Cubans took this to mean that the Americans were on our side, which meant that they were not. For the pair of Harriers that I was leading, this resulted in some awkward dialogue between our airborne tanker and Cuban air traffic control. We were aware of this, and that the Royal Navy would not be in the area, so we became somewhat concerned by the sight of a purposeful line of naval ships heading our way between Cuba and Florida. A short time later, our Radar Warning Receivers began to light up with all kinds of threats, which seemed to indicate that Cuba was indeed becoming distinctly less friendly. However, we later learned that the convoy below us was Soviet, and intent on seeing what all the fuss was about by checking us out with their radars. The third pair had now become a singleton (leaving one behind unserviceable in Canada) and, when the lone Harrier and his refueller reached Cuban airspace, the tanker was denied permission to enter. This meant that, without US clearance, it had to divert to the West Indies, so the Harrier pilot made the bold decision to take a last top-up from the tanker and head for Belize on his own, by following the US/Cuban airspace boundary.

After 6½ hours of flying (and with the tanker long gone), I called up Belize, only to be told to hold off if possible. This sounded ominous as no reason was given, and we were forced to wait offshore on an unusually gloomy day for that part of the world. While I was wondering what might have happened, I saw another big military ship below us. We decided that we really ought to let people know about this, so we went down for a slightly closer look and, sure enough, it was the Royal Navy frigate that we had been told would arrive some days later. After an hour of waiting, we were cleared to recover to Belize International Airport, with a detour to overfly Belmopan, the capital city, to reassure the locals that the Harriers were back. It later transpired that we had been delayed to give the ground-crew time to remove the ferry tanks from the first pair, so that they could launch to join us in some 4-ship flag waving. However, it was eventually decided that we had been airborne quite long enough – which indeed we had.

After landing, my first shock was to open the canopy and realise that clothing suitable for the sea around Canada is not ideal for the Tropics. A hasty change ensued, before I was met by my Wing Commander, complete with a chilled bottle and a cheery "Here we are again, another Belize panic over. Relax. It's been a long day so have a drink, off to bed and come in to work at 9 o'clock in the morning". Having followed his advice, I was a little surprised to find the same officer shaking my shoulder at 0300 saying, "Get up, they're coming, man the aircraft!"

Following a quick brief, we were authorised to get airborne before first light, fly outside the area covered by the airfield defences in the direction of the anticipated attack, and attempt to shoot down (we were still only armed with guns, remember) any incoming, hostile aircraft. The plan then was to land, re-arm with SNEB[2], which would hopefully be prepared in time, and attack the airfield where we expected the opposition to land. As dawn approached, I could make out sights, like an armourer with an unlit cigar hanging from the corner of his mouth, carrying arms full of SNEB rockets perilously close to the front of my loaded guns, and the squadron Regiment Officer wandering around carrying a GPMG[3], plus as many belts of ammunition as possible. Yes, this was Belize again.

We got airborne in the dark with the fifth aircraft which, by this time, was carrying a hydraulic problem that led to random undemanded, control movements; fortunately, that was one for a Flight Commander to deal with, not a Flying Officer! However, the raid never came and tension subsequently eased. Deterrence had triumphed again, but this time, unlike the previous year, we were not able to relax completely.

The commitment was to remain for many more years (during which time I completed no fewer than ten deployments to Belize), but I never did find out what happened to all that duty-free we abandoned in Denmark!

---

[2] SNEB (French: Societe Nouvelle des Etablissements Edgar Brandt): A forward-firing ground attack rocket system fired from pods carried on wing pylons.

[3] GPMG: General Purpose Machine Gun.

A Black Moment

The following story is taken from COLD WAR, HOT WINGS by kind permission of the author, Chris Bain, and Pen & Sword Publishing Ltd.

Christmas 1966. I was twenty-one years old, and I'd been serving in Aden for just under two years, playing my part in the downfall of the British Empire!

This was our first dusk scramble. As we took off, the afterglow of sunset had dissipated, as it does in the lower latitudes, and the dim of night had suddenly crept up on us. Diving now into 7,000-foot mountains, at 30 degrees at night in a day-fighter plane, on the blackest night of the year, with 23mm tracer shells coming up and filling the windscreen, was not conducive to longevity. This remarkable, life-threatening event would be incomprehensible, but for the fact that just before dusk a British Army patrol had been ambushed by a party of Yemeni dissidents. I was No 2 in the four-aircraft formation responding to their crisis call, and we certainly earned our flying pay that night!

This was no ordinary dive. It was three days after Christmas, and I was at 12,000ft in a single-seat Hunter fighter over Awabil in the Radfan mountains of southern Arabia, extremely close to the Yemeni border. What was I doing at the time? 420 knots, and I'd just learnt the meaning of the phase: 'The fog of war'!

They came at me from low on the left, bright flashes out of the dark. I was bloody frightened, probably more so than ever before. It was a black night, and all the lights had gone out, but all the time these numerous vivid white flashes were coming languidly straight up at me. Regular winking specks, always appearing to move lazily in my direction, but then astonishingly, at the last possible moment, veering off rapidly and whizzing through in a hurry of whirling motes, momentary darts of fire through that black night, zipping past and just missing with a final incandescent burst. These stunning white flashes were not good news, and I had no idea what the other three were up to or what they were thinking – one in front of me and two behind, diving into this unfathomable murk. The customary feeling of invincibility one felt when in a fighter cockpit had dissolved into something decidedly shaky.

Unfortunately, on arrival at the target area, the leader called as briefed to switch off all nav lights, and then throttled back as he tipped into his rocket dive.

His lights and the glow from the back-end of his jet pipe went out, and abruptly all went impenetrably black. That hadn't been briefed! I had nothing to formate on, and couldn't see the ground, the leader or anything, never mind the target. The only part of the universe moving outside the warm red glow of the cockpit was the white-hot tracer coming up lazily from below.

With a flash of passion tipped with the courage of panic, I slotted in behind him. By now I was down to between nine and ten thousand feet, with my leader just in front of me, having disappeared into the cold black night below, and the third and fourth aircraft just behind, diving in line astern, rapidly and steeply into the charcoal unknown, only two thousand feet from the volcanic mountain tops. I had this panic thought: I'm not paid enough to do something so stupid as this, and whose bloody idea was it anyway? It was turning into one of those situations over which I had no control!

Yielding to a calmly normal but irresistible impulse, an overwhelming desire for self-preservation, I decided it was time to get out of there in a hurry, so I screamed on the radio and pulled like mad. It was then that I saw the fireballs of the first twelve rockets detonate as they hit the target area. Being young and rash, I decided to complete a timed circuit and go in behind No 4. After seeing 3 and 4's rockets go off, I slotted into the usual 30 degree dive and, still completely unsighted, pickled off my rockets and, with an enormous release of tension, headed home.

These uncontrolled events had occurred in response to the usual army grievance, kicking up a fuss about no air support at night from the RAF's day fighter/ground attack squadrons. So someone with no day/night fighter experience decided we ought to be able to do the job twenty-four hours a day: Christmas present 1966: do it at night!

This first dusk scramble on that night just after Christmas did not cover me in glory. The following day, the political officer from up-country came waltzing into the crew room with the words, "Which silly bugger put his rockets 5,000 yards over the border then?!" Welcome to Night Fighter Ground Attack using Day Fighters, inaccurate World War II rockets and no proper sight! A typical cobbled-together RAF shoestring operation, which is probably why we got away with it!

Thank goodness someone quickly came to his senses! Night attack didn't last! We soon went back to our normal daytime war – life was simpler and longer, that way!

Inadvertent Flight

A first solo in a Lightning was always a pretty exciting experience – and that was after some dual instruction! Wing Commander 'Taffy' Holden, an Engineering Officer, flew his first solo by mistake, and survived to tell the tale.

Some Background Considerations:
In attempting to write a more detailed personal account of my unfortunate flight in Lightning XM135 back in July 1966, I think I should add some of the reasoning and reasons why I attempted the test in the first place. This might re-move some of the erroneous facts, misapprehensions and misconceptions which I have seen in some accounts of the event.

First, I should explain that I was a qualified pilot, even although I was an RAF Engineer Branch officer. I joined the RAF as an apprentice in 1943, from where I gained a cadetship to university. At the university, I read mechanical engineering, and learnt to fly on Tiger Moths with the University Air Squadron. On graduation, I was given the option to continue with an engineering career, or to follow a General Duties (Flying) career. I chose the former path, and the Air Ministry, at that time, considered that there was merit in allowing me to qualify to 'wings' standard as a pilot, in the belief that an engineering officer with a pilot qualification could more easily see the pilot's point of view in aircraft maintenance matters. I, too, thought this was a very good idea.

I qualified on Harvards, but my early engineering duties only allowed me to keep in flying practice on Chipmunks. Whilst I was at Kinloss, I managed to get checked out on Oxfords and, on occasions, assisted a qualified test pilot to air test twin-engine Neptunes. My only jet aircraft experience was as a passenger in the second seat of a Javelin T3, and again in the 'rumble' seat of a Canberra. In my service, one of my postings took me to 33MU Lyneham where, as the CO of a civilian-manned aircraft storage unit, I had Canberra, Meteor and Light-ning types, which were gradually being prepared for despatch to various flying unit tasks. When the Meteor and Canberra types had been cleared, the powers-that-be decided that the MU should close after the last Lightnings had been despatched. Up until the last Canberra, I had a qualified and current test pilot on my staff for those aircraft, but he was not a current Lightning pilot. When a Lightning needed test flying, I had to call for any available pilot with a current test pilot rating. Most times, I would find one who could be spared within a 24- or 36-hour period. So much for my personal and RAF unit background.

Lightning Mk 1A XM135:

XM 135 was being prepared for despatch to a Target Facilities Flight but, over a period of weeks, it had been giving no end of trouble. Each time it was being flight tested, the pilot found that, on the initial few yards of a take-off run, the inverter supplying power to the primary flight instruments would cut out, and the standby inverter would have to cut in, clearly an unsatisfactory state of affairs. Electricians were using every trick in their trade to establish the cause, each time thinking that they had removed, replaced and tightened every likely component. With nothing out of order, they would seek another test flight. It was a Boscombe Down pilot who next attempted to fly the aircraft, found the same problem persisting, and refused to fly until a more positive explanation could be determined.

Back to the drawing board; electricians decided to devise some tests which might isolate the fault, and indicate roughly where and which component was at fault. They intended to ask the next test pilot to switch in and out parts of circuits, using trailing wires from the likely circuits to temporary switches in the cockpit, and to do these electrical switchings before and after each few yards of a simulated take-off run, when the fault was manifest. The temporary wires from internal circuitry required the cockpit canopy to be removed and, in this state, the aircraft was made ready for another air test. Being a pilot, it was easiest for me, as CO, to request the services of a qualified test pilot from wherever I could find one but, for the next test on XM135, no pilot was available for at least another week. With my unit closing down, many civilians being made redundant, a timetable of clearance being upset by this 'rogue' aircraft, there was much tetchiness and irritation amongst my staff. The intended Boscombe Down pilot, knowing I was a pilot, suggested I might try the test myself. He suggested using an out of use runway (Runway36), as I would only be using 30 or 40 yards at a time. He suggested using a Land Rover to communicate with Air Traffic Control, and to get their clearance for each movement of the aircraft. However, there was one remaining minor problem. I had only sat in a Lightning cockpit once before, and I had no idea how to start its two Rolls Royce Avon engines! The Foreman of Engine Trades gave me a 5 minute briefing on how to do this, and XM135 was towed out to Runway 05 on 22 July 1966 for my electrical tests.

It was by way of extraordinary good fortune that my engine Foreman explained that, although I would not be needing reheat, reheat needed the throttles to be pushed past a reheat 'gate', and one had to feel for the gate keys, behind the throttle, to unlock. My only other knowledge of the Lightning was what I could remember from pilot's notes. At each test flight by the qualified pilot, I would be in ATC with a copy of pilot's notes, should he need any aircraft figures to be relayed to him. One or two figures stuck in my mind, namely that the undercarriage had a maximum speed above which it should be retracted, and I had an even vaguer figure of about 150 knots for a landing speed. Some extra knots would be required for each 1000 lbs of unused fuel, but I did not need to bother with any such figures for the test which I was to undertake.

The Ground Test:
I was correctly strapped into the cockpit (seated on the in situ parachute and ejector seat) and, after starting the engines and holding the aircraft static on the brakes, I did the necessary preliminaries for the electrical checks in the cockpit, checking the notes I had scribbled on a notepad, which lay on the coaming in front of me. All seemed ready for the first test, and I indicated to the Land Rover to obtain ATC clearance for use of the short 30 or 40 yards of runway. Holding the brakes, I gradually opened the throttles to about 90%. My feeling at the time was the unexpected heavy vibration of Avon power, held against the brakes. I did a quick check of the temporary electrical switches and circuitry lights, then released the brakes. That initial punch from the thrust was quite remarkable, and I moved the expected 30 to 40 yards, before I throttled back and applied the brakes. So far, so good. I made some notes, altered some more switch positions, noted the on/off lights and prepared for the next test. This was done in a similar fashion, and I was leaving the 'fault' diagnosis to my electrical staff, who would have to interpret my notes. I needed to do one more test, and ATC had noted that I had only used about 100 yards total, so they were quite happy to clear me for a similar short distance. ATC had also been holding up a fuel bowser and trailer, with 3600 gallons of AVTAG to refuel a

C130. They then decided to allow the bowser to cross the runway. On opening the throttles for that final test, I obviously pushed them too far, misinterpreting the thrust because of the unexpected heavy vibration, and they got locked into reheat. Yes, I did use some expletives, but I had no time to think of getting out of reheat because, in front of me, the bowser and trailer had just crossed the runway from right to left, so my thoughts were to make sure I was missing them by sufficient margin. No, I couldn't steer to clear them; reheat takes you in a straight path like a bullet out of a gun. The time between finding myself in reheat and just missing the bowser was less than half the time I have taken to write this sentence.

Before my thoughts could again return to getting myself out of reheat, I was gathering speed and about to cross the main duty runway, where a Comet had just passed on its take off run. I then had no time to look for reheat gate keys, my eyes were on what next lay ahead. Two things, the end of the short runway 07, and just beyond was the small village of Bradenstoke, which I just had to miss. There was no chance of stopping, none whatsoever. I had gained flying speed (that is what reheat is for, short, sharp take offs) and I had no runway left. I did not need to heave it off the runway, the previous test pilot had trimmed it exactly for take-off, and only a slight backward touch on the stick and I was gathering height and speed. Then my thought was to get my speed back, in case I should damage the undercarriage. Incidentally, I could not have raised the undercarriage; the ground servicing locks were in place for safety reasons. With only clear blue sky in front of me, I could then search and feel for those gate keys. Yes, I found them, and thanked my lucky stars that my engine foreman had quite incidentally told me of their location, and I was soon able to get the speed back to (I am guessing now) about 250knots. My next thoughts were to keep Lyneham airfield in sight and where had the Comet got to, the one I had missed a few seconds ago? Then I asked myself, should I eject and where and when? No, I could not; the safety pins were in the ejection seat and safe for servicing, not for flying. My only alternative then was to attempt a landing, but how does one interpolate or extrapolate Tiger Moth, Chipmunk, Harvard flying to a two-engined, 11 ton beast like the Lightning?

After regaining my bearings, a little composure and simply by observation, making sure that the Comet had been warned away, I decided I should attempt a landing on the duty runway and direction. I was trying to combine all my limited flying experience into a few minutes of DIY flight 'training' on a Lightning. It wasn't easy, but I must admit that some of the elementary rudiments of my proper flying training and flight theory were coming in useful. I needed to get the feel of the aircraft, if I was to get it back on the ground. My first approach was ridiculous, I could tell that my speed, height, rate of descent, even alignment weren't correct, and my best plot was to go round again. This time making sure that my throttles would be well below reheat position. A second approach was no better, I had some aspects better, but as the duty runway 25 is on the lip of an escarpment, with a valley floor beyond, my rate of descent took me below runway height, and I found myself adding power to get back to the right level. More power also meant more speed, and I was trying to get to something like 150 knots for landing, but the uncoordinated attempt was becoming a mess, so I abandoned it, took myself away on a very wide circuit of Lyneham, and decided to land in the opposite direction. This, I thought, would give me more time to get the 'feel' right and, if I made a mess of the landing, I would overrun the runway and just drop (crash) into the valley beyond. In that direction, with a messed up landing, I would have no fear of crashing into Lyneham village.

The long final leg of this approach gave me the thinking time that I needed, and I gradually got the feel that speed, alignment, rate of descent, height and approach angle were better. I plonked it down at about the right position off the runway threshold, but just forgot that I was in a nose wheel aircraft, and emulated my best three wheelers in a Chipmunk or Harvard. The result was that I crunched the rubber block which encases the brake parachute cables. However, I had got down, but I then had to stop. I obviously knew the Lightning had a brake parachute, but where was the 'chute lever, button or knob? There, I found it marked Brake Chute, and I pulled it, and I could then look ahead and concentrate on keeping straight and somewhere near the centre line. I hung on to the brake lever, I wasn't slowing as much as I would like, so I just kept up my hand pressure on the brakes. I had about 100 yards of runway left when I stopped and, even then, I didn't know that the brake parachute had dropped off as soon as it was deployed, because the cable had been severed as a result of my super tail-wheel three pointer.

Events Immediately after the Flight:

XM 135 was towed back to the hangar, and I was taken to see the medical officer, who gave me some pills to calm my nerves. I felt reasonably calm, because I had almost killed myself on five occasions in that 12 minute flight, yet I had miraculously survived. What is more, I would see my wife and young family again. Two or three times in that same 12 minutes, I thought I would never ever see them again. My only priority was to save my own skin, I was not thinking about the non-insured loss of a Lightning Mk 1A aircraft. The minor damage to the aircraft was repaired with a new set of brake shoes and a new rubber chute block. As a memento, I have kept that rubber block; one day it might be returned to XM135 at Duxford.

The Fault:

Although the tests I did, and the ensuing flight, did not immediately provide a reason for the initial electrical fault, my electrical staff, with additional assistance from English Electric, Salmesbury, eventually did. Apparently, in early versions of the Lightning, there was to be a ground test button fitted into the standby inverter circuit. It was never fitted to the Mk1A, but the wires were left in the looms. It was one of these redundant wires which shorted onto the UHF radio, as it moved on its trunnions when the aircraft nudged forward on take off. Who would have thought I should risk my life to find it, in the way I did?

Events Subsequent to the Flight:

There was a subsequent Inquiry, to find out what had happened and why, and to make recommendations for it never to happen again. As I was the Commanding Officer of the Unit, I was responsible for my own as well as the service actions of all my staff. I was not acting against any orders in the Flight Order Book, which I religiously kept up to date. But those orders did not cater for engineering officers doing investigative checks on Lightnings. They were later amended. After the Unit Inquiry, I had to go up in front of the Commander-in-Chief. That was when I thought my career would be placed in jeopardy. I even thought that my coveted 'wings' would be taken from me; I had no idea how the incident was being regarded by Command or indeed Air Ministry. But, as I stood in front of Air Marshal Sir Kenneth Porter, he read the proceedings, asked me if I agreed with his view that "With the limited flying experience that I had, the test would have been better left to an experienced and current Lightning test pilot." I agreed of course. He then told me to remove my hat and sit down, and proceeded to tell me some of his unfortunate flying incidents in Mesopotamia in the Middle East. I was thankful that nothing more was to become of the incident, and that I still had a job to do back at 33 Maintenance Unit, Lyneham.

I coped with all the official communications regarding the incident, but what I was unprepared for was the release of the story to the public. I had had very little experience of working with the press, certainly none with radio, TV, national and world press. I had no training in how to deal with their quest for news. My Command Headquarters suggested I went away on leave before press releases were made by Air Ministry. This I did, and took my family off camping to Jesola, in Italy. Imagine my complete surprise when, on the first day of camp, on my way to find some ice, someone shouted "Hello Taffy, I've just been reading about your Lightning flight!!" The world seemed a very small place. On returning to the UK, I was overwhelmed to find that the incident was still front line news. People wanted to write articles in newspapers, books and magazines, and there were interviews on TV and radio, and underhand attempts to hear my account of what had happened. Having admitted that I had made an unwise decision to do the ground tests, I decided that the unwanted publicity that I had attracted was in no way going to be for financial gain. I steadfastly refused offers although, for a two page article in the Sunday Express, I requested the editors to make a contribution to the RAF Benevolent Fund. Despite prompts, no moneys were ever handed over, and I became very disillusioned with all publicity media. Some friends thought I had gained reward for an article in 'Mayfair'; it was written without my knowledge and authority but, because it was factually correct, I had no redress from the Press Complaints Board. Nonetheless, I was extremely annoyed.

Some years after the incident, my hidden fears of high speed flight came to the surface, and I had to spend two periods in hospital. I had not come to terms with the emotional side of the event. To return to my wife and family, after five close encounters with death, was indeed a miraculous experience, but I had not been honest with myself to accept it as such, so I needed psychiatric help. I could recall the technicalities of the flight without any hang-ups, but was unwilling to talk about that emotional side of the ordeal, until I was placed under medical drugs to bring those emotions to the surface. That was a rewarding experience, and it gave me a much better understanding of people who might need that same kind of help, after similar unfortunate occurrences.

Forty Years On:

I am now retired, and living with my wife in Cheshire. Apart from being an active DIY plumber, carpenter, electrician, handyman, my main pastime is involvement with family history. My inadvertent flight is still very vivid and, in writing this personal account, I needed little prompting. Over the intervening years, I have received many letters and reminders from people whom I did not know, all praising my efforts to return myself and aircraft back to the ground safely. Yes, I have basked in some glory, when accounts of what happened, have been retold in social gatherings. I have never sought publicity, but whenever it became impossible to suppress, I have had to live with it. I enjoyed my career in the Royal Air Force, but not because of XM135!

Lightning XM135 (Credit: John Malley)

It Was Just One Of Those Days

It was one of those days that made flying a joy, not just a job. The sky was clear, and the countryside spread out below in a patchwork of greens and yellows, typical of an English summer. The Navajo groaned its way along at 5000 feet, and the 7 passengers seemed to be enjoying the experience as much as I was. RAF Marham passed beneath, and I could see a squadron of Tornados on the line outside the hangar. I reflected on the days when I used to climb hot and sweaty from its cockpit, after air combat or low-level evasion missions, or the buzz of air-to-ground strafing on the Holbeach Range. But no more white-knuckle flying for me, I mused. This is the life, shirt-sleeves and a lightweight headset.

Suddenly, my daydreams were shattered by an almighty bang, the aircraft shook violently, and the groan of the engines died simultaneously. Looking through the front windscreen, I could see a line of jagged metal, and a hole where the baggage compartment had been. My first thought was that we had hit a bird, but there were no bird remains on the windscreen, and it would have had to be a flying dinosaur to have done that much damage; maybe we'd hit another aircraft. There was no time to ponder the cause. The aircraft rolled rapidly to the right, entered a steep spiral dive or spin and, as it tumbled uncontrollably out of the sky, the passengers started screaming! I tried to control the manoeuvre, but the rudder seemed lifeless and the ailerons only made matters worse. I thought about many things in those few seconds, "Christ, I am not going to get home tonight - 24 years flying fast jets - Green Flag, Tactical Bombing Competitions - and all those day and night carrier deck landings. Now this p*** thing is going to get me!!"

I put out a Mayday on the Marham frequency, but I couldn't hear any response, due to the noise from the passengers and the wind whipping through the gaping fuselage. As the aircraft rolled towards the vertical, I noticed that the right hand engine was missing. At first I thought that I must be mistaken but, no, it definitely was not there. A glance to the left confirmed that all was not well on that side either. The engine was still attached, but the propeller blades were bent back like the skin of a peeled banana. This was not going to be a good day!

I tried to control the aircraft, but it would not respond and we continued to hurtle earthwards. The countryside spun round violently, and I frantically tried to apply some sort of anti-spin control. After what seemed like a lifetime (and it almost was), I felt some air resistance on the rudder, and gently eased the control column forward, not knowing what would happen or what effect it would have on the damaged aircraft. By now we had probably spun twice, but I wasn't counting. I was aware of trying not to make any dramatic inputs to the controls, in case the aircraft was so fragile I caused more damage. If the front was an indication of its general condition, then I shuddered to think what the other bits were like that I couldn't see.

Then the aircraft stopped spiralling, and entered a steep dive. I knew at this point that I had a good chance of getting it back on the ground with us all in one piece, hopefully. I just had to find a flat and big enough field. I shouted to the passengers "I've got it!!", in an attempt to reassure them and, subconsciously, enable me to express relief. However, I almost immediately thought it was a stupid remark to utter, and this was later confirmed by one of the passengers, who told me that he had wondered what I had got, because from where he was sitting things didn't look that good.

OK, things seemed to be back under some sort of control, but it wasn't over yet. The thought of being the last one pulled from the hole started to fade from my mind, and I set about trying to find a suitable landing area, and easing the aircraft out of the dive. I wasn't sure of the best glide speed, so I initially started to reduce the speed towards 100 knots, and put out a second Mayday to RAF Marham. As the speed decayed towards 110 knots, the aircraft started to roll again to the right. I quickly pushed the nose down to gain speed and, at about 130 knots, I had adequate control to enable me to carry out gentle manoeuvres. The noise in the cockpit was still quite deafening, and I didn't hear the response from Marham to the second Mayday. Also, the control column was vibrating violently, and I was concerned that the right hand windscreen, which was cracked, would fail and shower the passenger who was sitting in the co-pilot's seat with broken Perspex. I forced myself to stop thinking about the "what – ifs", and concentrate on getting us on the ground. We had lost a lot of height, and we were running out of time.

I had already started a turn to the left to look for somewhere suitable to land, and we were now down at 1500 feet, having spun or spiralled for about 3000 feet. I could see a barley field, but there was a set of power lines on the approach and it didn't look long enough. I continued the left turn, looking for somewhere more suitable, but none of the options looked bigger than the barley field. So I had to go for the barley field, but I couldn't make it safely from my position. I was too close, and there appeared to be a ditch in the over-run end of the field, so I would have to put us down as close to the pylons as I could. I continued to turn away from the field, conscious of the fact that if I turned too far away then we would be plucking Amazing Grace on the power lines. When I judged that we could make the field, I turned back and lowered the nose of the aircraft to aim just beyond the pylons.

My concern now was how the aircraft would react as the speed decayed during the flare, and just prior to touching the ground. I already had almost full rudder applied, to counterbalance the asymmetric aerodynamics of the damaged airframe, and there was very little additional control left to compensate for any late roll during the landing. The only option was to maintain the speed until the last minute, and then virtually fly the aircraft onto the ground at a fairly high speed, and hope the wing tip did not drop and dig in. I picked the spot and aimed for it. As we crossed the pylons, I told the passengers to brace, and looked over my shoulder to check them. I am not sure if they had read the literature, or were merely saying a few words to their Maker, but they seemed well prepared for the landing.

As the ground rapidly came up to meet us, I levelled the aircraft to skim the top of the barley. I could hear the vegetation rubbing on the underside as we started to sink to the ground and, at the same time, the aircraft began rolling to the right. We landed softly but firmly, and slid across the field. I felt a huge sigh of relief but, just as I thought it was all over, the aircraft swung through 90 degrees, and continued across the field sideways. We were still travelling at a fair speed at this stage, and appeared to be heading towards a brick building. Then, just as quickly as the panic had started again, it was all over. We came to a halt some distance from the building, and the aircraft rocked gently, as if to say "phew".

The passengers didn't need any encouragement to leave the aircraft, and they were outside before I could turn round. I eased myself out of the seat and joined them. There was a mixture of verbose joy and stunned silence, and some wandered around in a semi-daze for a few minutes, before settling down to the reality of it all. I looked at the wreckage, and marvelled that the aircraft could still fly in such a condition. The damage to the front of the fuselage was extensive, with the baggage compartment having been ripped open by a blade, shed from the right hand engine due to failure of the hub assembly. The blade and baggage had then continued across the aircraft and through the left hand engine. The rear elevator horns were both severely damaged, and bent through about 80 degrees. The loss of the blade from the right hand engine had caused severe imbalance on that side, and the vibration had ripped the engine from its mounting, leaving only part of the firewall and broken pipe work.

A farmer and his tractor arrived at the scene a few minutes after we clambered from the wreckage. He came over to speak to us, thinking that we were spectators who had arrived on the scene before him, and was stunned to be told that we had all been in the aircraft.

RAF Marham had responded to my Mayday quickly, and we were very soon joined by the search and rescue helicopter from RAF Coltishall, which flew us to Norwich and the end of our journey. As I was climbing into the helicopter, I thought that the face of the winch man looked familiar, and wondered if it was the same crewman who had rescued me several years before, when my Tornado caught fire and crashed. But that's another story.

The Piper Navajo (Credit: Author)

'Keep It Simple Stupid' Works

A Starfighter Wing was preparing for the Change-of-Command ceremony for the General of the Air Group. The routine was for a large formal parade to be held on the airfield, with a military band, an Advance in Review Order followed by General Salute, and then march pasts in quick and slow time – a 17-ship fly past was expected to coincide exactly with the General Salute.

The briefing was thorough, with pilots chosen equally from each of the 3 squadrons across the Wing. The senior squadron boss was the leader – Colonel Ferguson. The whole event has since become known as Fergie's Folly.

The positioning phase of the flight was low key and lasted some 45 minutes, with 4 x 4-ships flying in relaxed 'fighting wing' formations, following the Colonel as a singleton lead. The final run was about 8 minutes long and, half way through, a 90 degree turn was flown, with the formation in a big VIC – 8 on either side of the leader. The turn was necessary because of airspace restrictions, coupled with high terrain. At 5 miles to go, the leader called for the gear to be lowered, so that the landing-lights could be seen from the ground and, for further effect, the formation spacing doubled, making life pretty difficult. The 'whip' aircraft would break away at 4 miles to go, and the formation would hopefully be steady, and fly past on time!!

Because the ground rose very steeply some 6 miles beyond the parade, the plan required the formation to break quickly into 18 single aircraft for very high-speed, very low-level, opposition fly-pasts, separated by the width of the runway. Since all aircraft would be pretty low on fuel, the aircraft would then re-group in their 4-ship sections to land without delay.

The break itself was a complicated affair. On the leader's call of 'Break Break Go', all pilots were to raise the gear immediately and then, from the outside, aircraft were to break away at 2 second intervals, before accelerating and positioning for individual flypasts.

On the practice day, the visibility was good, with a high cloud-base and no low-level turbulence; the wind was 10 knots down the in-use runway, and the whole detail went without a hitch, and was enormous fun! However, on the day of the parade, the weather was quite different. Close to the airfield it was hazy, the cloud-base much lower at 1200ft, the wind stronger, and the turbulence significant - making things much more testing all round! Although the flypast was deemed a great success, inside the formation things were frenetic; I should know as I was flying near the outside of the VIC, with 7 aircraft inside me on my left, and just one other outside on my right. There was just a mile to run from the flypast datum before the formation had finally settled enough to allow the outside aircraft to maintain a steady position. All of us were pretty tense, and frankly quite stressed.

In my case, things nearly went really wrong on the break, when everything seemed to go into slow motion. I raised my gear on cue and looked right to see the No 8 start his break. I immediately looked to my front again to count 'one potato, two potato' to time my break, and saw No 6 to my left already had 90deg of right bank on, and was about to head my way. Rudder, bank and reheat saw me out of there in amazingly quick time – self preservation is a funny thing, and I think he had a bit of a rough ride through my slip-stream – ha!

The sortie debrief was something to behold. It was clear from the outset that others had had even more of an exciting time than me. Showing no inhibitions, pilots of all seniorities ripped into the Colonel for his over-ambitious, naive plan; one that could so nearly have ended in disaster. The corporate view, as ever, was that to ignore the KISS principle with so many aircraft was folly – in this case FERGIE's FOLLY!!

Mid-Air Collision

Back in 1966, I was a Qualified Flying Instructor, based at RAF Syerston, where I taught basic training on the Jet Provost. Early one May morning, I briefed my student for an 0800 take-off on his first spinning exercise and, as we entered the engineering hut to sign for our aircraft, I saw that another instructor was doing likewise. A little later, as we settled into our aircraft (a Mk4 Provost) and started our checks, I noted that the other instructor appeared to be in a hurry to get airborne. We were not the first aircraft up that morning, as the RAF Syerston aerobatic team, call-sign Viper Red, had been aloft on a practice sortie since 0730 but, being a highly competitive young man, I hastened our preparations, and we duly taxied out in front of the other aircraft, which was a Mk3.

The cloud-base was around 1000 feet, so I elected to depart under Instrument Flight Rules, which required us to climb on a heading of 315 degrees, as opposed to the much slower Mk3 Provost, which headed 305 to ensure separation. We duly took off and, after some 4 minutes in thick and turbulent gloom, shot out into a circular area of bright blue with a piercing sun blazing down. Almost immediately, my student, who was seated on the left side, yelled that a formation was about to hit us. I instinctively pulled back hard on the stick (an action that I later realised had saved our lives), after which there was an almighty bang and then total silence. Some time later, the Board of Enquiry evidence showed that Viper Red were halfway through their aerobatic sequence, when I popped out of cloud and ruined their (and my) morning.

Meanwhile, back in my aircraft, things had gone from bad to worse. We were heading rapidly downwards in a high rotation spin, and the standard recovery actions were having no effect due, as I later discovered, to the fact that we no longer had a tail. We had been cut in half, just behind the cockpit, by Viper Red leader's starboard wing. I shouted, "Eject, eject" to my student, but he just looked at me because the intercom was dead, so I took my hands off the controls to rip off my mask. As it happened, my student had been asking me if he should eject so, when he saw my hands leave the controls, he interpreted this as an intention to imminently vacate one of Her Majesty's aircraft, and duly went for the bottom handle of his seat. There was a blinding flash, and he departed in a cloud of dust at a subsequently recorded height of 4000 feet. I eventually exited in similar fashion at around 1000 feet.

While the ejection was quite violent, it all happened very quickly, and I was soon dangling from a parachute and looking downwards to see where I might land. To my horror, I saw that the strong surface wind (which was actually twice the normally permitted maximum for parachuting) was blowing me towards the centre of a small village on the outskirts of Nottingham. All too soon, the final hundred feet of flight arrived, and I realised that I was destined for a playing field with some adjacent power cables and a spiked metal fence, a main road or, potentially worst of all, a v-shaped roof. Of course, I landed on the roof (of a pub called "The Four Bells") and, in spite of my parachute training some years before at Cranwell, I was dragged across the tiles, which removed lumps of flying suit and skin. The parachute remained inflated by the strong wind, and plucked me sideways off the roof, whereupon I fell directly to the ground just short of the main road. It then collapsed, like a very large bed sheet, and completely enveloped a car that was travelling along the far side.

I gingerly picked myself up and, to my astonishment, felt no serious pain, or evidence of broken bones. I unbuckled the parachute and started walking towards the now stationary car, still dressed in a tatty, bloodstained, light blue flying suit, white leather gloves and the rest of my gear. The latter consisted of a bulbous blue helmet, with dark visor across the front, while my lower face was enveloped by a black oxygen mask, with the supply tube dangling below. I approached the driver's door, and lifted the parachute silk. The car contained a doctor, his wife (also seated in the front), and eighteen-year-old daughter. His account of the incident is as follows:

I was driving peacefully along this road at around 0810 on a Monday morning, accompanied by my wife. We were taking our daughter to Nottingham University, and travelling at approximately 35mph, when we suffered a sudden and complete white-out. I slammed on the brakes, we skidded to a halt, and were sitting in shock when the whiteout area by my window was lifted by a pair of large, white pigmented hands. I saw what I can only describe as a Martian from outer space. It had a blue head, large black eyes, elephantine features and was bleeding red blood."

As I lifted the parachute clear of the window, I saw the driver sitting transfixed, with his hands glued to the steering wheel. According to the doctor, who kindly visited me in hospital some time later, I then removed my oxygen masked, beamed at his daughter and exclaimed, "How lovely to see such a beautiful face!"

Having successfully terrified an innocent doctor and his family, and declined the offer of a glass of whisky from the publican, I looked down the road to see my student being dragged backwards by a parachute, to which he was still firmly attached. I rushed to assist him with disconnecting the harness, and quickly realised he was suffering severe back pain, which is a common injury associated with cartridge-fired ejection seats. There was a butcher's shop next door to the pub, so I dragged him through the entrance and, with assistance from the staff, he was laid on the slab to await the arrival of an ambulance. It was a uniquely comical sight, with the customers on one side, the butcher on the other, and my student in the middle, only missing a price tag.

The formation I had rudely interrupted fared little better. The leader's aircraft burst into flames, the controls failed, and it then collided with the one next to it. The leader ejected safely, but the pilot of the second aircraft, escorted by another member of the formation, managed to land back at Syerston, where it became apparent that the fireball had stripped the dayglo red paint off both aircraft and restored them to their original, pristine metallic silver.

Meanwhile, my aircraft had spiralled earthwards, causing havoc where bits of it landed. A man had gone to collect his bicycle from the shed, only to find that one of the tyres was flat. He returned to the house to collect his pump, and was exiting the back door for the second time when there was a loud "whumph", and the shed and bicycle disappeared before his eyes in a large ball of flame. The gentleman was later quoted as saying, "I had no bloody idea what had happened, but I ran into my house, grabbed a hot cup of tea and put some brandy in it." Another cyclist, beset by lumps of metal raining from the sky, plunged into a ditch, where he was severely stung by nettles and needed urgent medical treatment. Wreckage was spread over a wide area and, a mile from the main crash site, four young men took the opportunity to abscond from their Borstal when 'confusion rained down' on the premises. Fortunately, they were caught after a few days on the run.

Post Script

In time, both my student and I returned to flying duties, and the ejection incident was a distant memory when, some years later, I was one of a number of parachutists sitting in the back of a C-130 Hercules. As we approached the Drop Zone at Weston-on-the-Green, the aircraft captain appeared to check that preparations were complete and, to my surprise and delight, I realised that it was my former student. After exchanging pleasantries, he wasted no time in telling me, with a broad grin, that this time I was most definitely the only one of us who was leaving the aircraft while it was still airborne.

Jet Provost Mk4

Not Me Guv'

At the time, I was on the Queen's Flight at RAF Northolt flying the HS125. This was the civilian version of the RAF Dominie, with an immaculate interior of white leather and mahogany in great abundance. Besides transporting Royalty around Europe, we also positioned just about anyone within the military, as well as VVIPs such as the PM and Cabinet members.

As part of the job, there was a generous allowance of training hours, to ensure we had a chance to experience some of the airfields most likely to be visited, along with more glamorous locations - like Venice - that just happened to have the best luncheon allowances! Each pilot was allocated seven hours training so, with two pilots on board, that made fourteen hours. By taking a piece of string 'fourteen hours long,' we could pin European airfields on a chart and spread the training over three days, by flagging three or four destinations each day. We'd then fill the cabin with any cabin crew under training, and offer the spare seats to other departments within the station.

Brussels airport was a frequent destination for us, and so we duly found ourselves in the descent there. I was in the left hand seat, with another captain in the right and our training captain, Jim, on the 'jump seat', watching the proceedings. After we had landed, we were handed over to the ground controller, who gave us our taxi instructions. I might add here that it was often crucial to deliver our VIP to the reception area, and ensure that the aircraft door opened as close as possible to the expected time. This meant we had to work out which runway was in use, and the distance we would need to taxi, in order to calculate how much time we should allow. Training flights were ideal for this.

On this occasion, Jim remarked that our routing was unusual and that we would now be a couple of minutes early, but we were not to delay and just carry on taxiing. After a few turns, we saw where we were going to be parked, and slowed down for the last 100 feet or so. As we approached, I noted, to my surprise, that there seemed to be a lot of activity on the pan, and mentioned it to Jim. He couldn't see this from where he was sitting until we were nearly there, whereupon he made some exclamation, told me to only shut down the left hand engine, and promptly got up to open the door.

I stopped the aircraft and, when I looked down to the left, I saw lots of shiny black cars, men and women dressed ever so smartly, a brass band, a guard of honour, police and the Prime Minister of Belgium! Just before Jim opened the door, the Prime Minister stepped forward in anticipation, the band started playing, and all the military arms and swords came up for the salute. By then I sensed that all was not going to plan, and have to say that a Peter Sellers scene comes to mind when I recollect what happened next. The door had integral steps and hinged down from the top, and Jim was having a lot of difficulty getting it to fully deploy. He couldn't see that he'd dropped it directly onto two guys who had just unrolled the last 10 feet of red carpet, and were on their hands and knees smoothing out the end underneath the aircraft. Jim eventually lowered the door, and waved his hands back and forth in a 'not me guv' gesture. The salutes faltered, the band gently crumbled and stopped, and someone ran up to the aircraft. Meanwhile, I heard another "Ascot" call-sign taxiing in and realised that the tower had confused us with the following, similar, aircraft that had Margaret Thatcher on board. I managed to pass this information to Jim, who hastily closed the door, and we taxied off on the remaining engine in time to allow Maggie's aircraft to take our place. She was, of course, on time!

HS125 (Credit: John Malley)

Running On Empty

It started as an uneventful night practice intercept sortie, from our base at RAF Wildenrath in Germany, the one slightly unusual aspect being that we were working over the North Sea instead of over land. The weather forecast was for a cloud base of about 700 – 1000 feet with slight rain, so I was a bit surprised when, after the fourth practice intercept, we got a weather recall. "What's the problem?" I asked our Intercept Controller. "The weather is clamping in from the west, and Wildenrath's forecast has changed to YELLOW TWO[1], and possibly AMBER, within the hour," he replied so, without further ado, we headed for home. There was still no cause for alarm but, by the time that Dutch Military Radar handed us over to Clutch Radar (the British military area radar station covering the RAF airfields in Germany), the rot had really begun to set in.

My wingman was a bit lower on fuel than me, so I sent him down first and, after a lazy orbit for separation, was about to follow when Clutch asked for our fuel state. They were handling some diverted traffic from further west that was hurting for fuel, and wanted to get into the radar pattern ahead of us so, after confirming that we still had a bit to spare, we went into a delaying dog-leg. Eventually, it was our turn to enter the radar pattern but, when we contacted Wildenrath Approach, the controller gave us the uncomfortable news that my wingman had only just scraped in, and the airfield was expected to deteriorate to RED within minutes. Realising that we couldn't shorten our radar pattern because of the diverted traffic in front of us, I elected to go to RAF Laarbruch (to the north of Wildenrath) instead, and we turned onto our new heading before being handed back to Clutch.

We were on finals to land at Laarbruch when the airfield went RED, and the ants started to crawl up the back of my neck as I overshot and asked for local airfield weather states. Clutch told me that the German Air Force base at Norvenich was YELLOW ONE and, although it was south of Wildenrath, we decided that it was probably our best bet. The weather recall had left us with a bit more

---

[1] NATO airbases used a colour coding system to indicate the prevailing meteorological conditions in relation to cloud base and visibility. Starting with the best they were BLUE, WHITE, GREEN, YELLOW, AMBER and RED.

fuel than we would normally have had at this stage and, in any case, a night in a German Officers Mess with a few beers, and maybe a bratwurst, would make a pleasant change. "Yes please Clutch," I said, "And we'll be fuel priority."

We turned on to heading, and had begun heading south, when Clutch informed us that we were number one to land at Norvenich. I started to relax at this news but, just as we got onto finals, Norvenich went RED*, and the ants were back with a vengeance! B----y hell what next? Stay calm, no good panicking. "Not our night," came the somewhat anxious voice from the rear seat, "Any bright ideas?" Before I could reply, the Norvenich controller told me that Wildenrath had improved to YELLOW TWO, and everywhere else was either AMBER or RED. No time for vacillating. If we continued our approach and had to overshoot, we might not have enough fuel to get back to Wildenrath, whereas, if we abandoned it now, we could just about get there. I told Norvenich we were going to Wildenrath and were also declaring a 'Pan'. This meant that we were now officially an aircraft in an emergency situation, and would therefore acquire high priority as we tried to get back on the ground in one piece.

As we headed back to Wildenrath, we discussed our situation. There was enough fuel for an approach, but not much more and, if we missed this one, it was Martin Baker time - we would have to eject! What a change in fortune, compared with the routine sortie a short while earlier, from fat, dumb and happy to OMG in about 45 minutes. We considered jettisoning the underwing tanks, but were over a fairly densely inhabited part of Germany and, at the speed we were now flying, it wouldn't have made much difference anyway. Our collective state of mind wasn't helped by the Wildenrath controller who, on handover, informed us that the weather had deteriorated again; it was back to AMBER. "We haven't got the fuel to go anywhere else," I told him, "If we miss this approach we'll have to eject." There was a distinct pause before he acknowledged.

The next piece of bad news from Wildenrath almost seemed inevitable. It was RED again, with occasional improvements to AMBER but, from our perspective, there was no further decision to make, and we had to press on in the hope of landing. If I didn't see the runway, we would have to overshoot and eject, so we discussed where to 'dump' the aircraft to minimise the collateral damage on the ground. However, we certainly would not get very far, as our fuel gauges were now in the range that the Aircrew Manual described as 'unreliable'.

We reached Wildenrath without further mishap and, as we approached decision height to land, I stared through the windscreen into a grey blanket, with my heart in my mouth.

Please, please let me see the lights – wait a second, what's that?

A bright blue and white luminescence just off to the right.

It's the Aral garage just outside the perimeter fence!

So we're lined up OK, the lights must show up now... pause... there! An approach light, good grief it's close! Threshold lights, runway, thump – we're down! Brake, deploy braking parachute, nosewheel steering, more brake – I can hardly see enough to keep straight... ah, there's the centreline of the runway. Thank you, God.

We slowed to taxying speed and turned off the runway. Air traffic asked us if we needed any assistance, and my back-seater suggested they could arrange for a change of underpants. "No thanks Wildenrath, we're fine," I responded. Of course we were fine; a bit shaken maybe, and a bit wiser certainly, but still fine.

Post Script

The following day, the Squadron Senior Engineering Officer quietly took me to one side and told me that, when our aircraft had been refuelled, the amount of fuel put in had equalled what an F4 in that configuration was supposed to hold in total. Quite sobering really!

Who Would Be An Engineer?

Back in the 1970s, the RAF ran full page advertisements in the press for Engineering Officers. The following article is an abridged version of a spoof advertisement that appeared in the RAF Lossiemouth Station Magazine, when the venerable Shackleton was still, just about, providing Airborne Early Warning (AEW) cover for the United Kingdom.

You can't fail to notice that there's something radically different about it! A direct descendant of the wartime Lancaster, the bulbous profile of the Mk2 AEW Shackleton betrays its totally un-aerodynamic nature. Very simply, this archaic flying radar station is Britain's oldest contribution to NATO's air defence network. A network that can sometimes detect high or low-flying, potentially hostile, aircraft or missiles, in time to actually do something about it.

The AEW Shackleton is jam-packed with technological antiquities. For any electronics engineer, it'll be like a trip back into pre-history, filled with some of the most ancient radar, primitive hardware and non-existent software you could hope to find. Yet that is exactly what you could be doing after a 12 month, fully paid, post graduate aero-systems course, following your commissioning as an officer. And don't forget that the training you receive could count towards your Chartered Historical Engineer status.

There are over 2000 Engineer Officers in the RAF, and some of the far-ranging opportunities open to them will give you new insights into rapidly disappearing technologies. In the communications and electronics field, you could find yourself working on one of the most complex and baffling military data processing systems in NATO: the Shackleton intercom system. You might command our line servicing flight, where a blood, sweat and tears-driven operation links hammers and big spanners with the oldest flying radar in the World. You too could become an expert in guesswork fault tracing, random valve exchange, and inaccessible component replacement. Along the way, you will gain the satisfaction of ensuring the continued airworthiness of a bona fide museum piece, so old that the pointed bit is at the back, and so slow that birds collide with the trailing edge of the wing.

You may have built the Airfix model when you were young; well, now you have the opportunity to work on the real thing! But, if we've whetted your appetite, don't delay, because we're quickly running out of spares and patience.

RAF Engineering Officer. The job has never been so important.

Avro Shackleton AEW Mk2

One Less Landing Than Take-Off

It was in the summer of 84; I was a Jaguar flight commander at an idyllic base in East Anglia, which was separated from the rest of the air force by an invisible 'happiness barrier', whose exact position on the A11 was indeterminate, but certainly east of Marham. We, I hasten to add, were on the good side. All 3 squadrons were participating in an offensive support exercise, which involved targets in Wales. I had drawn the shortest straw possible, which involved sitting in the tower as duty pilot all morning, and then leading a formation comprising all the jets we could muster in the afternoon. The weather in the target area was extremely average, but the met-man promised the standard 10Z[1] clearance. Well, 10 became 11, and eventually it dawned on the exercise controller that it might be 10Z the next day. Salvation, however, was at hand; some bright spark unearthed a slot at Otterburn and, without so much as a 'by your leave', we were re-tasked to the north. The extra good news was that the TOT[2] at Otterburn was earlier than the original in Wales, which would make the planning process even more relaxed and orderly. Out went the Ho Chi Minh Trail[3], to be replaced by the leapfrog of lightships up the North Sea, and the standard Red Flag 'gorilla'[4]. There was no time for finesse, so the individual element leaders were given TOT brackets for deconfliction and a basic routeing, and left to get on with it. Due to late turnrounds from previous sorties, the planned 8 aircraft from each squadron became a marginally more manageable 6 and, more by good luck than good judgment, 18 aircraft taxied out at the appointed hour. So far, so good – but not for very long.

In order to reduce radio transmissions after take-off, I had briefed an uncalled change from Tower to Approach. This worked fine for 5 of the first 6 aircraft; however, my No 2 (a fine gentleman, whose name shall remain a secret – but let us, for the sake of the story, call him 'Frog') had been distracted by a

---

[1] Z = GMT

[2] Time on Target

[3] A standard low level routing from Norfolk to mid-Wales

[4] The 'same way, same day' formation, beloved of participants in Red Flag and other major exercises; it simplified planning, deconflicted different elements, and saturated defences

problem on take-off, and remained on Tower frequency as we bravely headed out in the general direction of Sheringham on the north Norfolk coast. At this point, Approach picked up a contact ahead of us, coming in our direction – the thot plickens! We were flying in a formation called Card 6 for obvious reasons – 3 pairs in 3-mile trail, each pair in one-mile line abreast. Unfortunately, Approach were confused about which was which in the lead pair, and called the contact in front of No 2 instead of No 1 – with me so far? This would not have mattered, since the eagle-eyed Frog had a bead on the contact, and called it 'down the throat', a common but non-standard term for another aircraft approaching head-on. We would have known what he meant if, of course, he had been calling it on the same frequency as the rest of us were on.

Meanwhile, I had got tired of scanning the sky ahead of Frog, in a vain attempt to acquire the contact, and resumed my normal lookout forward just in time to see my entire windscreen full of Tornado. I ducked instinctively (probably well after he passed) and felt a thump on the airframe. At first the aircraft flew sort of straight, and I thought I'd got away with it. Then it yawed violently, and I jabbed the appropriate rudder pedal (normally a footrest in the Jag). This seemed to do the trick, and I started congratulating myself again, just as a bigger thump from the back heralded the next phase of my flight – a rapid roll and nose drop, accompanied by an eye-catching assortment of the available lights on the warning panel. This was pretty academic, since it was becoming clear even to me that I wasn't likely to be around long enough to deal with any of them. Photographic evidence later indicated that this was the point at which the tail fell off.

I had been flying at about 1000 feet at 450 knots, so a roll and nose drop didn't take long to translate itself into a windscreen full of sea. I recall pulling the ejection seat handle, more out of curiosity than hope, and I had adopted the recommended ejection posture, to the extent that my left hand was still on the throttles as I left the aircraft like a sack of spuds. I was conscious of severe tumbling, and then an almighty deceleration (at those heights, there is no time for niceties in the functioning of the seat automatics). About a swing and a half in the parachute, and I hit the sea like a flounder rejected by a trawler, and headed for Davy Jones. I had not even thought about my emergency drills, but I must have done the one that counted – inflating my lifejacket - because I popped back out again pretty smartly. I struggled out of my harness, pulled the dinghy towards me and inflated it. Getting into it wasn't that easy, since I seemed to be a bit tangled up in straps and cords and things, but I even remembered to sling out the sea drogue (designed to hold the dinghy into wind) as I made my undignified entrance.

Things got a little less hectic then; it was a warm and sunny July afternoon with a light breeze, so I did a spot of sunbathing. I was having difficulty in hauling my survival kit on board, and the dinghy seemed to be trying to sink itself, but I couldn't get too bothered about that. I could see the remains of the smoke from where my jet had hit the water, and inland another tell-tale plume of smoke bore witness to the fact that the Tornado hadn't done much better than me. I could see the helicopter getting airborne from base, and rejoiced in the knowledge that they would always attend to a survivor in the water before one on land.

Meanwhile, back in the air, confusion reigned. The 4 of my formation who hadn't seen the Tornado, and didn't really know what had gone on, were broadcasting their best guesses on Approach. Frog, on the other hand, was telling it like it was on Tower. In the midst of this mayhem, in an exemplary display of either devotion to duty or lack of situational awareness, the leader of the last formation – which was still on the ground – called 'Cresta, stand by to hack[5]'. His only reward was a response from the duty pilot, 'Sid, you're going nowhere'.

My exciting afternoon wasn't quite over yet, though. The helicopter approached, and I tried to disentangle myself, so that I could be winched up. I remember feeling that something was not quite right about this, but it wasn't until I was pulled clear of the water that I realised that, contrary to every dinghy drill I had ever done, the chopper had come from behind me instead of from in front. As I dangled on the wire, it became apparent why this was. From the front end of my dinghy hung a limp 6" drogue; from the other end billowed a nicely deployed 18-foot one – the result of my never having been able to jettison my parachute, which remained attached to the dinghy through my harness.

Once in the helicopter, I was ordered by the lovely (she - it was a she!) but quite forceful doctor to sit in the corner and behave myself, while we went to fetch the Tornado crew. As I sat there, I became aware that a spare comms lead

---

[5] A synchronisation of timing reference within the formation

was dangling from the bulkhead. Keen to find out what was going on, I plugged it in. Error! With a helmet still full of water and lots of static, the wiggly-amps took the path of least resistance – straight through what had, until take-off time, been my brain. The perfect end to a perfect sortie.

There are a couple of footnotes to this saga. The first involves the reaction of the Tornado pilot (a friend then, but an even better one later, as we pounded the AOC's Wilton together)[6]. I stumbled, regardless of the Doc's orders, from the helicopter to see how he was, only to be greeted by a look of complete bewilderment (he was not aware at this stage that he had hit another aircraft). What was said then has been reported apocryphally more times than I can shake a long stick at. Suffice to say that it had something to do with "how long has he been on helicopters?" The second occurred at Ely Hospital where, having trailed around from department to department carrying our flying kit (in case we had sustained back injuries in our ejections), we were pronounced fully fit, and then immediately told by the sister that we were to stay in our beds and not to get out even for the potty.

So, that is the tale of how I came to share ownership of the north Norfolk Coast 'flow arrows'[7]. How I subsequently acquired a 50% interest in the Hexham arrows is another story...

---

[6] A reference to the 'interview, with hat, without coffee' with the Air Officer Commanding, consequent on being found wanting by a Board of Inquiry

[7] Mandatory 'one way streets' in congested airspace

One Of Your Bolder Attempted Interceptions

A bonus of night flying is the opportunity to enjoy the view of the night sky. If you know your stars and follow things astronomical, as I have always done, it becomes a privilege and a joy. So one night, around 1974 or 75, I was cruising slowly across the North Sea in a Lightning Mk 3 towards the Lincolnshire coast, enjoying the view. It was gin clear, moonless and with a rare alignment of the planets occurring in the west.

My task for the first part of the sortie was to provide a target for our Squadron Junior Pilot, 'Cockney Lad'. He was everything a young fighter pilot should be: bold, brash, confident, good enough to earn the respect of his peers and with the sharp repartee that you'd expect of a cockney.

As far as 'Cockney Lad' was concerned, his task was to intercept and identify an unknown target. I was lights out. That called for a slow, careful approach on radar, stabilising at radar minimum range of 300 yards, trying to pick up visually an aircraft shape against the star background, and creeping in to identify it without bumping into it. It was not easy. For that reason, I was flying straight and level at medium altitude and about 300kts, to make it as easy as it could be.

I heard the fighter controller giving 'Cockney Lad' his intercept directions and his task, and saw his jet on radar, and then visually as he turned to drop in behind me. He called "Judy", meaning that he had control of the intercept.

Then a strange thing happened.

He appeared below and to the left, rocketing past in full burner! The burners faded off into the distance ahead of me.

Fighter controller, "Do you require more assistance?"

"No, I'll be complete shortly"

A minute or so later, "Identified, one Lightning, ready for next split, and make it a short one please." 'Cockney Lad' had thrown most of his fuel out the back end. I was mystified, and looking forward to the debrief.

The next short intercept was uneventful, and we returned to our base at RAF Binbrook as a pair.

Walking in from the jets, 'Cockney Lad' comes up. "What the f*** speed were you doing then?"

"What, me? 300 knots."

"B*******! I was doing 1.5[1] and not catching you, and you didn't even have your burners in."

CLANG. The penny dropped.

The Lightning had twin tail lights and so, from behind, you saw both, side by side. The rare astronomical event that evening was the closest approach of Venus and Jupiter for centuries, side by side low in the west! He had gone from radar to visual a bit prematurely. It would have been a long, long chase!

Sorry about that 'Cockney Lad', but it was a story worth telling in a good cause.

Lightning Mk3 (Credit: John Malley)

---

[1] Mach 1.5 (approx 1000 mph at 30,000 feet)

Tracing The Route

July and August 1974 were difficult months for those of us based in Cyprus, as we dealt with the evacuation in the wake of the Turkish invasion. At the time, I was Officer Commanding Kingsfield, which was the emergency airstrip for Dhekelia Sovereign Base Area, and our task was to fly out Service dependants and tourists to RAF Akrotiri, for onward transit to the UK. The passenger terminal was a dilapidated, corrugated iron hangar, and an important element of my job was to make regular rounds of the many people awaiting evacuation, to check that all was well and to answer any questions. On one such occasion, a dear old lady approached me and said, "Squadron Leader, you and your chaps are doing a marvellous job, and I don't wish to complain, but you haven't provided us with anywhere to mail our postcards".

On another occasion, a group of wives, who were dependants of a Scottish regiment, asked me what was going to happen to them. Squatting down in front of where they were seated, I used the bare knee and lower thigh of one lady to trace out their route back to the UK. Moving my finger to the left I explained that they would go from here to Akrotiri. I then went on to say that they would be repatriated to either RAF Lyneham or RAF Brize Norton, and moved my finger just above the lady's knee to the left and then the right to indicate the two, different routes. With a broad grin on her face she said, "It's a bloody good job you're not taking me to Glasgow!"

Wakey - Wakey!

As we slowed down on the runway at RAF Akrotiri, a female voice from Air Traffic Control announced, "Message for the co-pilot, bar at 1830". It was only an overnight stop so, while we were putting the aircraft to bed, I confirmed with my captain (who also happened to be my Flight Commander) that we were not due to depart until 1600 local the next day. This ensured that I could have a sociable evening, but still meet the 8 hour 'bottle to throttle' requirement with ease. Excellent! Time for a shower and change, before heading bar-wards to meet the mystery voice.

I should, perhaps, mention that, in those days, the Officers' Mess bar at RAF Akrotiri in Cyprus was a crossroads. It was almost impossible to go in there of an evening, or anytime over a weekend, and not bump into someone you knew. That occasion was no exception and, as I walked through the door, I was greeted with the usual diffident derision by a bunch of people I had known since flying training days. They were a mixture of resident Hercules and Vulcan drivers, with a couple of visiting Lightning jocks, all of whom were ready to hit a kebab house in downtown Limassol. How could I refuse?

Suffice to say that the evening was a roaring success. Copious quantities of local food and wine were consumed and, at one stage, I recall being handed a Bouzouki by the owner in the clear expectation that I could get a tune out of it. Fortunately (or perhaps unfortunately), we managed "Zorbas' Dance" and "Never on a Sunday", which generated much bonhomie with the locals and free brandy for as long as we continued to drink it.

I confess to not being entirely sober when I eventually arrived back in my room, to find a note on the pillow. "Sorry but take-off has been brought forward to 0900. Crew in at 0630". All I could do was set the alarm for 0600, down as much cold water as I could ship, swallow a couple of aspirins, and hit the sack. Five hours later, the alarm went off and I jumped out of bed feeling remarkably clear-headed. However, those who have enjoyed the delights of Cypriot red wine (the big K) will know what's coming next! Half an hour later, I arrived at the crew transport feeling like death on a stick. Luckily for me, the captain had already left to pick up the met forecast, and I was clearly viewed as young and foolish by the ancient operators who sat in the rear seats. "Come with me, young man", said the Air Electronics Operator (AEO), as he put a kindly arm around my shoulder, and off we set for the aeroplane. I was tasked with removing the engine intake covers, while the AEO did just about everything else. So I laboriously climbed up the step-ladder and extracted the large 'bung' that covered the front of numbers 1 and 2 engines but, having dropped it to the ground below, that was about the limit of my capability. The sun was already beating down, so I lay back in the engine intake.....and dozed off.

I was jolted from my slumber by a very loud and rhythmic clicking. "S***", I thought, "That's the bloody igniters, someone's starting the engines!" Ignoring the step-ladder, I dived out of the intake and, fortunately, landed in an ungainly heap on the 'bung' I had earlier removed. Looking up at the cockpit with a mixture of fear and anger, I saw the AEO's face grinning down at me. He had spotted my legs hanging over the wing, and guessed what had happened. He then climbed into the cockpit, switched on the Battery Master and pressed the Engine Relight Buttons for numbers 1 and 2 engines. It had the desired effect! I sharpened up considerably after that and, following a stout breakfast in the Aircrew Feeder and 10 minutes on 100% oxygen after strapping in, I was good to go. As we taxied out, I even consoled myself with the thought that I had managed the 8 hours 'bottle to throttle' and vowed never to touch Kokinelli again. Ah, the promises we make in haste!

Oh, the female Air Traffic Controller? She was the girlfriend of a pal who was flying the Hercules. They've been married for nearly 40 years now.

A Close Shave At Darwin

In the 70s, support to the SEATO Treaty saw regular rapid deployments of V-Force Vulcans from the UK to Darwin and Singapore. Aside from rapid aircraft regeneration on arrival, to demonstrate air power deterrence to the perceived Indonesian threat, one of the main aims of the deployment was to drop live ordnance on the unmanned Quail Island bombing range close to Darwin.

Some clever chap had decided that simulated bombing runs would be flown north-south, and live runs in the reverse direction, and our mid-day sortie included a simulated attack at the range, which was booked with our Duty Operations Officer. Unfortunately, shift change then occurred on the Ops Desk and, with no apparent record of our reserved range time, the new Ops Officer booked a live run for another crew, but with our overhead target time. Live sorties comprised a stick of 7 High Explosive 1000 lb bombs, dropped from a minimum height of 3500 feet for safe separation and to avoid fratricide from the explosions.

No other units were using the range during our deployment and, since it was unmanned, there were none of the usual radio transmission clearance calls. We therefore entered the range for a 500 foot simulated target run, completely oblivious to our fellow squadron crew, some 3000 feet above us and coming in the opposite direction! Luckily we were very slightly off the designated target run line, and all I can remember is a cry from one of the pilots of 'Jesus, I don't believe it!' This was followed by repeated heavy thumps, as our aircraft was severely buffeted by the impact of bombs exploding immediately beneath us, at a height well below safe separation altitude. When the pilots had recovered their composure, they told us that a stick of seven 1000 lb bombs had passed a whisker away from our starboard wing. Had we been closer to the precise target, that stick would have blown our Vulcan to pieces, and us with it!

Subsequently, our buddies' in-flight camera provided clear evidence of our aircraft, with a perfect stick exploding immediately below – a direct hit on the range target, but amazingly no damage to us. The Mess Bar was quickly opened for a post-sortie debrief, where our squadron 'adversaries', not to mention the Duty Ops Officers of the day, bought the beers!

Unsurprisingly, range procedures for Quail Island changed overnight, but I for one can vividly remember the experiences of that day some 37 years later!

Double Dutch

The Buccaneer was the only RAF aircraft capable of providing stand-off airborne target laser designation, from 1979, when PaveSpike was first introduced, until 1991, when the TIALD[1] pod finally came into service on the Tornado. Should the formation be engaged en route, the Buccaneers were well able to defend themselves, with their Sidewinder air-to-air missiles, chaff[2] packets (loaded into the airbrake), the ECM[3] pod and the 4 retard 1000lb bombs, which could be used as a 'last ditch' defence against a fighter carrying out an attack from astern. It is interesting to note that the Buccaneers' major operational contribution to the Gulf War of 1991 was as airborne laser designators, albeit from high level rather than the low level scenario for which we practised so much.

A by-product of this activity was the opportunity to become involved in the NATO squadron exchange scheme. A Dutch F16 squadron (No.322), based at Leeuwarden, was equipped to carry Laser Guided Bombs (LGBs) and, with the assistance of our man in NATO, we organised a squadron exchange with them. The Dutch were very keen to toss some of their LGBs at Garvie Island, the Cape Wrath weapons range, as there was nowhere in Holland where they could do this. We were naturally going to provide the laser designation for them, thereby giving a graphic demonstration of true NATO interoperability. Two Buccaneers and two F16s set off for Garvie, the weather was good and I had an expert PaveSpike operator, Norman Browne, as my navigator. The live toss bombing exercise was a great success, with all the F16s' bombs guiding well and impacting on target. Norman even managed to organise an HF radio link to our man in Germany, to tell him of our success. So far, so good. The plan was then to fly across the 'moon country' in the north of Scotland, escorted by the two F16s, to be bounced by a third F16. The 'bounce' duly turned up, and our two Buccaneers accelerated off, leaving the three Dutchmen to indulge in a bit of air combat. Half an hour later, we were sat in the debrief, watching the

---

[1] TIALD - Thermal Imaging Airborne Laser Designator

[2] Chaff – Air deployed radar countermeasure of small, thin pieces of aluminium or metallised glass

[3] ECM – Electronic Counter Measure

PaveSpike videos, when a broadcast from Air Traffic Control announced that an F16 was returning to the circuit with engine handling problems... it was our bounce aircraft, which had got airborne somewhat later than us. A few moments later, Air Traffic announced that the aircraft had landed safely, and we went back to our debrief. Suddenly, the door to the briefing room burst open, revealing an incandescent F16 pilot, gibbering away in what can only be described as Double Dutch. All the remaining Dutchmen immediately leapt to their feet and rushed upstairs to their detachment office, slamming the door shut behind them. Sounds of considerable altercation came from behind the closed door and, at this point, my Warrant Officer sidled up to me. '"I think you had better come out to the flight line and have a look at this" he said. There sat the F16 with a thin wisp of vapour coming out of a jet pipe that, on closer inspection, was riddled with 20 mm bullet holes around the back end. "Get it into the hangar as quick as you can", I told him.

By now, the Dutch had calmed down somewhat, and were able to offer an explanation. After leaving the bombing range, one of the pilots had failed to put his master armament switch to safe. Dutch F16s always flew with a full load of 20 mm ball ammunition, apparently to keep the Centre of Gravity within limits. Our pilot found himself in a position to claim a shot at the F16 ahead of him, he selected guns, air-to-air, pressed the trigger to film his opponent with the gun camera and, because his master arm switch was still live, the gun fired. Fortunately he was only tracking the rear of the aircraft ahead, not the cockpit as is normal. However, seeing that nothing appeared amiss with his opponent, he decided to say nothing and carried on with the fight! His opponent, unaware of what had happened, continued with his sortie and only became aware that something was not quite right when he rejoined the circuit.

The Dutch decided to lock up their miscreant pilot in the detachment office for the rest of the day/night, and I went to see the Station Commander to brief him on the affair. His immediate and understandable reaction was that we should tell someone; I urged caution. After all, the incident took place over moon country and was unlikely to have been witnessed by anyone, and the Dutch were doubtless going to take care of the culprit in their own way. If anyone brought in a dead sheep riddled with 20mm, or even a dead human, we could always claim that the incident was under investigation. Eventually, the

Station Commander agreed, and we left it to the Dutch to sort out. The culprit was flown back to Holland the next day in handcuffs, and the F16 underwent an engine change in our hangar. No one from moon country complained, and the incident was quietly forgotten. However, I could not resist mentioning, at the final Dining-In Night at the end of the detachment, that when the RAF shot themselves down they did it properly - earlier in the year a Phantom had shot down a Jaguar recovering into RAF Bruggen.

Our next squadron exchange with the Portuguese Air Force was an altogether much more restrained affair.

Buccaneer (Credit: John Malley)

Gibraltar Or Bust

My tale starts with a weather briefing, on 23 April 1976 at RAF Honington, for a deployment of 6 Buccaneers of 12 Squadron to 'The Rock', with air-to-air refuelling, en route for Exercise OPEN GATE. It was not a very positive weather briefing as far as the destination airfield was concerned; nevertheless (and with that typical can-do attitude), the launch decision was taken, in the sure knowledge that, as usual, the wind would abate at Gibraltar by lunchtime, and we would arrive in time for our first brandy sour at about 1400 hours. The 6 aircraft were split into 3 pairs to match the tanker bracket, and off we went with a firm promise from our leader, the Squadron Boss, that he would keep an eye on the Gibraltar weather and, if necessary, advise on High Frequency radio (HF) where our diversion would be. Well, we didn't quite launch successfully! No 2 went unserviceable on start, but thankfully got himself fixed in time to make up a 3-ship at the back. Thus, the daisy chain was a singleton, followed by a pair, followed by a 3-ship, at 20 minute intervals.

Following a successful refuelling bracket overhead St Mawgan, we were half-way down the Iberian coast when those fateful words came across on HF "Gib's Black – Grade 1 Diversion to Lisbon". Back down the stream, each aircraft discussed whether that message implied Lisbon International or Lisbon Montijo, the military base across the estuary of the River Tagus, and most concluded that it had to be the military option. However, once established in the descent, the landing details were passed, and a frantic searching of nav bags began in most aircraft for the Lisbon International approach charts! No big drama to professional aircrew of the Buccaneer - sure it was an international airport, but just follow the procedures and nothing can go wrong. Simple! The Boss, out front, did a Precision Approach Radar to land, and caused no panic amongst Air Traffic Control whilst the pair did a visual straight in to land without any problem.

Meanwhile, some 40 minutes to the rear, the 3-ship was preparing for a visual descent, over an azure sea, to an airfield that was clearly visible 34,000 feet below, just under the port wingtip. Things thereafter happened fairly quickly. The lead navigator barely had time to put away his flask, sandwiches and Telegraph crossword, before communications were established, clearance given for a tactical break to land, and he caught a vague glimpse, through the typically misted-up canopy, of the noble features of Chris Columbus, as the three Buccaneers charged up a big river. Perhaps, in retrospect, the fact that the Military Visual Controller continued to insist that he could not see them, even in the circuit, plus the presence of quite a lot of civilian aircraft on the ground, should have rung some alarm bells. Consequently, in retrospect, a 540 knot and 200 ft tactical break was not the most appropriate arrival to have employed! The penny finally dropped after landing, when the crews were surrounded by grim soldiers in armoured vehicles and escorted to a distant shed. Meanwhile, in one aircraft, a flight commander was observed frantically trying to generate enough saliva to wipe the classified vu-graphs he had thoughtfully prepared for the first exercise brief at Gibraltar! After arriving at the shed, the Lieutenant RN Observer exchange officer on 12 Squadron was despatched to contact the Naval Attaché (who was also the Air Attaché), to explain the situation. He later reported that what started off as a friendly chat deteriorated rapidly, when the nature and high visibility of the unannounced arrival at an international airport became evident. Thereafter, the crews were wrapped in borrowed civvies, driven to the Hotel Penta on the outskirts of town, given a bottle of whisky and 200 cigarettes each, and ordered to lie very low until they were collected the following morning for their onward flight.

At this stage it, should be explained that Portugal had just emerged from a dictatorial regime and, the following day, was due to hold its first democratic elections since before the military coup of 1926. Perhaps worse, the country was engaged in a dirty war in Angola, and the corridors of the Hotel Penta were strewn with the waifs and refugees from that (at the time) God-forsaken country. So, sensible aircrew that we were, we drank the whisky, smoked the cigarettes and put our minds to work! Unsurprisingly the Naval Attache's dire warning about the rise of the Communist Party in the run up to the elections, and his advice to stay in our rooms and depart from Portugal, unobserved or commented upon, the following morning, was beginning to drift from our minds. Cue the Lieutenant RN Pilot exchange officer on 12 Squadron, who announced to the assembled throng that this had potential for a great "run ashore", and subsequently proceeded to lead the motley band of badly disguised aircrew to join a riotously happy carnival in the centre of town. This lasted well into the early hours and, at one point, the aforementioned officer was observed riding in a truck and waving a hammer and sickle flag wildly above his head.

Next morning, we reassembled for the onward journey to a now calm Gibraltar. Dressed in the same long johns etc from the day before, and nursing thick heads but strong hearts, we were accosted in the hotel lobby by an American tourist, who enquired what the Brit military was doing there on the day of the national elections. Unfortunately, we had not escaped unnoticed, but worse was to come. The communist national newspaper ran a photo of our arrival at the airport under the headline 'BRITISH MILITARY ARRIVE TO SUPPORT CAPITALIST CAUSE'.

Thankfully, the journey back to Lisbon International and our subsequent departure, under the guidance of the resident Portuguese Navy detachment, was uneventful. As far as the Naval Attache was concerned and informed, we had all religiously observed his curfew and, headline apart, he was only too pleased to see the back of us without further diplomatic incident.

Hit And Miss

I was a young, second tour, ex-Hunter pilot on an F4-Phantom strike/attack squadron in Germany during the early 1970s, when we were tasked with tri-alling Inertial Nav/Attack System (INAS) weapon aiming. At our annual Armament Practice Camp (APC) in Decimomannu, Sardinia, it was therefore decided that we would divide into two factions for the strafe (air-to-ground guns) trial, with half the Squadron using fixed sighting and the other half INAS sighting. So far so good, but what hadn't been taken into consideration was the APC auction and its outcome – I will explain. At the start of each APC, the ground-crew would organise an auction, at which each pilot would be put up for sale to the highest bidder for each weapon event, and the winner would scoop the pool, to be divided between pilot and backer. With syndicates forming to raise their bidding power, the stakes could be quite high for fancied pilots and, during the APC, the ground crew line hut walls would have charts showing cumulative scores. Tension was palpable as the conclusion of each weapon event approached, and invariably there would be an anxious, 'How did it go, Sir?' from someone with vested interest, as you walked in after a sortie.

All went well until the strafe phase arrived, and it quickly became obvious that the INAS sighting needed more work from the 'boffins', because the fixed sight group was consistently getting far better scores. In fact, the common perception was that anyone using INAS was lucky to hit Capo Frasca range, let alone a particular target! It was therefore hardly surprising when a deputation from the auctioneers went to the Boss as the end of the phase approached, to report that there was a deal of unhappiness among those who had bought INAS pilots, particularly the more fancied shooters. What could be done, they enquired, to make the outcome fair? If things went on as they were, the strafe competition would have to be declared null and void, and no one wanted that, did they?

After met briefing the next morning, one of the Flight Commanders, OC 'A' Flight, announced the executives' decision – each pilot would begin his next range detail with one strafe First Run Attack (FRA) and, unlike the usual scoring system of percentage hits out of shells fired, the result would be based simply on the number of holes in the target. Previous scores did not count, and the strafe competition would depend purely on this one pass for each pilot. A simple solution that everyone seemed happy with, but there's always the unforeseen loophole that someone will try to exploit - isn't there?

In this case, the exploiter was me! When I went to 'sign out' my aircraft, the Armourer Chief informed me that I had over 400 rounds in the gun, which he deemed to be unfortunate because the jet had to go into the hangar after landing, so whatever I didn't fire would have to be downloaded. That was when a little bulb in the recesses of my brain began to glow. On the way from the line hut to the aircraft, I bumped into OC 'A' Flight. "Sir", I innocently enquired, "Can you just confirm that it's holes in the target that count and not percentage?" He gave me a withering glance. "Do you never listen to briefings?" he retorted, "What did I say this morning?" I gave him my contrite look. "Er, holes in the target, Sir." The withering look was undiminished. "Well, get on with it then." The little bulb was very bright now.

Taxying out for take-off, I discussed with my back-seater what sort of opening range would be required to fire 400-odd rounds before reaching the foul line (beyond which safety dictated that firing had to cease), and how high the sighting solution would have to be initially. "You must be mad," he opined, but then conceded that it might work. The next scene in our drama opened about twenty minutes later, as I pulled up on the FRA pattern and identified my target. "London 3, in hot", I called. 'Clear 'ot London 3', replied the Italian Range Safety Officer (RSO). On with the master arm switch, put the sight way, way high and, at a very long range, pull and hold the trigger. At this point, I should explain that half a second was the usual burst length, which was enough to do a lot of damage if you were accurate. After all, the SUU23A was a five-rotating-barrel Gatling gun, capable of an enormous rate of fire. In this case, it took over four seconds to empty the magazine and send all the shells on their way. It was the first time I'd ever seen them hitting the ground clearly before pulling out, and what a sight it was! The first ones impacted short of the target next to mine, then marched up to it, sawed off one of the legs, and finally drifted right to start making holes where I wanted them. At that stage, the amount of dust and dirt being thrown up obscured the rest of the proceedings, and the Gatling gun ran out of ammunition, so I pulled up and prepared to get on with the next event. The RSO, however, had other ideas. "London 3," he shouted over the radio,

"You crazy man, go'ome, leave the range," and other similar indications that my sortie was finished as far as range work was concerned.

The rest of the story doesn't take long. At first, the RSO didn't intend to score my target, as I was definitely in his bad books, but we had a Squadron Liaison Officer in the range tower each day, and he persuaded the Italian range party Warrant Officer to count the holes. By the time I landed, the complaints had reached the Boss. He quickly made it clear to me that Orderly Officer duties would feature quite prominently for a while, and this was accompanied by a detailed tea-leaf reading concerning my continued residency on the Squadron; but that was about par for the course really. And so an eventful day proceeded towards Happy Hour. The strafe contest? Oh, I won. Like I said, there's always a loophole.....

Phantom (Credit: John Malley)

The Central Flying School Course

The following story is taken from SILVERED WINGS, by kind permission of the author, Sir John Severne.

Having enjoyed my flying training towards the end of the War so much, and my first tour on a Mosquito night fighter squadron (No 264) just after the War ended, I decided that I would like to put something back into flying. Thinking this could best be done by becoming a test pilot, or by instructing, I soon realised I did not have the academic skills to become a test pilot, so I applied for the course at the Central Flying School (CFS) at RAF Little Rissington, to become a Qualified Flying Instructor (QFI). I admit there was a certain attraction in going to CFS at that time, because the course included flying the Lancaster, Mosquito, Spitfire and Vampire, in addition to the Harvard and Tiger Moth, on which one would learn the techniques of instruction. It would be a fantastic opportunity for an inexperienced pilot like me to fly three new representative front-line types.

It is important for flying instructors to have an understanding of the handling requirements of those aircraft which their students are likely to be flying. These four operational types were typical of the current heavy bombers (Lancaster), multi-role aircraft (Mosquito), piston-engine fighters (Spitfire) and jet fighters (Vampire). Most of the students on the CFS course would be experienced in at least one of the roles, but few would have had the chance to fly all of them.

I began the six-month course in January 1948, and again I was very conscious of my inexperience compared to the majority of the other students, who had wartime operational flying in their log books. I believe one of the best ways to improve a skill is to try to teach it, and certainly on this course one really did learn about the finer points of flying. I had had few opportunities to do any aerobatics since my flying training days, so I particularly enjoyed polishing up the various manoeuvres, and was very thrilled to be awarded the Clarkson Trophy at the end of the course for the best aerobatic pilot.

Aerobatics are very important skills for any pilot to acquire. It is not just a matter of being able to give an exciting display; rather they teach pilots co-ordination skills and, most importantly, they are a method by which pilots can learn how to recover an aircraft safely after finding themselves in an unusual attitude. This may be caused, for example, by some form of mechanical failure, losing control in a thunderstorm, or by simply mishandling the aircraft. By being competent at aerobatics, pilots know how to identify the problem quickly, and then recover quickly and safely from any attitude, even at night or in cloud, when flying on instruments. I consider that such training is essential, even for those civilian pilots who are training to be airline pilots, because it is unlikely that they will go through their entire careers without finding themselves in an unusual and potentially dangerous attitude at least once. Aerobatics also help students to fly very accurately, which is an essential requirement for a good pilot – and they happen to be fun, although some would question that statement.

I had, of course, already flown the Mosquito, but the other three were a very exciting prospect. The first time I flew a jet aircraft was when I flew the single-seat Vampire Mk3. It was a beautiful evening, and I clearly remember the wonderful view from the cockpit, the complete lack of vibration coupled with a very low noise level, and of wheeling this delightful little aircraft around the clouds over the Cotswold Hills. I am reminded of John Magee's remarkable poem, which describes the sheer joy of flying far better than I possibly could. I certainly 'danced the skies with laughter-silvered wings' on that occasion. Sadly, he was killed in a Spitfire mid-air collision in 1941. He was just nineteen.

> High Flight
> Oh! I have slipped the surly bonds of Earth
> And danced the skies on laughter-silvered wings;
> Sunward I've climbed, and joined the tumbling mirth
> Of sun-split clouds – and done a hundred things
> You have not dreamed of – wheeled and soared and swung
> High in the sunlit silence. Hov'ring there,
> I've chased the shouting wind along, and flung
> My eager craft through footless halls of air...
> Up, up the long, delirious burning blue
> I've topped the wind-swept heights with easy grace,
> Where never lark, or even eagle flew –
> And, while with silent, lifting mind I've trod
> The high un-trespassed sanctity of space,
> Put out my hand and touched the face of God.

It was very exciting for me to be able to fly the Spitfire, which must be one of the most charismatic fighters ever built. It caused much amusement in the crewroom to watch fellow students take off on their first flights, because they invariably wobbled a bit just after take-off, as the undercarriage was raised. The reason was because the lever to raise the wheels was on the right-hand side of the cockpit, so one had to change hands by taking the right hand off the stick to raise the wheels, whilst replacing it with the left hand which had been holding the throttle lever. As the elevators were very sensitive, the tyro's wobble was almost inevitable.

There is another reason why I remember that first Spitfire flight, and it is one that I am not at all proud of. One of the problems of landing a single-engine fighter is that there is a great big engine in front, which blocks the view of the runway when landing – which is why most pilots fly a curved approach, so that they can see the runway until the last few hundred feet. A fundamental rule of flying is that one must always keep a good lookout for other aircraft, but I failed to do so on this occasion. I was concentrating so much on making an accurate curved approach that I forgot to check that no-one else was flying a straight-in approach at the same time. The first thing I knew was when I flew under a Harvard that was so close I could hear its engine. Apparently, the runway controller in his caravan at the end of the runway could have fired a red Very light to tell me to go round again, but did not do so in case both aircraft took the same action and collided. I never ever made that mistake again.

My first solo in a Lancaster was memorable for a totally different reason. My instructor, Graham Hulse, wanted to send me solo, but the flight engineer had been flying all morning, and was due for a break and a bite to eat, so Graham said, 'I will be your flight engineer, but to prove that I can have no influence on your flying I will lie down behind you so that I can still see the engine gauges.' And he did! Graham made a name for himself when he subsequently baled out of a Meteor, when it broke up around him during a Battle of Britain air display at Little Rissington in 1950. Sadly he was killed in Korea, but not until he had shot down two Mig 15s.

The Perils Of Spinning

In April 1970, I was a student at RAF Chivenor in Devon, on the pre-Lightning course. This was intermediate training after the Gnat, and comprised 70 hours on Hunters, as preparation for the Lightning conversion. Those were the twilight days of the Hunter force, and many of the staff were very old school, and consequently viewed embryonic Lightning pilots as some form of pond life. Their general approach was 'kick the tyres, light the fires and get airborne' and, although some were excellent instructors, many were truly terrible.

One morning, I was flying a basic, 1 v 1 combat mission against one of the better instructors, who was teaching me the techniques for what is known as a 'slow-speed scissors', which involves flying a zig-zag path in an effort to get onto your opponent's tail. Meanwhile, of course, he is doing exactly the same to you. We were at 30,000 feet over a clear, blue sea, and I was working hard on co-ordinating my aileron and rudder inputs, which is the key to reversing direction at slow speed in a swept-wing aircraft. All went well for a while until, during a reversal to the left, my aircraft decided to roll to the right and enter an incipient spin. No problem, I thought, because, by all accounts, the Hunter was just a large Jet Provost, and would instantly stop spinning when I centralized the controls. At this stage, it's relevant to point out that I had all of 15 hours on Hunters, so I was disappointed and rather nonplussed when we quickly settled into a fully developed spin. Undeterred, I initiated the recovery action, full opposite rudder to the direction of spin, and stick centrally forward. It was still spinning!

From a lofty perch above all the action, my instructor could clearly see that things were not proceeding as briefed, and advised me to check that the flaps were retracted – at high speed, an inadvertent flaps selection put the Hunter into a dive from which it could not be recovered. I replied that I was in a spin, and set about re-checking my actions, opposite rudder and stick centrally forward. It was still spinning!

Things were now getting serious, and I was running out of ideas so, as a last resort, I decided to apply aileron in the direction of the spin. Initially nothing happened, but then I noticed the airspeed increasing through 450 knots rather than fluctuating around 100 knots as would be normal for a spin. I wasn't in a spin after all! The rotation I was now experiencing was due to the aileron input so I centralized the controls and pulled back hard on the stick to recover to level flight.....at 8000 feet.

Sometime later in the day, it dawned on me that I had become so preoccupied with trying to recover the aircraft and work out why it was not behaving in a way that Pilot's Notes said it would, that I completely lost track of my height. In so doing, I had lost 22,000 feet (almost four miles) and, if I had continued for another 30 seconds, I would not have lived to tell the tale.

Post Script

When, as a 50 year old, I became a Qualified Flying Instructor on the Tucano, teaching the next generation how to fly, I noted with some satisfaction the emphasis on height checks as part of the standard spin recovery actions.

Hunter (Credit: John Malley)

Spinning Again

Having learnt (nearly) the hard way about mastering spin recovery, I was to use the lesson fairly soon afterwards and, inevitably, become even wiser in the process. A few months later, I was off to do a spinning exercise with one of our foreign students, an experienced pilot who was being introduced to the RAF way of doing things. As mentioned in the earlier yarn, the control forces in the Jet Provost Mk5A during a spin could be quite high, and some of our more physically modest students could find that quite difficult.

On this trip, I demonstrated the spin entry, let my man have a go, which he did very successfully, and then I did a full spin and recovery, for him to see in real time what had been covered in the pre-flight brief. After that, I let him fly the spin himself. However, he inevitably encountered the aforementioned control loads and, after briefly struggling with this, he handed over control of the aircraft - but not to me, which was the approved method, but to his God. The deity appeared to not actually be paying attention because, for a (short) period of time, it was evident that no-one was flying the aircraft.

No worries, this was just the sort of thing I had prepared for, so I jumped to it, or I would have done if I could have got hold of the stick (control column for the purists). Having been left to its own devices, the stick was thrashing around the cockpit in a thoroughly demented fashion, and I simply couldn't get hold of it, or even anticipate where it was going next. At around this time, I became aware that my own whimpering had joined that of my companion. Finally, I grasped my left hand with my right hand, extended my left arm diagonally across the cockpit, and forced the stick into the far left corner, whence I could retrieve it in a normal fashion. Thereafter, the recovery went as briefed.

Once again, hindsight is a wonderful thing and, crucially, I should have shadowed the student on all the controls (including the rudder) far more closely than I was doing at the time. Does the learning ever stop?

Even More Spinning

In the early 1980s, I had the great opportunity of being the first Basic Jet Instructor to do an exchange tour with the French Air Force. As it was breaking new ground, nobody really knew what training I needed to fit into the French system so, although I was an experienced instructor (A2 for those who are interested), they took the sensible view that I should wander over to the French Ecole de Formation de Moniteurs (EFM) at Clermont-Ferrand, the French equivalent of the RAF Central Flying School. There it was planned that I would do the full six month course, which was required of French Air Force pilots to become instructors. We were flying the little Fouga Magister, a small, fully aerobatic twin jet basic trainer with a butterfly tail. It was a nicely balanced aircraft, very pleasant to fly although a little underpowered.

Anyway, after about a month at EFM, they got fed up with me, and decided that, if I could pass a flight test, then I could go to the French training base at Cognac (yes, I know, a tough posting). As this was the first event of its kind, they sent a Colonel from the Paris-based MOD to check me out. After a standard introduction, I was told that the main exercise that I would be tested on was the teaching of spinning. No worries, really, as I had spun the thing and it was vice-free. However, the 'How to Teach Spinning' section was further downstream in the EFM course than I had then reached. Consequently, I had not yet learned the French words for the key descriptions of the exercise. A quick flick through the course notes helped with some of them, and off we set.

It is perhaps worthwhile noting a couple of things, before we enter that spin. The exercise is quite complex, and is normally broken into separate segments. There is quite a lot of information to impart right from the start. This includes how to enter the spin, what to look for when you do, and then, once in the spin, to describe what is happening and what to look for, both inside and outside the aircraft.

Climbing to a comfortable height, I did all the safety checks, and started into the performance. The aircraft behaved itself perfectly, and displayed all the proper characteristics as we settled into the spin. All was going swimmingly, apart from one slight detail. The rate that things were happening was considerably greater than the rate at which my poor French could explain it. We had settled well into a stable spin, before I had finished describing how to enter the spin. I then continued with the script on the instrument indications, the visual references, the control inputs and so on. However, this commentary was taking some considerable time. A glance out of the front of the aircraft from time to time showed the map of the French countryside becoming clearer and clearer. I ploughed on. Eventually it got to the point when the picture through the windscreen was much more detailed than I really liked, so I initiated the recovery. A full 30 seconds after establishing straight and level flight I was still 'pattering' the spin recovery. Nothing was said from the back seat.

We continued with the rest of the flight, aerobatics, low level, circuits etc and landed. Still no comment! However the debrief was interesting. The good Colonel commented on the spinning, by noting that I had most of the right words and that they were in the right order, but just a little slow. He was reassuring – he said that he was sure that my French would speed up with a bit of practice, but that, in the meantime, I was unlikely to kill either myself or my student so I might as well pack my bags and make my way to Cognac – what a relief!

Know Your Enemy

The Support Helicopter Force of the RAF does what it says on the tin – supports the British Army, when it needs bigger helicopters than the Army Air Corps can provide. Not long after I had joined my first SH squadron, I found myself in an area of Salisbury Plain called "The Pennings". It came as a bit of a culture shock to discover that, instead of living in the 5-star hotels I had been used to in the V-Force, I was required to share a tent with another officer, and camouflage it so that it would be invisible to the "enemy".

This we duly did, and our campsite in The Pennings was almost invisible. The aircraft, however, were a different matter and, whilst you could throw cam netting over them, they tended to stick out like sore thumbs. There was an open area in The Pennings called the Walled Garden, from which our helos operated, and our almost invisible campsite surrounded it. On the third morning of the exercise, we received an unexpected visit from the Brigadier controlling everything, and he practically tripped over our cammed-up site before he even noticed it. Our aircraft had all departed on task about 30 minutes earlier, so the Walled Garden was empty.

The Brigadier was most impressed with our low level of visibility, and asked to see whoever was in charge. Fortunately, this was our Squadron Commander, who subsequently went on to greater things, despite, or perhaps because of, a propensity to stick his neck out.

The Brigadier duly congratulated him on the tactical disposition of our site, but went on to say:

"Tell me Wing Commander, can you camouflage your aircraft as effectively as you have your domestic and ops sites?"

Whereupon the Boss indicated the empty Walled Garden, and replied: "Well Sir, there are 2 Pumas in that enclosure – how many can you see?"

The Brigadier looked carefully, smiled and departed without another word, while we rolled about in the grass trying to suppress our mirth!

There's A Time And A Place For Everything

It was in the heady days of the early 70s, when the entry qualification to the Wattisham Wing appeared to be ownership of an MGB, and nobody would have contemplated looking for entertainment on a Saturday night other than in the Mess. I was at that sublime point in a first tour when the chasm between my perceived and actual ability had reached its widest – in short, just experienced enough to be dangerous. One sunny morning, I found myself over the North Sea, in the almost unknown situation for a Lightning F3 of having more fuel than I needed – the result of having been stood up by the electronic warfare training Canberra with whom I was supposed to be playing.

Wondering what to do with this surplus Avtur, I lit on the spiffing wheeze of simulating a proper crash diversion to the nominated airfield, just to see if the fuel figures we used really worked. So, on overshoot from the break at Wattisham, I declared my Practice Emergency, and headed off in the direction of Honington. Needless to say, no Air Traffic Control handover could be effected, and I had to free-call Honington, only to find that I was already in their instrument pattern, it was full of Buccaneers and I was definitely not first in line. A glance at the fuel gauges – who needed a stopwatch in the F3? – revealed that holding was not an option. No problem, I thought, I'll go for a radar-to-visual, and ackle[1] the fuel figures to see what would have happened. This change of intention resulted in a semi-guided tour of East Anglia, with the upshot that, on arrival at initials, it was apparent even to me that I didn't have enough fuel for a circuit, so I told the Tower that I would fly straight through and return to Wattisham.

Well, I ask you: what red-blooded fighter pilot could fly straight through the circuit at a Banana-Bomber base and do nothing? So, on the spur of the moment (most of my heinous crimes seem to have been committed on the spur of the moment), I elected to demonstrate my best slow roll. Unfortunately, my best slow roll that morning was an abomination; nose not high enough inverted, dished out of the last quarter, and required large amounts of back-stick and copious G to avoid the trees at the far end.

Breathing quite hard and hoping that nobody had spotted me, I snuck back to Wattisham, proving that at least my fuel calculations had been up to spec – I didn't have a pound to spare. Sadly, I had not reckoned with the fact that OC Ops at Honington happened to be in the Tower during my 'display', and had arranged a nice little welcoming party on the pan. There followed much dressing-down by the Boss, and buying of beer for the groundcrew doing the overstress checks and replacing the rivets in the wings.

As a footnote to this sorry saga, I was at least spared further pain, when my letter of application for additional uniform allowance - to compensate for the added wear-and-tear on my No 1 uniform during 2 weeks Orderly Officer - was intercepted by OC Admin, a wily old bird with command of a Spitfire squadron in Burma behind him and, therefore, ample experience of people like me.

The moral of this tale – try not to be such an a**e, I suppose.

---

[1] 'Ackling' was a word with many meanings, in this case an imprecise extrapolation of fuel figures. Ackling could also refer to use of the radar hand controller in the Lightning, and its use migrated with pilots converting to the Jaguar as manipulation of the navigation system hand controller.

Silence Is Golden

As a young single officer, I lived in the Officers Mess, along with the other unattached males and females. Most messes were built along traditional lines and consisted of a central core, providing dining and recreational rooms, and four wings of individual bedrooms. Ours was no different and, in accordance with the custom of the day, the female officers all resided together in one wing. This did not inhibit our social life in any way, although young officers were expected to behave with discretion and, to be fair, the code of conduct was seldom breached.

The running of the Mess was overseen by a committee of officers, who were individually allocated areas such as catering, entertainments and house. The latter responsibility fell to a friend of mine, who quickly became fed-up with responding to what he saw as petty entries in the Mess Suggestions Book which resided at reception. Complaints were frowned upon, so entries were worded along the lines of 'I suggest that the spider which resides in the top left-hand corner of the bar be offered the opportunity to spin a new web' or 'I suggest that we arrange a visit to the Mess laundry, so that I may see for myself the wondrous machine that rips the buttons off my shirts and fires them through my underpants'.

One particular Friday evening, my friend was late arriving in the bar (Happy Hour was originally a Service tradition) and, when he eventually did arrive, he looked rather crestfallen. Half-way through his first pint, I enquired what was wrong, and he told me that he had just been given a bollocking by The President of The Mess Committee. Apparently a visiting, senior, female officer had written in the book 'I suggest that the floorboards in the ladies' corridor are oiled, as they creak'.

With some trepidation, I asked him what his response had been.

"Well", he said, "I just replied that this would be done. However, if you walk slowly down the left-hand edge they don't creak".

Napalm

The following story is taken from SILVERED WINGS, by kind permission of the author, Sir John Severne.

Soon after I was appointed as a flight commander on 98 (Venom) Squadron at Fassberg, the station was tasked with carrying out trials and demonstrations of the use of napalm. I was one of two pilots selected for this interesting activity. Napalm is jellied petrol, which was carried in fuel tanks slung beneath the wing (I think they were 100-gallon tanks), and which could be jettisoned. The effect, viewed from the ground, was dramatic and, to some, quite frightening. We used a Vampire Mk5, and most of the trials and demonstrations were carried out on the range at Fassberg. The technique was to approach the target at 360 knots at a height of only 20ft, which itself was quite exciting. There was no bomb sight of any kind, and we dropped the 'bomb' by eye, simply pulling the fuel tank jettison lever when we judged the moment was right. After a little practice, we were able to achieve direct hits on most occasions.

Our practices were usually carried out with water in the tanks, but even that was quite impressive. I remember one of those demonstrations very clearly, when I flew from Fassberg to Tangmere, and from there to take part in a 'Firepower Demonstration' on Salisbury Plain. These demonstrations were regularly held, to show off the various military and air force weapons the UK produced; consequently, the large audiences included foreign senior officers, together with their military attachés. We had a rehearsal the day before, using water and, just after releasing the 'bomb', I flew over the top of the target tank and saw, out of the corner of my eye, two pressmen running away. They had been hiding behind the far side of the tank, hoping to get a good picture, but they must have got more than they bargained for – imagine the noise of a 100-gallon fuel tank hitting a very solid object at 360 knots, only feet away. I had no idea whether I had hit the target, or whether I had overshot it, and perhaps killed the pressmen, so I explained what I had seen on the R/T and asked whether the two idiots were safe. Thankfully they were, because I had achieved a direct hit, but I don't suppose they ever tried that trick again. I have never been particularly fond of the gentlemen of the press, but I have never considered trying to kill them.

On my return from Tangmere, the day after the demonstration, the weather over Germany was very poor and, as I started my descent, I asked for a bearing to Fassberg, as I was not sure where I was – this is given by an operator on the ground, who can tell the direction of the radio transmission from the aircraft. After a number of bearings had been transmitted, I became suspicious, because I felt certain that I must have passed over the top of Fassberg, and was therefore heading for the Russian Zone. After checking, the operator admitted he had been giving me reciprocal bearings; in other words, I was going in the opposite direction to that intended. After landing, we calculated that I must have been at least 20 miles into the Russian Zone, and I therefore waited for the inevitable diplomatic complaint. It never arrived, because we learnt later from intelligence sources that the Russian radar was unserviceable on that day.

Vampire

Law Of The Jungle

A few decades ago. Wednesday, mid-afternoon. Forty thousand feet above hot, somnolent Belize. All alone, the only jet airborne. Just finished the high level part of a test flight on a Harrier GR3. Roll inverted and pull steep nose down to descend for the lower level part of the test schedule. And there, perfectly framed in the Head Up Display, is APC (Airport Camp), the main British military base, just north of the civil airport.

Mischief floods the soul .... Aha!! ..... steepen the descent ..... the devil rises .....Tally ho!..... steely gaze narrows, sunshine flashes off the grinning pearly whites ..... we'll just sharpen up the Army a bit...... show them not all of us are asleep at our desks on these tropical afternoons ...... hold APC steady in the screen...... ooops.... looks like the jet has slipped through the sound barrier - a moment of inattention - for about 20,000 feet of the dive....... Throttle back, pull out, carry on with the schedule.

A few moments later, our friendly RAF radar controller comes on the air: "Holy macaroni, Zero One, did you just drop a boom?"

"What?? Who?? Me?? Come on!!"

Silence for a bit, carry on with the schedule. Then he's back again, different tone of voice: "Zero One, we need to know. This is a serious question. Did you drop a boom? We have to know."

"Well...... all right then..... maybe just a little one...." End of conversation.

Finish the whole test schedule, land. Hilarity amongst the hide team on signing the jet back in: "Jeez, boss, what a boom! .... real cracker, that one .... whoo hoo, that's got to be the best bang ever.... Oh, by the way, call the Air Commander...."

Aahh! Rats.

Call the Air Commander, a nice non-Harrier wing commander chappie: "Hello, sir, it's me. I plead guilty". Astonishingly, he completely ignores that, and goes off at a tangent: "Airtest OK? Jet fit? Good! Now, about that admin thing we were discussing this morning.... "

Not a mention of the boom, never a hint, not a squeak, not even over a beer or two over the next couple of days. Unreal! Can't believe it. Scot free......??

Until Friday. Head to the joint RAF / Army officers' mess for TGIF. Packed as usual, during which, at a suitable moment, a fairly recent RAF weekly ritual will be enacted; the awarding, to the most deserving candidate, of the POW trophy. This is a quite magnificently upstanding ethnic woodcarving, fashioned, most appropriately, from a local hardwood. As accessories, it sports a couple of well used squash balls in a tastefully colour-coordinated mesh net. POW does not exactly stand for Prize of the Week.

Eventually the Air Commander quells the hubbub, and gets around to it. "Eventful week etc, etc, lots of things happening, so several candidates for the POW today."

'First, on Monday, the Army finally got its team away to Antigua, to aid the Governor and police with the civil unrest we've been hearing about. Major Rupert of the Guards, after days and days of planning and coordination, at last got his transport Hercules here on Sunday. Loaded the heavier stuff that night. Made sure the deploying team, led by Captain Jeremy, was fully prepared and briefed up to the eyeballs. Even went over to the airport to see everybody and everything away on the Herc, late Monday morning. Then, well satisfied with his efforts, came back over here for a bit of a purr and a well earned lunch. Went back to his office mid afternoon and, um ...... found all the keys to all the vehicles they'd loaded onto the Herc the night before were still sitting on his desk. So, to Major Rupert, for masterful leadership, deploying your team abroad with no keys for their vehicles, third place!' Much hilarity and laughter. Good old Army, again!

'Now we move on to Wednesday.' Uh oh! Uh oh!! 'Wednesday afternoon, sports afternoon, lot of you probably flat on your backs on your scratchers. Suddenly there was that massive great BA-BANG. Buildings shake, spiders fall from ceilings, feet fall off desks, everyone suddenly bolt upright, awake, wondering what the hell happened. I was at the swimming gala with CBF (Commander, British Forces) and DCOS (Deputy Chief of Staff, an Army major). The Brigadier turns to me and says "Air Commander, what on earth was that?" I knew exactly what it was, and who. "Sir, that was a Harrier going supersonic." The DCOS turns to us both and says "Don't be ridiculous, Air Commander, Harriers can't go supersonic!".............. To DCOS, theatre intelligence expert, second place!!' Huge hilarity and laughter. The Army, again! ..But.... uh oh..... what next?

The Air Commander continues, 'Anyway, back at the swimming gala, we carry on presenting the prizes, when we see a runner panting across the sports field towards us from the Force Ops Room. He comes up to the platform, apologises, and gasps to the Brigadier "Sir, the bomb dump has blown up!"'

'We all turn to look towards it; no plume of smoke, nothing. We tell the runner that's rubbish, it can't have blown up. "But sir, the pressure alarms have all gone off. Ops Officer says to tell you he's activated the recovery plan and is getting our disaster team and the Belize Defence Force team over there. Oh, and he's sending over all the fire trucks from the airport and has called out the Belize City Fire Brigade from downtown......." '

The Air Commander couldn't be heard any further. He just handed me the trophy.

Harrier GR3

Near Mid-Air No 1

I was No3 in a Hunter 4-Ship, flying from RAF Brawdy on a low-level Tactical Weapons Unit training mission in mid-Wales. The late morning weather was perfect, and the sortie was going exactly to plan. Off the 2nd target, I was to assume the lead for the return to base in battle formation.

As I manoeuvred off that target onto a southerly heading, with my No2 properly positioned, I noticed the other pair was in my 7.30 position, albeit a little stretched. I was checking my map for a moment, to confirm the route, when there was a radio call from the other pair about an AIRMISS – a Buccaneer had flown between the two of them, and was breaking up in flight – the tail-plane and fin had come away.

As I looked back, what I saw was in slow motion. The Buccaneer had pitched up, and was clearing a ridge; it then rolled slowly over onto its back, and was plummeting nose first into the middle of a reservoir. I saw the glint of a canopy as it left the aircraft, about 5 seconds before impact. Two parachutes deployed a second or so later – the last one had just fully opened when the person hit the water. How lucky was that?

The only injury to the crew was a broken wrist, due to the high speed nature of the ejection – the aircraft had been close to 500 knots on a simulated attack run in a valley bottom, when the pilot saw a Hunter very close on a collision course, crossing the ridge at the end of the valley. He had to pull hard to avoid the ground, whilst also rolling aggressively to reduce the collision risk on the second Hunter that appeared from nowhere. Unfortunately, in an aircraft with a T-tail, you can make either one of these control inputs individually, but not both at the same time – or the fin can come off!

My formation leader had more fuel than me, so he stayed overhead the scene and transmitted a MAYDAY Relay while I took the 2 wingmen home. Because I was shaken by events, I sensibly pulled out of low-level. Unfortunately my mind was racing so much that I nearly took all 3 aircraft straight into Sennybridge range. There is a message there somewhere!

Near Mid-Air No 2

In the summer of 2007, I was piloting a Dominie with a total of 6 crew members. We were returning to base after a 2 hour detail, along the centre of the Lichfield Radar Crossing Corridor at FL140, on an easterly heading in clear weather. As normal, prior to the Radar Control Service being downgraded to Radar Information Service by the Swanwick Controller as we exited the corridor, we had requested an immediate descent for recovery into RAF Cranwell. This had been denied because of the number of aircraft close by.

Minutes earlier, a Tornado F3 had conducted a flypast at Cranwell and, on completion, it had climbed very quickly and checked in on our frequency. Although Cranwell had suggested that the Tornado be kept 1000ft below us at FL130, Swanwick allowed him to climb to our level for entry to the southern side of the corridor. He was currently north of the centreline.

The Swanwick controller was very busy making traffic information calls, while also endeavouring to monitor the air picture, and accepting and handing over traffic to/from other agencies. We were called as a target to the F3, but somehow were misidentified by the crew; this of course confused the controller. The F3 was consequently released from its hold, and converged on us unsighted from behind my canopy arch.

It only became visible to me when I made a small heading change. It was co-altitude, stationary in my windscreen (therefore on a collision course), and closing fast. I pulled up and, at the same time, it fortunately bunted and, some 5 seconds later, I passed some 250ft above the F3. Far too close for comfort, that's for sure!

After a thorough investigation the Swanwick Controller was sadly suspended.

Some time later, I met the F3 navigator, and we toasted our survival with a beer – or perhaps it was more than that. Had the Dominie been equipped with TCAS[1], this close call most probably would have been avoided. It is sobering to think that 8 aircrew could have perished that day, had luck not been on our side and the weather not been fine.

---

[1] TCAS - Traffic Collision Avoidance System

Mr Vice

When undergoing pilot training at RAF Acklington, Northumberland, in 1966, I was designated Mr Vice[1] for a Dining-In Night in the Officers' Mess. At such functions, it is customary to toast the Queen, and the Heads of State of any foreigners attending, after the meal and before the speeches start. It was my luck to have some Malaysians in attendance, and the President of the Mess Committee (PMC) told me their Head of State was the 'Yang di-Pertuan Agong'. I foresaw that, after copious amounts of sherry before, and wine during, the dinner, this would be beyond me – so asked if I could call him simply 'The King of Malaysia'. The PMC said no, but did write the toast down for me on a bar-chit. During the pre-dinner sherry drinking competition, colleagues inspected the bar-chit, and handed it back after suitable commiserations over the tricky toast.

When the time came for the toast, the PMC stood, thumped his gavel, and said, "Mr Vice, the Yang di-Pertuan Agong of Malaysia". Full of confidence, I stood, took out my piece of paper, to discover that written on it was 'The Ying Pong Po of Yantee' – a 'friend' had switched it before dinner. Desperately trying to remember the title, my delivery of the toast was along the lines of – 'Ladies and Gentlemen, the Ying, the Yang, the Ping the Pong of Malaysia'. A week's Orderly Officer taught me to be more careful about sharing notes with friends while drinking.

---

[1] The Vice-President of the Mess for the Dining-In, whose role is as 'right-hand-man' to the President.

Terremoto!

It's 27th February 2008. The time 0056 hours. From a deep and tranquil sleep in peaceful Lincoln, I'm jolted into awareness by sudden ferocious thunder. This thunder, however, comes not from the clouds but from deep underground, a rumbling, rolling subterranean growl felt as much as heard as the house shakes violently around me. For ten, long seconds I hear the tiles above my head clatter and, half expecting chimney pots, I warily eye the ceiling as the overhead light swings in the streetlamps' orange glow.

'Terremoto!'

After years of repressed distortion, it's Mother England who is abandoning her maidenly restraint and bellowing in a bucking, quaking orgasm of tectonic relief. But I'm not in Spain, so why does the Spanish word for earthquake spring to mind? I know why. I'm transported back thirty-eight years.

It's 1970, and I'm a sergeant avionics technician serving on 543 Squadron operating Victor SR2s out of Jorge Chavez International Airport, Lima, Peru. We're spying on - sorry, monitoring - the French atmospheric nuclear weapons tests on Mururoa Atoll, way out in the Pacific, and sending the fusion debris collected back to AWRE Aldermaston for analysis. The operation is deemed 'Secret' (though how operating two camouflaged, one hundred and ten foot wingspan aircraft out of an international airport – an aircraft that streams a thirty-foot braking parachute each time it lands - can be kept secret is beyond any of us). If questioned, we are told to say we are working for the World Health Organisation. Nobody believes us, least of all the French, whose ambassador greeted us on arrival with a bottle of champagne.

It's the squadron's second detachment to Peru, the first, two years earlier, memorable if only for the international incident caused when, after ten long hours airborne, one of our Victors, short on fuel and highly radioactive, was forced to land in Chile after chasing a cloud of debris too far south. 'BRITISH SPY-PLANE FORCED DOWN BY OUR FIGHTERS' screamed the Santiago press. After two face-saving days, it was allowed to return to Lima.

But it's a quiet Sunday afternoon, and we non-comms are spending a few relaxed hours in the foyer-cum-lounge of the 'Hotel Riviera', enjoying a cervesa or two and what few English language newspapers we can find. The officers are at the 'Crillon' half a mile distant. The date is May the thirty-first and, although Lima is but twelve degrees below the Equator, it is blanketed by cloud throughout its winter months. I suddenly feel cold; I need a jacket.

'Ocho, pour favor'. Although the two young lift attendants exchange grins as its doors slide shut, I'm proud of my Spanish pronunciation and, eight floors up, with the key to my room in hand, I give them some more. 'Una momente, OK?' Then dash along the corridor to return seconds later pulling on a jacket. The doors again slide shut.

The 'Hotel Riviera', or most of it, has thirteen storeys, its zenith five floors higher than the one on which the lift, like a giant pendulum, now hangs suspended. Suddenly, everything goes berserk. Yo-yo like, we're bounced, battered and ground against the shaft walls, the din reverberating throughout the whole of its thirteen storeys. Debris cascades onto the fragile roof just feet above my head and, as the word 'earthquake' has not yet entered my mind, when a much heavier object slams onto us, I imagine it's the cable and that we're plummeting earthwards. Seeing the lift boys down on their knees, their right hands a blur as they make the sign of the Cross, convinces me. I'm no Catholic, but my knees are bending too - for a different reason. Hope really does spring eternal! Do I honestly believe bent knees can cushion an eighty foot drop on to concrete? This was not meant to happen! This was not how it was supposed to end! Then I look at the control panel; the floor numbers are counting down at their usual slow pace; we're not plunging earthwards after all. My finger hits button number five as it lights up and moments later, we're out of our animated steel box. But suspended on cables now extending eight storeys, its vigorous bouncing persists. Only now do I realise what's happening.

The young lift-boys do too. 'Terremoto!' Wide-eyed, they mouth the word in unison. Silently. Just the one word.

In an earthquake zone, all edifices more than six storeys high have to be built on concrete rafts. The thirteen-storey part of the Hotel Riviera complies with this regulation. Its six-storey extension, however, does not. Two buildings with a shared wall; one of them rocking to the rhythm of the earthquake, the other rigid and unyielding. And here, on the fifth floor, with daylight winking at me through a crack in the wall opposite, their junction is only too obvious. To my layman's eye, it would seem the bigger one is about to knock the smaller one down! Shouting to be heard, I tender yet more of my dreadful Spanish and, pointing to where we're standing, yell 'Peligro' then, 'Esquina' before ushering them into what I think will be the safest corner. I detect no exchange of grins this time.

Records will state that the Great Peruvian Earthquake of 1970 lasted forty-five seconds. I do not believe that. It lasts an hour, at least. Or that's how long it seems, as I stand squeezed into a corner with two teenage lift attendants.

Without having lived through the experience, the power of an earthquake is truly beyond man's imagination. I watch piles of plaster dust grow on the carpet; as the crack in the wall lengthens vertically, I hear glass breaking and women screaming. And I wait for the inevitable collapse. Surely this building will fall! Surprisingly, I accept it. Although convinced I am about to die, the emotion I feel is disappointment more than fear. I think of my children nine thousand miles away; they'll never see me again.

Forty-five seconds? No, I don't believe it. But as suddenly as it started it's over. Instantly. No fade-out. It's as though a switch has been thrown. All that mighty power turned off at the mains. The floor under my feet stops shaking, and it's so quiet I feel I've gone deaf. The relief is instant too. How long have I been holding my breath?

We've survived and, seeing the smiles on the faces of my two companions, I need to demonstrate my feelings. I sense they do too. We've shared a very special moment in our lives, one we will remember always. So what to do? They are very young, very junior members of staff; I am a patron of the hotel they serve. It's up to me. But a mere handshake won't do. In a very un-British display of emotion I extend my arms for a hug. Laughing, they respond enthusiastically.

The bar is six floors down, and I need a drink. Do we use the lift? Is it still serviceable? We take a chance and, although our ride is attended by a discomforting clatter from mechanisms overhead, we make it to the ground floor safely.

With the hotel staff having deserted en masse, there's no one at the reception desk and the lift-boys, no doubt following standing orders, join them outside. But there's a party underway in the bar! With no barman on duty, my RAF comrades are helping themselves. I'm greeted by a huge cheer. But, in discussing our respective experiences, our voices are just that little bit too loud, our laughter more prolonged than it should be. There's a hint of hysteria in the air.

And it's not yet over. At a sudden after-shock, the standard lamps distributed around the lounge rock in unison, the one close to where I'm sitting almost toppling. Instant silence. Only one man moves: a young corporal rigger leaps to his feet, and is half way to the door before the jeers of the rest of us stop him in his tracks. Sheepishly he returns to his seat.

Will it make the papers back home? What none of us realise yet is that our exciting, eight-point-one on the Richter scale earthquake experience has killed, or will kill, more than seventy-five thousand people, that three million others will be rendered homeless. We do not yet know that a natural dam high in the Cordilleras to the north of Lima has burst its banks after half a mountain slid into it, that the result is a drowned town, its adobe houses reverting back to mud. Twenty thousand of its inhabitants drowned in what were their own homes. Or do you suffocate in mud? The Peruvian government will allow no excavation at the site and the dead of the town of Yungay lie undisturbed still, a memorial to that tragic day.

So of course it makes the news back home and, in a few hours time, once every squadron member has been accounted for, police Landrovers will be broadcasting our survival throughout RAF Wyton's married-quarters.

Over the next few days, and despite television assurances to the contrary, Peruvians, agitating against nuclear weapons testing, convince themselves that we are responsible for the earthquake - they think we're French because of the 'tricolor' painted on our Victor tail fins (all RAF aircraft have them in 1970), and a protest march to the airport is planned. Only after Union Jacks are procured from the Embassy and prominently displayed can they be persuaded otherwise.

Despite world-wide protest, the French would continue testing their nuclear weapons on Muroroa, so we were back in Lima the following year and again in 1974. With earth tremors common along the whole length of that western seaboard, I was to experience many more of them. On every occasion, just as in England on February 27th 2008, it was 'terremoto' rather than 'earthquake' that sprang to mind.

Editorial comment

On a lighter note; the squadron boss was hosting a drinks party for the aircrew and staff from the British Embassy in his hotel suite at the time. He had just gone to the bathroom when the earthquake struck and did not appear again until it was over. As he re-entered a now silent room, one of the squadron wags quipped, "Christ boss, I hope you feel better now!"

Victor SR2 543 Sqn   (Credit: John Malley)

But How High Does It Really Go?

"Coming down from above 60, you need to be careful not to let the nose get too low, or something funny happens to the Q feel and you run out of tail-plane authority. Then the speed just increases.....and don't get too vigorous with the controls because of roll-yaw coupling." Jim was an old and not too bold Lightning pilot, so I was sure he knew what he was talking about. I made a mental note that, if I ever tried to go high, then I'd be careful about that, but to me the important message was that he'd been up there. The risk was putting your faith in the pressurisation system, but then it always seemed to be reliable.

So it was, on an early evening in the summer of 1974, that I'd just filled off the tanker, I was wearing a pressure jerkin and my target had gone u/s. This could be a boring flight - or an exciting one! I told air traffic that I was going for a high speed run before returning to Binbrook, turned northeast to make more room and, as I was already well east of Flamborough Head, immediately plugged in the burners. At Mach 1.3, I turned about and pointed it towards The Wash, some 150 miles away. Plenty of room, I'll go high over the airway to miss all the civvies, and turn left before I get within 35 nautical miles of the coast (the minimum clearance distance for supersonic flight).

Mach 2 would have been the ideal speed to start the zoom but, at 1.8, Flamborough was already appearing on the right edge of the boglescope (radar) at 60 miles, so I thought I'd better get on with it. I pulled the nose to 20 degrees above the horizon, and up we went. I knew that, above 50,000 feet, we were depending mostly on kinetic energy to take us up, but there was a lot of kinetic energy! With a pressure jerkin, the aircrew limit was 56, but it would be nice to go above 60. That was the published aircraft limit that I had so often heard mocked.

As I went through 60, I realised that my actual maximum altitude was clearly going to exceed my expectations, and a pitch angle of 20 degrees had been way too high. At 68,000 feet, both engines flamed out. I cancelled the burners, throttled back and hit the crackers (engine relight buttons). Fortunately, the engines were windmilling so fast at 92% that the electrical and hydraulic systems stayed on line, and fluctuating jet-pipe temperatures showed they were trying to relight.

It all seemed to be happening in slow motion, except that my brain was in overdrive, wishing that events would speed up, because I realised that I had got the scale of things significantly wrong, and was desperate to do something about it, but couldn't. On the one hand, I wanted to take in the awesome view (the black sky, the white sun, the curvature of the earth) but, on the other hand, I wanted to get the hell out of there, because I could see some dire consequences pending. Essentially, the aeroplane was ballistic, and I was afraid that, if I got back to Binbrook and the Boss heard of this exploit, he too would go ballistic. The last thing I was going to do was turn, and I was trying to let the nose come down towards the horizon..... but not too quickly.

We topped over at Mach 1.3, 160 knots IAS and 74,500 feet.

I stopped the pipper (gunsight) on the horizon, and let the aeroplane mush down, maintaining 1.3. I knew I'd blown the airspace issue. At 68 the engines relit. At 65, with IAS building, I began a gentle left turn, now maintaining 220 knots to let the Mach number decrease.

Staxton Wold radar called, "Are you still supersonic?"

"It's quite turbulent up here, I think I might be in a jetstream." I replied. The newly discovered phenomenon of jetstreams was much in the news at the time. No response from Staxton; that's good!

45 degrees of bank doesn't do much at Mach 1.3, but I'd already chanced my luck enough and, at just 220kts, I didn't want to push for more. As I crossed Norwich, still above 50, having gone well south of Marham and Kings Lynn, I finally came subsonic!

I called Staxton. "I'll go home now please."

I emerged from this adventure a bit chastened, but the Lightning was unblemished so, luckily, nobody knew. I did hear later that the engine trick is to throttle back to minimum burner above 65, and the engines will stay lit... according to folk lore of course. But I never tried it again!

The Day The Air Turned Purple

Late in 1965, I was serving on 100 Squadron at RAF Wittering as a Nav Radar, flying the Handley Page Victor B2. Our crew was scheduled for a high-low-high profile, with fighter affiliation arranged with a pair of Lightnings from RAF Coltishall, and several Blue Steel[1] runs planned and booked with two RBSUs (Radar Bomb Scoring Units). As the end of the six-monthly V-Force training period was fast approaching, this was a very important sortie for us as a crew, because we needed to complete a number of activities and procedures to ensure we retained, or improved, our "Select Classification" rating. I vaguely remember that we had been on QRA (Quick Reaction Alert) the day before, and had spent the afternoon preparing the sortie in detail, with only the weather and last minute NOTAMs (Notices to Airmen) to worry about the next morning. An Andover from the Royal Flight, carrying a VVIP, was due to land mid-morning with the usual Purple Airspace[2] restrictions, but we planned to be airborne long before that!

Next morning, as soon as we handed over the Squadron's QRA aircraft to another crew and returned our war target bags to the vault in the Operations Block, we completed our flight planning and headed for the aircraft. Unfortunately, we found a snag, which our Air Electronics Operator said would affect the sortie, and had to call for 2nd-line ground-crew to change one or two black boxes. In the meantime we returned to Ops, to re-plan the sortie and re-book the RBSU slots and low level route. At this stage, I think we had to bin the fighter affiliation that had been originally planned. Anyway, after nearly two hours, we finally got word from the engineers that all was ready, and we headed back out to the aircraft, but now the Royal Flight was due. We duly started up, but were held in dispersal, with engines running, while the Andover trundled (very, very slowly) down the glide-slope on an ILS (Instrument Landing System) approach. Back in the Victor, we were getting desperate, as any further delays would blow away our bookings and badly affect the success of the sortie, and kept badgering the controller in the tower. He finally let us taxi to the runway threshold, just as the Andover touched down.

Of course the Andover only needed a fraction of the 10,000 feet of runway to land, and it turned off to the right onto one of the access track, where the Station Commander was ready to greet the VVIP, and a Rolls Royce was waiting to collect her. As the Andover came to a stop, the rear door opened on the far side of the fuselage from us, and steps were rolled into position by airmen dressed in bright white overalls, as befitted a Royal Flight arrival. However, it was parked only some 25 yards from the runway edge, and we had finally got permission from Air Traffic to roll! Just as the dear lady stepped out of the rear door of the Andover, we came past with four RR Conways at full throbbing chat, and she rushed back inside, deeply distressed!

We continued the sortie, blissfully unaware of the chaos we had caused on the ground but, as we taxied in some six hours later, we were told to report to the Station Commander's office ASAP! Evidently, the dear lady had refused to move for nearly an hour, and the Commodore of the Queen's Flight had been lecturing the Group Captain down the blower. We arrived at the Station Commander's office, and were joined by the SATCO[3] and the young controller who had cleared us to roll. Over the next twenty minutes, we too received a stern, rather blue in places, lecture on royal etiquette! After that, nothing moved at Wittering during a Royal Flight arrival until after the Roller had gone through the gates!

---

[1] Blue Steel - A British, air-launched missile, built to arm the V bomber force
[2] Purple Airspace – Temporary controlled airspace to facilitate the movement of VVIPs
[3] SATCO – Senior Air Traffic Control Officer

A Pizza Good Luck

So there we were: a Hercules 'K' crew based at Kandahar, flying tactical air transport sorties in Afghanistan during the Spring of 2008. It was my first time in-theatre, but the rest of the crew were experienced operators. We'd had about a week to settle into our detachment, and everything had gone to plan, the aircraft had stayed serviceable, and we'd got the job done without incident.

One day, we flew up to Kabul with a cargo of something or other. It could have been anything; water, ammunition, mail, blankets, toilet rolls, food – we flew everyone and everything everywhere. Having off-loaded at Kabul, we waited around while the aircraft was refuelled and re-loaded for the return trip. Due to complications with the load, it became obvious that we wouldn't make it back to Kandahar before the canteen stopped serving dinner. Not to worry; we could order take-away pizzas from the restaurant in the ISAF compound at Kabul. They were cheap, tasted good and could be eaten on the way back to Kandahar - job done.

Unfortunately, our load wasn't the only thing which was delayed that night; the restaurant was running behind with our order. No problem, we had plenty of crew duty left, this was the last leg of the day, and the aircraft wasn't needed back at Kandahar in a hurry. So we decided to wait for our pizzas.

We eventually took off 10 minutes late. Weaving between the mountains to the West of Kabul, we climbed into the clear, moon-lit night and set course for Kandahar.

By and by, the lights of Kandahar airfield appeared on the horizon. We copied the latest airfield information from the automated radio transmission, bade goodnight to the Australian controller who'd followed our progress for most of the journey, and began a tactical descent towards Kandahar. Almost home and dry!

I checked-in with Kandahar Approach ... and the plan began to unravel. The controller advised us that Kandahar was under rocket attack. As if to verify his words, the familiar attack alarm could be heard in the background. We were directed to hold over the desert until the extent of the damage could be ascertained. Eventually, though, with no news from Kandahar and dwindling fuel reserves, we diverted back to Kabul, where we bedded-down for the night.

Next morning, we returned to Kandahar to find the engineers retrieving pieces of shrapnel from our parking slot. After we'd shut down, they explained that one of the previous night's rockets had landed only a few yards from our slot, at precisely the time we would have been crewing-out of the aircraft if we had been on-time. As it was, our delay in leaving Kabul (entirely down to the overdue pizzas) meant that we were still airborne when the rocket landed.

Some might have chided us for allowing our departure to be dictated by late-running rations. Thankfully, on that occasion, our consciences had allowed us to wait. Had we been on time, engineers and aircrew would have been milling around the aircraft when the rocket landed, and the result would probably have been rather different.

Air Racing

The following story is taken from SILVERED WINGS, by kind permission of the author, Sir John Severne.

Each September, most RAF stations hold annual Battle of Britain cocktail parties, to which our civilian friends in the locality are invited. At the 1951 party at Little Rissington, I met Lord and Lady Sherborne – Charles and Joan – who lived about 5 miles from the airfield. I had a fascinating conversation about their time as ferry pilots with the Air Transport Auxiliary during the War. Although Charles was a pilot, he had not joined the RAF because he only had one arm, but still managed to ferry Spitfires, amongst other aircraft. Joan currently owned a Vega Gull, which she kept at Kidlington, about 30 miles away and, apart from the distance, her main concern was the high cost of hangarage which she had to pay. At that time, RAF pilots were allowed to keep aircraft, free of charge, on their stations, provided space was available in a hangar and, since I was reasonably sure we had room at Little Rissington, I offered to look after the Vega Gull for her.

The Percival Vega Gull was a delightful four-seat touring aircraft, of the same parentage as the Mew Gull which had fascinated me as a boy. A military version, the Proctor, was produced during the War for communication duties. After a short time, as a 'thank you' for looking after her aircraft, Joan said, 'Would you like to enter the Vega in the King's Cup Air Race?' It is not difficult to imagine what my answer was, because I realized I would then be able to achieve one of my boyhood ambitions. I was newly married and had little spare cash at the time (what's new?), so I then had to set about trying to get some sponsorship. I managed to persuade Shell to give me the fuel for the race and some practice, while De Havilland at Hatfield agreed to give the engine a top overhaul. The latter was important because the race is a handicap race, and the handicappers calculate your speed on the basis that it is a standard aircraft in perfect condition. If you make any modifications to make it go faster, you have to declare them on the entry form and your handicap is then adjusted accordingly. Unfortunately, they don't make corresponding allowances for clapped-out aircraft.

The King's Cup was presented by George V, and was first flown in 1922 from Croydon. It is still being flown each year, and has become the longest-running major air race in the world. Before the War, civil aircraft were as fast as, if not faster than, the military aircraft of the period; consequently, the King's Cup had a national following not unlike that of Formula One motor racing today. In the weeks running up to the race, The Times would list all the entrants and their expected speeds, and give details of the pilots and aircraft, all of which I used to study with great enthusiasm as a small boy.

The 1952 race was to be held at Newcastle Airport, and the Commandant agreed that I could enter the Vega Gull as a CFS entry, so we painted the CFS crest on the engine cowling. I contacted Air Commodore Allen Wheeler, who was then Commandant at the experimental establishment at Boscombe Down, to seek his advice about air racing in general. I did not know him, but I knew of his reputation as a light aircraft enthusiast and an experienced air racer. He gave me some excellent advice along the following lines:

Prepare the aircraft as far a possible as if it was new. The handicappers will inspect the aircraft in detail, and compare it with what you have written on the entry form. If you win, they will also inspect it after the race to make sure there has been no cheating.

Navigation must be spot on. If you wander off course, you will lose time.

Turns must be as close as possible to the pylons, but if you clip the corner you will be disqualified. For safety reasons, you must not climb or dive during a turn.

Fly as low as possible into wind, where the wind is least strong, and then climb to about 200ft downwind to gain the maximum benefit.

The race was to be flown over four laps round a course with four turning points, each lap being about 32 miles long. I did several laps at about 1,000ft in an Anson a week or so before the race, to memorise the details of the course in case the visibility was poor on the day. We were given the opportunity to fly several practice laps the day before the race, and were given our handicap times the next day shortly before the start; I thought mine was very fair. Shortly after the event, I wrote an article to record my impressions at the time:

I glanced at my watch; eight minutes to go before we were to be flagged away. Two Tiger Moths and the Avro Cadet had passed overhead and were already on their second lap, and there were still six others to take off before me.

Why couldn't I fly a nice slow aeroplane, I thought, and avoid all this expenditure of nervous energy. 'Can you start up now please' shouted one of the marshals. 'Can I stay another couple of minutes, I have no oil cooler and she gets a bit hot? No? Oh very well!' The next worry is, will she start? One push of the button and she fired first go, I saw satisfied smiles from my crew, Ian Scott and my brother Dick, who were standing by my wing tips. A moment or two later, we were marshalled forward to fill the gap of the last competitor away. The starter held up two fingers, which I hoped meant two minutes to go (this I checked with my watch and I found it to be so). The last Proctor had been flagged away, and beside me was Ron Paine's beautifully polished Miles Hawk Speed Six which was not due off for some time.

Whilst I was noting all this, I suddenly realised the starter's flag was up, which meant I had ten seconds to go, so I opened up the throttle as far as I could against the brakes (no point in checking the magneto switches for fear of frightening myself) and, as the flag was whipped down: throttle fully forward, brakes off, tail up and the event we had looked forward to for so long had actually arrived.

Shortly after crossing the airfield boundary lay the first turning point of nearly 180°, which then set us off on the first leg towards St Mary's Lighthouse. This turn safely negotiated, we settled down on our first leg, which we flew at about 200ft to get the most out of the tail wind. There was no difficulty in staying on course, because one kept an enormous slag heap slightly to the left of track until we could see the lighthouse dead ahead. It was interesting to watch the turning techniques of the experts. Some rolled rapidly into the turn, hauled the aircraft round and rolled out rapidly. This looked impressive, but it did result in a loss of speed. Others took a more gentle approach to avoid losing too much speed; I had no option but to take the latter course because the Vega's ailerons were fantastically heavy at full speed and it was hard work to roll at all. The second leg was a straight forward run over the sea as low as one dare, but the third was more difficult, being a climb of some 500ft over coal mining country. The fourth leg led straight towards the airfield and, again, meant a few more minutes of glorious legal low flying.

All the four legs were about eight miles long, and each took the Vega about three minutes to complete, but the Vampire, flown by test pilot John Wilson, only took four minutes to complete the whole lap. Since the handicappers had aimed to have us all cross the finishing line at the same time, there was not much excitement until the third lap when we began to bunch up a little, and we could see it was going to be an exciting finish. As I was starting the last lap, I noticed that all the other aircraft except the Vampire had taken off. It subsequently overtook me four times, before finishing three places in front of me.

It was on the third lap that I hit one of the biggest bumps that I had ever experienced, as I came round the lee side of a wood. My head hit the roof, and there was a most alarming noise from the wing like a revolver shot. However, we were all in one piece so we pressed on. Inspection later revealed a flabby piece of canvas which seemed to have absorbed much of the shock. I now feel confident to fly the Vega through the most violent of storms (or do I?).

The last leg was incredibly exciting. We were overtaken by several others, but we on the other hand had overtaken even more. As the finishing line loomed ahead, I saw one of the two Miles Messengers just in front, but I failed to catch it before the end of the race. In fact we started 16th out of 23, and finished 11th at an average speed of 155 mph. The Vampire had flown at 460 mph. After nearly an hour flying at full throttle, I checked the oil after landing and, as I lifted the filler cap, there was a puff of blue smoke! The next day the engine ran sweeter than ever and a previous 'mag drop' had disappeared.

On looking back, an air race seems to be a series of individual battles; you win one and then sort out the next fellow. All the competitors seemed incredibly friendly, and would give you a cheery wave as they overtook you. They helped one another on the ground, with advice on flying the race and even assistance in preparing aircraft. There was no feeling of cut-throat competition – just everyone out for a good sporting race.

This was written over half a century ago, but the memory is as vivid as ever. The achievement of my boyhood ambition was every bit as exciting as I had hoped it would be. A few years later, I was to get another chance to fly in the King's Cup.

PS. In 1960 I won the King's Cup flying a Turbulent of the Tiger Club entered by HRH the Duke of Edinburgh, an honorary member of the club.

Dedication To Duty

One November day, we flew back across the Atlantic from Goose Bay, Newfoundland, into a gradually deteriorating weather situation, as first our base and then our alternate airfields disappeared under a blanket of autumnal fog. Ultimately, the only RAF base that could take us was Machrihanish, which is near Campbeltown, in the southwest of Scotland. Even there the weather was pretty dire, with heavy rain and strong winds, but we bumped our way down through the clouds and eventually made an uneventful landing.

After closing down the aircraft for the night, we were transported to the Officers' Mess, and were in the process of signing in at reception when the telephone rang. The receptionist answered the call, and then asked if one of us could take it. Being the nearest to hand, I took the telephone and the voice at the other end said:

"Hello, are ye a member o' the crew that's just landed fae Canada?"

I confirmed that I was.

"Well, noo", continued the voice, "It's Customs and Excise here fae Campbeltoon. I dinnae fancy comin' oot on such a night.....so I was wonderin' if ye have anything tae declare."

After a quick discussion amongst the crew, I confirmed to him that we did not.

"Well, in that case we'll just keep this between oorselves and I wish ye all a guid night!"

High Speed Tricycle

The first sortie of the Lightning conversion programme was designed to impress the student. It began with a full reheat take-off, which meant that the engines were run up to 85%, the brakes released, full "dry" power selected and, after a short pause, maximum reheat engaged. The latter had the effect of increasing the thrust of each engine (the Lightning was unconventional in having two engines mounted one above the other) from 12,500 lbs to 16,000 lbs, which gave a thrust to weight ratio of almost 1:1. Once airborne, the instructor immediately retracted the undercarriage and, at 230 knots (which was reached very quickly), pulled the control column fully back before centralizing it. The net result was that the aircraft would rotate through some 60 degrees, and then continue to accelerate upwards.

In this situation, things happened very quickly and, during take-off on the sortie in question, the instructor did not notice that reheat on the lower engine had failed to light. However, he subsequently became aware that all was not well when he pulled the control column back and the aircraft stayed glued to the runway. With time and runway fast running out, he centralized the control column and moved it rearwards again, but the aircraft still refused to fly. At this point, he exclaimed "SHIIIIIIT!" which the student, sitting in the left-hand seat, and keenly aware that all was not well, interpreted as "chute". The braking parachute was the Lightning's primary method of slowing down so, given the situation, the student, not unreasonably, reached forward and pulled the handle to release it. The parachute deployed directly into the jet wake of the upper engine, which was still at maximum reheat, and promptly melted into a blob of nylon, before detaching and falling onto the runway.

As the Lighting arrived at the far end of the runway, it was probably setting a new land speed record for tricycles so the safety barrier, which was designed for a maximum entry speed of 100 knots, stood no chance. It was torn from its mountings, and accompanied the Lightning, like some enormous fishing net, through the airfield boundary fence and a long way into the adjoining potato field. The aircraft came to rest virtually undamaged, which was more than could be said for the reputation of the instructor or the confidence of his student.

Never Assume – Check!

Cold is not a word usually associated with South Carolina, but cold it was on that February morning in 1960, when I took off through snow flurries for my third conversion sortie in the RF-101 Voodoo. On an exchange posting, I was training to become an instructor pilot on the 4414th Combat Crew Training Squadron, at Shaw Air Force Base.

With 30,000 lbs of thrust from the two mighty Pratt and Whitney J-57 engines in afterburner, the big Voodoo was always ready to leap off the ground at 175 knots, but today the ground run would be very short indeed. I also knew that my peers were watching, expecting (and hoping) that their new 'Limey' would fail to get his 'gear in the well' before reaching 230 knots, after which the nose-wheel would be left, very visibly ,'hanging'. I was determined not to give them that pleasure but, in the event, we all got more than we had bargained for.

Everything went well on take-off, until the Voodoo was airborne at 180 knots, with the gear already travelling, at which point the heavy nose cone covering the aircraft's camera compartment reared up on its top hinges, warning that it was about to depart. Depart it did, but not before I had time to duck my head, as it smashed through a side panel of the canopy and flew back over the aircraft. My helmet visor was down but, even so, my face was peppered with flecks of Perspex and dust from the cockpit floor, some of it finding its way into my eyes. I now had no airspeed indicator, my eyesight was impaired, and I could hear nothing on the radio for the roar of the airstream. I was also concerned that the flying cone might have damaged the tailplane, but the robust Voodoo seemed to be flying normally so, on the assumption that the pitch-up warning system would alert me to dangerously low speeds, I cancelled the afterburners and set the power we used in the circuit. Having declared an emergency, I asked for a 'shepherd' to bring me in to land, and received a 'green' from the tower to acknowledge my transmissions; I then dropped my two 450 gallon external fuel tanks into the swamp.

Meanwhile, my squadron commander, Major 'Grumpy' Brittain, not normally known for his speed over the ground, scrambled to my aid – probably seeing the rest of his career crumble before his eyes. He need not have worried; having inspected my aircraft to his satisfaction, he gave me my first formation lesson in the Voodoo. Using hand signals, and with me peering through the one remaining side panel with my one useable eye, we landed safely.

My hopes that the Crew Chief would confirm that he had checked the two lugs which secured the nose cone to the airframe were quickly dispelled when he, and the photographer who had installed the camera, both admitted that they might have missed this vital check. However, there was no escaping the blame; the pilot always has the ultimate responsibility. Mea Culpa!

After a trip to the flight surgeon, and a one-sided session with 'Grumpy', things returned to normal, with both the aircraft and pilot soon back in the air. It might have been worse; I had checked that it was clear below before dropping my tanks, and made the warning call, but I was not aware that an over-zealous T-33 pilot, anxious to help, was joining me fast from behind and below. Greeted by the two huge tanks, spewing fuel as they tumbled either side of him to their watery grave, he decided to take no further interest in my plight!

This was not the first time, nor the last, that an RF-101's nose cone caused a scare in flight. It had happened before, at Laon Air Base in France, and would again at the start of an operational sortie during the war in South East Asia, in which all these tactical reconnaissance Voodoos were involved. In the first incident, as in mine, the cone broke off, but in the second it remained attached. Captain Harry Runge recovered the aircraft to Udorn Air Base, Thailand, with his wingman as shepherd, and landed very gingerly – at which point the cone flopped back into place.

In all three cases, the pilots lived to tell the tale and their aircraft flew again – but it could have been otherwise. Never assume – check!

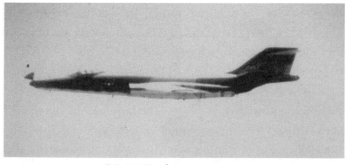

RF-101 Voodoo (Credit: Author)

Never Assume – Check (Again)

In almost ten thousand flying hours, my most memorable aviation experience has to be when I qualified for membership of the Goldfish Club. I should explain that the Goldfish Club is rather exclusive, and is open only to aircrew who have survived an aircraft ditching and subsequently been rescued from the sea. I became eligible to join on Tuesday May 16th 1995, and this is the story of that day.

Although stationed at RAF Waddington, I was at RAF Kinloss at the time, along with six squadron colleagues, to conduct a post-major servicing air test on one of our aircraft, Nimrod R1, XV 666. I had only returned from Cyprus the previous Friday after a three week stint, so I really didn't want this detachment, as short as it was; however, I had been assured by the Squadron that, as Pilot Leader, I was the only one qualified and available. In my haste to get to Kinloss, I forgot to pack a service hat, an omission I became aware of just before walking down to Operations for briefing. However, as we left the Mess at about 0900, I noticed an old and very worn 'chipbag' hat hanging on a peg in the cloakroom. That will do I thought to myself. If the owner was still alive (which I very much doubted, given the state of the hat), I would have it back on its peg within a few hours, with a signed bar chit inside as explanation and recompense for any inconvenience caused. As I donned the hat, I forgot to ask if it could swim....

Briefing, crew-in, start-up, taxy and take-off were all normal. As we climbed up to Flight Level 150, and turned out over the Moray Firth to start the air test, I recalled the words of an old and much respected ex-instructor of mine who, on beautiful days such as this one, would turn and utter the immortal words, "Almost a shame to take the flying pay today!" The weather was marvellous, with unlimited visibility, a light breeze and, most importantly, a sea state of less than one, with a swell of no more than a couple of feet.

We had just started the air test checklist when the problem began with the air start valve light illuminating on the centre console. This, in itself, was nothing to worry about as, to my knowledge, it had happened a dozen times before on Nimrods. I viewed it as more of a nuisance than an emergency, because in the past it had always been a false alarm. But on this occasion it wasn't. Unbeknown to us, a short circuit in a wiring loom across the number four engine had allowed power to the number four engine starter motor. The turbine within the starter, under no load because the engine was already running, wound up to in excess of 100,000 rpm in a second or so and, in so doing, imposed stresses on a £5 nut holding the starter turbine in place. The nut failed, and allowed the spinning turbine to exit the starter motor casing before coming into contact with the engine. Needless to say, a catastrophic explosion followed, which blew the lower casings off the engine and penetrated the adjacent fuel tank, which was fortunately still full. Two hours later, it would have been empty except for vapour, and the outcome would have been dramatically different.

On the flight deck, we remained unaware that all this was going on only feet from where we sat, until the fire warning for number four engine activated. The co-pilot and flight engineer immediately began running through the checks, and I started to turn the aircraft and commenced a descent back towards land and Kinloss. The fire spread rapidly through the engine, and was quickly followed by a fire warning (false as it turned out) on the adjacent, number three engine. All four fire extinguishers were quickly discharged, but to no avail because the contents were venting directly overboard although, obviously, we didn't know it at the time.

One of the safety team in the back of the aircraft began reporting on the state of the fire. Grey smoke at first, which quickly turned to black, then the first flames and numerous reports of panels breaking away as the wing appeared to be melting. His accuracy was nothing short of inspiring. I saw the fire through his eyes, and subsequently made the most dramatic and important decision of my thirty odd years of flying, based on someone else's reports. I had heard and felt a major explosion, experienced the whole aircraft shudder and, with the reports coming from the back, I really thought the aircraft was about to blow up. However, as the minutes passed and we got closer to land (and to the sea), I began to fear that the wing would collapse, and I would lose control of the aircraft, so I told the crew to prepare for a possible ditching.

At about 1000 feet, I allowed the aircraft to slow down, and requested 20° of flap in preparation for ditching. Fortunately for us, the flaps failed to lower due to loss of hydraulic pressure. I say fortunately, because I would have ended up with asymmetric flap plus no starboard aileron to assist with controlling the resulting roll, as the hydraulics to that had also gone. So, I had no option but to go for a flapless configuration ditching. Unfortunately, no one had foreseen this eventuality, and therefore no trials had been conducted, it was not practised in the Simulator, and there were no advisory speeds written down anywhere. We were literally going into unknown and uncharted waters.

The flat calm sea-state, and the flapless, nose-high attitude of the aircraft, made it extremely difficult to judge height during the last hundred feet or so. The radio-altimeter helped, but my eyes were firmly outside, to ensure that the wings were level on impact. We finally found the water at 127kts, two knots higher than I planned; not bad, under the circumstances, looking back on it. The flight engineer described the actual ditching as the biggest log flume in the world, but personally I don't remember much about events after we touched. We bounced twice, I've since learned, and, as we slowed, pivoted about 80° degrees around the port wing, and came to rest roughly parallel to the shore, about 3 miles out.

After the noise of the ditching, the silence when we came to a halt was almost deafening. There was about a foot of water and fuel in the cockpit and, without my headset (lost in the impact), I just shouted at everyone to get out. I don't think anyone on board needed telling twice! We exited through the port over-wing escape hatch, and boarded the dinghy on the wing. Of the two wing-root-mounted dinghies, one had been burnt and the other had inflated on impact, and was floating, upside down, about 400 yards astern of us. I can honestly say that the only part of me that got wet was my flying boots. Consequently, I always feel guilty when speaking to other members of the Goldfish Club, and hearing of their feats of survival and endurance in open dinghies in the North Atlantic in winter.

As we pulled away from the still-floating fuselage, I remember the all-pervading smell of fuel, and praying that a stray spark would not trigger an explosion. However, the good old waters of the Moray Firth had succeeded where we had failed in putting out the fire. Within seconds, we heard the whoosh-whoosh of the approaching rescue helicopter and, ten minutes later, we were all aboard, en route either to hospital for the injured or the Scruffs Bar for the remainder.

The application forms for membership of the Goldfish Club arrived at my hospital bed four days later. And the hat? I must regretfully report that it failed to vacate the aircraft before she sank, and now resides on the bed of the Moray

Firth, approximately three miles off Lossiemouth. Much to my surprise, the owner of the hat, a very junior navigator on one of the Kinloss squadrons, contacted me shortly afterwards. I apologised profusely for losing his hat and, despite his protestations, insisted on buying him twenty tickets for the Christmas Draw, none of which won a prize!

And the lesson to be learnt......never assume, always check. Not all hats can swim and, as they say in Yorkshire, "One is never too old to learn about flying from T'Hat!"

Nimrod R1 (Credit: John Malley)

It's The Way You Say It

Many years ago, when both RAF Wyton and RAF Alconbury (the latter a USAF base) were active airfields, their proximity to each other meant that, in poor weather conditions, aircraft returning to either airfield were controlled from the same place, to avoid conflictions. That duty was carried out by Wyton Radar and, on one particularly dark and dirty evening, a young, recently qualified (but nevertheless highly competent – or so she told me), female controller was on watch.

At around 9.30pm, the silence was broken by Bluewater One, a USAF F4 Phantom inbound to Alconbury from Germany, and the resulting exchange between the crew and the controller went something like this:

"Wyton radar, good evening, this is Bluewater One inbound Alconbury, requesting radar service".

"Bluewater One, this is Wyton Radar, you are identified on handover. Maintain heading, set the QFE 998 and descend to 3000 feet."

"Bluewater One, maintaining heading, 998 set, commencing descent for 3000."

"Bluewater One, roger, do you have the latest Alconbury weather?"

"Bluewater One, yes thank you Ma'am, and we're levelling at 3000 feet"

"Bluewater One, maintain, shortly handing you over to Alconbury, intermittent radar contact as you enter my dark area"

"Bluewater One, wriggle honey, wriggle!"

Post Script
My apologies to the lady in question who, it so happens, subsequently married an F4 pilot from Alconbury!

The Blackburn Beverley

The Blackburn-built Beverley aircraft came into service in 1957 as a heavy lift, short-range, tactical transport aircraft. At just under 100 feet long, and with a wingspan of 162 feet, it stood some 40 feet high and was affectionately known as 'The flying block of flats'. In addition to the spacious crew compartment, it had a large freight bay, capable of accommodating a standard RAF fire tender, and could also carry over 30 passengers or paratroops in the tail boom. It was powered by four (not-so-reliable) Bristol Centaurus engines, which consumed large quantities of oil, such that each engine had to be replenished in-flight by the engineer from a reserve tank in the wing root (known colloquially as the 'dog kennel' – rather cramped and not easily accessed). Thus, the engines were known as 'oil burning/petrol cooled'.

The Beverley served in the RAF for over 11 years, with two squadrons in the UK at Abingdon, and further squadrons in Aden, Nairobi and Singapore. While the overseas squadrons used the aircraft in its intended role, the UK squadrons were employed more on medium-range transport operations. While at base, a fair amount of squadron time was spent training the Paras and doing practice parachute drops of various sorts of loads. Exercises also claimed some time. As a transport squadron, we did get around Europe and the Middle East a fair bit, although it was not an easy journey - five days to get to Bahrain from the UK: Abingdon/Orange (France)/Malta, night-stop; Malta/El Adem, night-stop; El Adem/Khartoum/Aden (a very long day), night-stop; Aden/Sharjah/Bahrain – sometimes hopping up the southern Arabian coast - Salalah/Riyan/Masirah - sometimes night-stopping at these outposts, which could be quite fascinating (turtles coming in to lay their eggs on Masirah island, one of the few places in the world where this happens). But these journey times seem almost incomprehensible against today's flights - one hop to Bahrain now.

Unpressurised, slow (cruising at around 150 knots), with a fixed under-carriage and rather ugly, the Beverley was the subject of many adverse comments. With the rear clamshell doors removed, it looked something like a huge, pregnant dragonfly. Thus, as much as the aircraft was loved by the crews that operated it, and as efficiently it could do the job for which it was intended - for some tasks by no other aircraft before or since - it was the butt of many jokes.

My favourite concerned a Beverley, in the circuit at Heathrow for a 'touch and go', which the RAF could do in those days (early 1960s). An arriving American aircraft was told by Air Traffic that he "...was number two to land behind the Beverley". His drawled, rather laconic, reply? "I have no idea what a Beverley is, but I have a goddamn combine harvester in front of me!"

The previously mentioned route to Bahrain across Africa was from El Adem - then an RAF staging-post in Libya - almost due south to skirt around Egypt, which we were not allowed to overfly in those days, to Khartoum on the Nile in the Sudan. No 47 Squadron, one of the UK based Beverley squadrons, was stationed at Khartoum for many years before WWII, and has the motto 'Nili nomen roboris omen' - 'Let the Nile be an omen of our strength'. Flying south, it was sometimes possible to see parts of the route, laboriously ploughed into the desert before WWII to be followed by the then low-flying mail run aircraft. But by and large, with very few electronic navigation aids, it was a straight navigation exercise, in which the bubble sextant played a large part. At the bottom left hand corner of Egyptian territory was a large rocky outcrop, which we nicknamed 'Nasser's Corner'. It was the point where we would turn eastwards to head for Khartoum. We would normally pass this rock outcrop on our left-hand side, but sometimes it was on the right if we had cut the corner – but who could check so far out in the desert? The usual navigation technique then was to deliberately aim to one side of Khartoum so that, when we approached the Nile, we could turn on to the known direction of Khartoum – the so-called 'Chichester Technique' after the famous round-the-world sailor. However, on this occasion, we were flying with a navigator who had eschewed this technique, and had opted to aim direct for Khartoum. The only problem was that, when we crossed the Nile, Khartoum was nowhere to be seen; and, with the radio compass going round in circles, our erstwhile navigator had no idea which way to turn. Now this could have been a major problem, as our fuel reserves were quite low on such a long leg of the journey. However, the experience of our very senior captain came to the fore. As mentioned previously, the Beverley was unpressurised, so we were flying at around 8-9000 feet, and our airspeed was not greater than 150 knots. So it was possible for the pilots to open a small window to the side of the cockpit which, among other things, would allow them to give hand signals to the ground crew. In this instance, when we were again over the

Nile, the captain opened his window and turned the aircraft to fly north, sniffing the air as he did so; after a while, he turned south and did the same thing again. Swinging the aircraft round to the north again he said, "It's this way, I can smell it". And he was right! Guess who bought the beer that night!

Blackburn Beverley (Credit: Adrian Pingstone)

Priorities

I was once sent on detachment from Calcutta to the Imphal Valley, and an airfield that was quite high. When we landed there my pilot, Jack, remarked on the detrimental effect that the altitude had on our aircraft. The Beaufighter was not renowned for its gliding characteristics, but I had good cause to trust his ability. A couple of months previously he had achieved the first, ever, successful ditching of a Beaufighter – with me in the back!

Two restful days passed, without any flying, and we were tasked with taking an aircraft back to base for servicing. It was just before Christmas so, in addition to the usual detachment orders, we were expected to return with whisky and beer for the festive season. Once back in Calcutta, the aircraft was duly serviced, and loaded with so many supplies that I had difficulty getting into the rear cockpit. Unfortunately, our departure was then delayed for various reasons, and it was much later in the day when we eventually got airborne.

The return flight to Imphal went smoothly but, by the time we arrived, it was almost dark. Undeterred by the gathering gloom, Jack carried out his usual tight fighter circuit, side-slipped down finals, but completely forgot about the effect of the airfield altitude when we had first arrived. The starboard undercarriage hit first, very hard. So hard that the wheel departed from the axle, bounced over air traffic control and disappeared. This was followed by the starboard wing-tip which, to our alarm, sent a spectacular shower of sparks around the wing fuel tank before trailing behind us down the runway.

Eventually we ground to a halt, still in one piece but rather keen to evacuate the aircraft. This was particularly difficult for me, as the exit was a panel on the lower surface of the fuselage, and I was surrounded by the additional stores we had carried. Jack, meanwhile, was busily shutting everything down when the rescue services arrived. On this occasion they consisted of a petrol bowser, driven by a very anxious armourer. He stopped a respectable distance from our battered airframe, leaped out of the cab and ran across to us with concern written all over his face. Pausing to catch his breath he shouted, "Is the beer alright?"

Timed To Perfection

One dark night, my captain said that I could do the landing when we arrived at Goose Bay (Newfoundland) at the end of our transatlantic flight but, before we arrived, he impressed on me that the runway at "Goose" was twice the normal width and, therefore, it was easy to misjudge height on finals. However, I was an experienced and responsible co-pilot, 22 years old with, um, dozens of hours on the Vulcan - so no sweat.

As we came down finals, I was concentrating hard on getting everything right, probably too hard. I raised the nose to achieve the touchdown attitude when I was still too high, with the result that, as the Vulcan's undercarriage finally met the runway, the planned-for 'kiss' was replaced by a teeth-jarring 'thump'. We rolled down the runway in awkward silence, until my captain switched on his microphone, and asked the rear crew[1] if anyone had noted the time of landing. "Bloody should have", was the reply. "All the clocks have stopped back here".

---

[1] The Vulcan, in common with the other V-bombers the Victor and Valiant, carried a crew of 5. Pilot and co-pilot in the front, navigator plotter, navigator radar and air electronics operator in the back.

Kill's A Kill But...

On this occasion, I was flying a Jet Provost aircraft with a student navigator from the Air Navigation School, during a detachment to RAF Lossiemouth. I had previously served as operations officer on a Buccaneer squadron in Germany, so knew several of the crews on the maritime Buccaneer force stationed there.

Our flight was planned as a low-level formation exercise in the Highland training area and, before arriving in the exercise area, we were transiting at 'medium level' (two to three thousand feet). We were the number 2 aircraft at that stage of the flight, with little to do except watch out for, and advise the leader of, possible collision threats. There were no planned 'enemy forces' for our training exercises, although we took every opportunity to instil as close to an operational attitude in our students as we could. Indeed, as a squadron, we had developed an unofficial tradition of deviating from planned track during the navigation exercises we flew from our English base, to intercept the USAF A-10 'Warthogs' which had a similar performance to our own Mark 5 Jet Provosts and trained in the same areas. We felt a proud sense of achievement if we were able to place our aircraft in a simulated gun-firing position behind an aircraft in an American formation, without their crews spotting us!

As we crossed Findhorn Bay, I noticed two Buccaneers well below us, and my student informed our leader of their position. Surprisingly, they seemed to be flying relatively slowly, and I calculated that, even though their level flight cruising speed would be faster than we could ever achieve, from our position on the right of the loose formation, I might just be able to get on their tails for a few seconds. The little devil on my shoulder took over, and I requested permission to break formation "to practice a rejoin procedure".

Permission granted, I peeled off and accelerated in a curving descent, describing to my student as I did so what I intended to achieve. I warned him to expect our targets to take avoiding action as soon as they saw us, when we would have to return to our formation. However, as we approached from the traditional up-sun position, there was no change in the Buccaneers' course or speed, which remained a little less than we had built up in the dive. I rolled out of our descending turn exactly where I had planned (to be honest, rather to my surprise) and, for a few seconds, the Buccaneer formation included a Jet Provost in short trail behind the leader. We were of course unable to maintain the speed we had gained in the dive, so we soon fell behind and climbed back up to rejoin our leader. The planned exercise continued with, I hoped, my student having been suitably impressed by my skill as an interceptor.

That evening, as was traditional after work, we went to the Officers' Mess 'Bothy Bar' to slake our thirst. Soon several members of 12 Squadron walked in, including their Boss whom I had known at a previous station. Anticipating a free beer, I enquired (less than subtly) as to who had been in the formation at such and such a time over Findhorn Bay. Even before I had the opportunity to call the said formation's lookout into question, the Wing Commander accepted responsibility. "I was leading, and you're entitled to your beer, Dave, but perhaps a few words in explanation. Did you happen to notice what was going on underneath us as you slipped in behind?" Of course I hadn't, I'd been far too keen on getting into position! "Oh, so you didn't see the chap standing on the deck of the launch?" WHAT LAUNCH? "So you wouldn't have seen him returning the salute as we flew past to welcome him as our new Air Officer Commanding!"

Footnote

Knowing that particular Air Officer's reputation, and having previously met him, I'm pretty certain that incident had no bearing on my subsequent lack of promotion. There must have been some other reason!

A Really Short Landing

After completing my first tour of productive service as a Movements Officer, at RAF Khormaksar in Aden, I was lucky enough to be selected to join the Far East Air Force Mobile Air Movements Squadron (FEAF MAMS) as one of the 3 team leaders, and duly arrived at RAF Seletar, in Singapore, in early December 1967. My work with FEAF MAMS took me and my team all over the Far East, to such luxurious locations as New Zealand, Fiji, Australia, Hong Kong, Thailand, Korea, Japan and the Maldives. In the course of all this, we spent many hours in Beverleys, Hercules, Belvederes, Belfasts , Whirlwinds, and Bristol Freighters belonging to the RNZAF.

Of all the flights undertaken during my 4 year tour on FEAF MAMS, the most memorable was during a 2 week detachment to Kathmandu in Nepal during the late 60s. The task was to provide equipment and supplies to the Gurkhas, located in various parts of Nepal, and our team flew from Singapore to Kathmandu in an Andover of 52 Sqn (outbound via Rangoon and Calcutta and returning via Calcutta and Bangkok), to await the arrival of 2 or 3 Hercules from 48 Sqn. The Hercules brought the equipment and supplies which, on one occasion, included hundreds of live piglets and a thousand ducklings and baby chickens. However, the re-supply strips at Pokhara, Bhairahawa and Biratnagar were too small for the Hercules to operate from, so the Andover was used to move freight in-country. Kathmandu airport was high and short (elevation 4000 feet plus and a main runway only 4500 feet long), which caused a number of operating problems. The Air France Caravelles had to use a very large brake parachute when landing, and a fully-fuelled Andover could only offer around 1000 lbs of payload for the first trip of the day. As a result, on subsequent Gurkha resupply tasks, the Andover was replaced by a RNZAF Bristol Freighter, as it was able to carry more cargo on each trip.

On the day of my memorable flight, we had flown directly from Kathmandu to Pokhara and, after unloading the freight (which did not take very long with the help of the Gurkhas), the Captain invited me to sit on the jump seat for the return flight. Having always had an interest in flying, I asked him if he would demonstrate a tactical, short landing for me when we got back to Kathmandu, and he said that he was more than happy to do so. I was quite looking forward to the experience and, as we lined up on the approach, I noted that the runway started on the edge of a cliff, with very little scope for an undershoot. As we reached the cliff edge, the Captain changed the pitch of the propellers to obtain reverse thrust, while we were still some 50 to 80 feet above the runway. The retardation effect was quite marked and, soon afterwards, we had touched down and stopped in a very short distance. I was most impressed with the short ground run, but had spotted that, just after landing, the Captain was having great difficulty in keeping the aircraft straight and on the centre line of the runway. After coming to a halt, the Captain asked the loadmaster to jump out and see if he could determine what had caused the steering problem. He duly lowered himself to the ground through one of the rear doors, while remaining in contact with the flight deck via a very long extension lead on his headset, and it wasn't long before we heard him exclaim, "F****** H*** Sir, you have blown all 4 main tyres!"

The Captain shut the aircraft down, and we all got out to 'review' the situation. At this stage, it was quite unnerving to be standing by a stranded aircraft, some 600 to 700 feet from the end of the main runway, with flights still taking off and landing over the top of us! On closer inspection, it became evident that only 3 of the 4 main tyres had blown and, as we walked back along our landing track, it was possible to follow the skid marks and see precisely where they had failed. Not far from where we had initially touched down!

It was then that we discovered that the aircraft spares pack-up had only one spare wheel. As the Captain was under considerable pressure from the tower to remove his aircraft from the main runway, he decided that, if we could put the spare on the side with 2 flats, it would be possible to taxi the aircraft with one good wheel on each side. We then removed the aircraft jack from the pack-up and discovered that, with 2 flat tyres on one side, it was not possible to get it under the oleo leg. Undeterred, a committee convened and agreed to place vehicle ramps – designed to take the weight of a land rover – in front of the 2 flat tyres. The Captain would then start up the aircraft, and taxi up the ramps until the oleo leg was high enough for the jack to be placed underneath it.

To this day, I can still remember standing behind the engine, struggling to stand upright, while the Captain inched the aircraft up the ramps. As you might have already guessed, the vehicle ramps were not strong enough to take the weight of the aircraft, and started to buckle. However, luck was on our side and the Captain managed to get the aircraft high enough for the rest of us to manoeuvre the jack under the oleo leg. The wheel change was then completed without further drama, and a very relieved Captain was able to taxi off the main runway, and out of the way of other aircraft which had continued to use it throughout the entire escapade.

The task of resupplying the Gurkhas was delayed for a couple of days, while we waited for additional spare wheels to be flown in from Singapore. When we eventually returned, no further mention was made of the incident, and I am pleased to say that, after retiring from the RAF, the Captain in question had a very long and successful flying career with a major civilian airline.

Andover

No Going Back

Many years ago, representatives of the Air Secretary used to run a programme of annual visits to RAF stations, to brief personnel on current issues relating to pay, allowances and terms of service. Invariably, these were dry and slightly tedious events, with the only incentive being that the bar would open for attendees once the briefing had finished.

One particular year, the Squadron Leader in charge of the team was getting a lot of flak from the floor, having just announced that we were to get one less free travel warrant per year. Now, while free travel might be viewed by the public as an unnecessary perk, I would point out that many cold war RAF bases were situated in remote locations, so a reduction in warrants was not viewed kindly.

Things were getting rather heated so, in an attempt to close off discussion, the Squadron Leader said:

"To conclude this matter, might I point out to you all that the original reason for introducing free travel warrants was to allow personnel to return whence they came, and spread the word on how good Service life was. Effectively, it was a recruitment tool, and I would ask you to remember that".

He then swiftly moved the presentation on to pensions, which was the last item on the agenda, and finished by asking if there were any final questions, clearly hoping that the lure of the bar would work in his favour at the end of a particularly lively afternoon. After a pause, one of our squadron Air Electronics Operators (AEO) raised his hand.

"Sir, I was just thinking about what you said earlier about travel warrants being for personnel to return whence they came, to spread the word, as it were, and wondered if that was still the official view".

The Squadron Leader rolled his eyes and replied that, yes, they could be viewed that way.

"That's interesting", mused the AEO.

"Why do you say that?" snapped the Squadron Leader, clearly becoming irritated.

"Well, it's just that I was born in India".

Silent Night

When Blue Steel[1] was introduced at RAF Wittering, any sortie flown without a live or a training missile loaded was rather a waste of effort for the navigation team, as nearly all our training activities and procedures for the six-monthly V-Force classification scheme involved practising operation of the missile systems. Wittering held half a dozen training missiles, basically shapes containing only the navigation and guidance packages, which met most of the daily training needs of both 100 and 139 Squadrons. However, there was also a Bomber Command requirement to fly the live (or operational) missiles on a regular basis, to prove their reliability and airworthiness. On these occasions, the missile tanks were loaded with kerosene and HTP (High Test Peroxide) but, I hasten to add, the Red Snow nuclear warhead was not installed. My crew was due to fly such an operational missile on a 6-hour high-low-high profile one winter's evening in 1963, but the missile failed on loading and was removed.

We quickly re-planned a sortie, using night astro-navigation on two high-level navigation legs up the North Sea, around Iceland and back. In a 6-month training period, we were required to complete a number of 1,000 mile navigation stages, using three techniques. The 'primary technique' assumed all navigation systems were serviceable, including the H2S radar for fixing and, with this capability, the accuracy required was easily achieved. The 'secondary technique' assumed that the H2S had failed, or couldn't be used because of the need to minimise high-powered electronic emissions which would reveal our presence. Accuracy along track was still pretty good, because the Green Satin Doppler radar provided a continuous input of groundspeed and drift to the Ground Position Indicator (GPI) Mk 6, which was probably the most accurate analogue navigation computer ever built. 'Limited technique' assumed that the Green Satin had failed, and we would then resort to the use of airspeed and calculated wind velocities from astro-fixing, a much more difficult exercise if we were to meet the criteria specified by Bomber Command. Achieving the high accuracy required for Select Star/Command classification was not easy at the best of times but, without the very good true heading provided by the Blue Steel inertial navigation system, it was even more difficult.

---

[1] Blue Steel - A British, air-launched missile, built to arm the V bomber force

This was because the two gyro-magnetic compasses of the Smith's Military Flight System suffered from dynamic errors of up to two degrees in flight.

We decided to improve our chances of success by flying a 'secondary' stage first, recording the wind velocities provided by Green Satin inputs, and then flying a 'limited' stage back through the same air mass. So we took off and climbed out over The Wash, to start the first 1,000 mile leg up the North Sea and across Scotland towards Iceland. The auto-pilot was in, of course, and we took a series of sextant shots just for practice, although we knew the position lines they provided were not worth using because, for at least the first hour, the "dead-reckoning" of the GPI Mk6 would be better. We cleared Scotland and relaxed, as there was still some 500 miles to go to the first NTP (Navigation Terminal Point) off the North East coast of Iceland. I kept myself busy by heating a can of tomato soup from my ration box and cleaning the sextant optics. It was a clear, calm, star-lit night, and all cockpit lighting was dimmed to preserve night vision. I glanced to my right and noticed, to my amusement, that both the Nav Plotter and Air Electronics Operator were fast asleep. So I turned on my microphone and, with a chuckle, reported this to the guys up front...but got no reply. They were both asleep! It then dawned on me that, had I dozed off too, we could have ended up very close to the North Pole and very short of fuel – or even worse! I woke them all up, raised hell and made sure that nobody on my crew ever fell asleep after that.

Navigator On Top

In the late 70s, I was a pilot on a Canberra squadron that was frequently tasked with towing aerial targets, known as 'banners', which were used by fighter crews to hone their shooting skills. A bonus of undertaking this task was that we were often deployed to the Mediterranean to do it, and the tale I am about to tell happened off the coast of Malta.

It was a clear, calm afternoon, as we got airborne for the final trip of the day. Air Traffic confirmed that our banner was 'flying' correctly behind us, so I turned south away from the island and headed towards the range area. The sting had gone out of the sun's rays, and cockpit temperatures that late in the afternoon were quite bearable, so we had agreed to take a cadet passenger along for some air experience. He was safely strapped into the right-hand rear ejection seat, next to my navigator and, by top of climb, they were heavily into aerial charts and navigation equipment. The cadet had expressed a keen interest in photography, so I had agreed to let him come forward onto the Rumbold seat (a fold-down seat adjacent to the pilot's position) during our recovery to base, but there were three F4-Phantom crews to be served first.

By the time I had reached the range and found a ship-free area, never an easy task in the busy waters to the south of Malta, our first two F-4s were circling anxiously overhead. We had reached the phase when crews needed to get bullet holes in the banner to qualify as operational, and our role was to afford them every opportunity to do as well as possible. Unfortunately, our passenger was not prepared for the smelly, humid hovel that a Canberra cockpit soon becomes in such climatic conditions and, by the time our final customer was complete, he had focused his attention on the sick bag that was poised a few inches from his face. I sympathised with his predicament, but there was nothing I could do, apart from fly as smoothly as possible for the remainder of the trip. The crew of the final F-4 asked if they could carry out a banner inspection, and I readily agreed. We had lost an 'Op Shoot' banner the previous day during recovery, and I was keen to know how many of the attachment cords were still in place.

We settled down at 1500 feet and 200 knots, and I cleared the F-4 in on our starboard side. Meanwhile, a couple of minutes of gentle flight had revived our passenger sufficiently for him to ask my navigator to take some photos, even though he wished to stay firmly in his seat. Once the banner had been confirmed safe, I invited the F-4 pilot to come past slowly so we could get some airborne shots. He agreed, and was soon perched down-sun on my starboard wingtip, looking highly photogenic. My navigator, meanwhile, had unstrapped and moved forward onto the Rumbold seat to take the photos. He snapped away for a couple of minutes, at which point I thanked the F-4 pilot, and cleared him to depart the range and call Malta approach. That was when things started to go wrong.

Instead of breaking away to the right, the F-4 pilot slid forward and left, selected full power, lit his afterburners and pulled up directly in front of us. My navigator had meanwhile turned round to hand the camera back to its owner, and was completely oblivious to events, until he heard my muffled oath just before the slipstream hit us. The Canberra rotated violently left, and my navigator fell across me as we passed 90 degrees of roll. Two things saved us. Firstly, both engines kept going and, secondly, my navigator was physically much slimmer than me and about four stones lighter, so I was able to support him with my right arm, while trying to move the control column with my left.

We regained straight and level flight, somewhat closer to the water than was comfortable, my navigator hauled himself off my lap and, after collecting up as much debris as he could find, strapped into his seat again. Once we were back at 1500 feet and 200 knots, the power required indicated that the banner was probably still attached, and our passenger was more interested in examining the contents of his sick bag, so we elected to 'suck it and see'. In the event, the aircraft was undamaged, the banner intact, and a loose article check of the cabin revealed nothing. However, a very apologetic F-4 crew paid for an expensive dinner that evening, and we all agreed that it was an experience not to be repeated.

Smoke Without Fire

I was on a tactical check in a Hunter FGA 9, being chased by my Flight Commander on a high-low-high profile out of RAF Wittering, with two simulated attacks in southern Scotland followed by a first run attack on the range. It was a cracking day, with the odd thunderstorm, and the trip went well until we started recovery to Wittering. Unexpectedly, in front of my very eyes, on came the fire warning light, bold and bright. My wingman was duly advised. The bold and bright fire warning light remained illuminated. We pulled up from low level, and set up for a precautionary forced landing at Wittering. Inside the cockpit, the engine gauges were normal, with no smells and no red glow in the mirror. Must be a hot gas leak or a fire, methinks! Getting close for a forced landing, so press on, methinks! Flight idle was selected on the throttle, but still that very bright fire warning light was there. I transmitted a Mayday and, when certain of being able to land, I carried out the full fire drill - but still that red light shone brightly, dammit! The next call from my wingman (Flight Commander, don't forget!) was "Lots of smoke –EJECT, EJECT, EJECT!!" Thus, believing that all Flight Commanders are near perfect and God-like, I reached for the handle.

The "boom-bang" sequence went well and, in a very short time, I was laying in a ditch with the helmet visor though my nose and a damn sore back. The jet disintegrated in the woods a few hundred yards up ahead, and it quickly became apparent that I had explored the limits of the Martin Baker Mk4H ejector seat, with a combination of late ejection and high rate of descent. In addition, my first parachuting experience had been in high winds and heavy rain, and I had landed in a filthy, water-filled ditch. Nevertheless, the ejection was successful and I did not break anything else that day.

After a spell in the hands of the Medics and the spinal injury unit at Headley Court, I was back flying again within three months. The only long term damage was to my golf swing as, since that day, I have developed a nasty slice left to right. It has been caused by my T11/T12 spinal fracture and, so far, no golf professional worth his salt has been able to correct it. Thus I am doomed to forever play off a 19 handicap!

Finally, there was the Board of Inquiry and the bollocking from the Station Commander. You see, the fire warning light was spurious, caused by serious corrosion in the Triple Fault Free Fire Detection Circuits around the jet pipe. My wingman kindly reported smoke but, in fact, what he saw proved to be hydraulic fluid being dumped as the hydraulic flying controls reverted to manual when the engine was shut down. The engineers conducted a fleet check of all aircraft, and corrosion, some quite serious, was found in the fire detection circuitry of a good number of jets.

The rollicking from the Station Commander was gentlemanly and polite, and I did get a cup of coffee - but no biscuit. I was guilty of misidentifying a spurious fire warning, and had thus made an error of judgement, something my wife tells me I do all the time now that I have retired. All of this happened over 35 years ago and, despite amassing over 16000 hours on Phantoms, Jaguars, Tornados and Boeings in military and commercial aviation, I still think about how I might have played it better. Regrettably, my Flight Commander, who reported the smoke, died in a flying accident two years later; but I remain indebted to him for his advice in the circumstances.

Inverted Leader

The following story is taken from SILVERED WINGS, by kind permission of the author, Sir John Severne.

By 1952, CFS no longer had a variety of operational aircraft for the students to fly, but we did have a flight of two-seat Gloster Meteor Mk7s so that the students could experience jet flying up to solo standard if they had not already done so. I was keen to get on to the Meteor flight, not just because I wanted to instruct on jets, but because I thought that it would enhance my chances of being posted back to an operational jet fighter squadron after my time at CFS. In fact, I was able to join the Meteor flight some eight months after arriving back at Little Rissington, and this proved to be one of the most interesting periods of my flying career. At about the same time, I was appointed PA to the Commandant, Air Commodore 'Mark' Selway but, as this was a part-time appointment, I was able to continue instructing on the Meteor. The Commandant had been one of the pre-war CFS formation aerobatic pilots, and one day a photograph arrived in my in tray. It was of the pre-war team, flying AvroTutors with the leader inverted, at a Hendon air display. There was no note attached to the photo, but the Commandant had simply written on it: 'Re-do Meteors'. So we did.

I had always been enthusiastic with a camera, so I asked if I could fly the MOD chief photographer, Mike Chase. He produced a photograph in March 1952 which hit the world's press, because it was the first time this formation had been attempted with jet aircraft. The problem was that Meteors were only cleared to fly inverted for 15 seconds so, once the leader had turned his aircraft upside down, we only had 15 seconds for me and the other two to get into position and for the photographer to take his picture. In fact, we found the engines would keep going for much longer than 15 seconds if full power was not used, but I was subsequently told that this did not do the oil pressure much good. Our flight commander, Caryl Gordon, went one better by leading the four Meteors with himself inverted, and even led the team in the first half of a loop in this configuration.

Red Flag Buccaneers

RED FLAG is an advanced aerial combat training exercise. Its purpose is to train aircrew from the United States and other NATO countries. In a typical Red Flag exercise, Blue Forces (friendly) engage Red Forces (hostile) in realistic combat situations.

There was nothing very sophisticated about the Buccaneer when it came to navigation or navigation aids, particularly over land and more so over the arid wastes of the Nevada desert. The aircraft was, of course, 1950s vintage by its design, and the navigation system, in the 1970/80 era, was very much analogue or "steam-driven", as described by the crews who flew it. Thus, reliance was very much placed upon the Mark One Eyeball, particularly in the overland role where the Blue Parrot radar, specifically designed to find a needle in a haystack or rather a soviet Sverdlov cruiser in a blue water battle, was virtually useless. The Doppler system (Blue Jacket) was equally unreliable, as its analogue cogs and pulleys had a tendency to drive the Lat/Long counters one nautical mile in an unpredictable direction as soon as the navigator selected 'RUN' during the take-off!

Mission Planning, therefore, followed the tried and tested principles of visual navigation, as adopted by single-seat pilots in the good old days of Day Fighter Ground Attack. For Red Flag, with its operational environment, clear skies and 'need to survive' personal policy, this meant 'big feature' navigation; ie from one ridge line to the next, avoiding the salt pans, using the ridges themselves to terrain mask from either GCI[1], SAMs[2] or the ubiquitous Red Air! There were no AWACS[3] in those days, with an ability to look behind ridges, and the principle adopted by the Buccaneer aircrew to avoid detection and attack was 'low and fast'. As low as you could go, and as fast as the 2 RR Speys would take you and the airframe would tolerate, whilst operating west of the exercise 'entry point' of Student Gap. This equated to an authorised height of 100 ft and a

[1] GCI - Ground Controlled Interception
[2] SAM - Surface to Air Missile
[3] AWACS - Airborne Warning And Control System aircraft

maximum speed of 580 knots, although the radio altimeter height-warner was notoriously unreliable below 100 feet, and unusable below 50!!

The daily routine depended very much on which wave a crew was assigned to. My first experience of Red Flag was in October 1978 (RF 79-1), as an instructor on the Buccaneer Qualified Weapons Instructor (QWI) Course. Thus, we took a dedicated 4-ship, embedded within 208 Squadron, on what I believe was the second Red Flag that the aircraft had participated in. We arrived at Nellis amidst tales of infamy about the Buccs' ability to outrun and out-fly at low-level any fighter that got within range! It was a story that we were happy to use to our advantage, and to embellish as and when the right number of Budweisers had been consumed by both us and the 'enemy' in the Officers' Club! The QWI course was designated the afternoon wave throughout RF 79-1 and, therefore, we were able to enjoy the delights of the 'O' Club and Las Vegas in the evenings, prepare our missions in the mornings, and fly in the afternoons. We were also, occasionally, privileged to be appointed Mission Commander for the Blue Force, which would involve additional preparation time but, once the de-confliction aspects had been resolved, the planning of each mission was fairly routine and simple. The lead pilot and his deputy planned the target runs and selected the Initial Points (IP) with the lead navigator, who primarily concentrated on the preparation of the navigation route to and from the target, the split to ensure safe separation over the target, the hold to guarantee the de-conflicted 'push' time through Student Gap (which was invariably a 'timing trombone'[4] in Caliente East), and the avoidance of the SAM threats and Dreamland[5]! Other members of the formation would have been tasked with threat analysis, map drawing, and providing drinks to water the fevered brows of those directly involved in the preparation which, if my memory serves me well, took about 4 hours from the end of the Mission Commander's brief to the end of the sortie pre-brief.

Of course, the Bucc had no self-defence capability other than a Westinghouse jamming pod and a one-shot Chaff[6] option taped into the airbrake!

---

[4] A racetrack pattern, which could be cut short or extended to adjust the timing

[5] Dreamland – Commonly used alternative name for Area 51, a secret military base in the Nevada desert

[6] Chaff – Air deployed radar countermeasure of small, thin pieces of aluminium or metallised glass

However, we did adopt a 'Bomb in the Face' (BIF) tactic, codenamed 'knickers' for some obscure reason, if a fighter was fortunate enough to get within 1000 yards of the stern. The hope was that a retarded 1000lb bomb falling from the aircraft would be enough to force his tracking to wander if not ruin his day completely. It was a tactic acknowledged by the Aggressor pilots to be realistic, and one that would definitely force a break-off from an attack!

After take-off, the 4-ship (or 8-ship when tasked) would form up in the climb out of Nellis, to be in the designated formation (normally 2000 yard Card[7]) at 15, 000 feet by the north end of the corridor, prior to entering Caliente East and the timing trombone. The idea behind the hold was that, suitably marked with minutes during planning, the trombone could be shortened or extended as required to guarantee a successful 'push' at Student Gap on time. The formation would always 'hack' their stopwatches through the Gap, and the responsibility for navigation from that point on became the lead navigator's. All other eyes were outside the cockpit, with pilots taking primary responsibility for their forward arcs from 10 to 2 o'clock, and their navigators attending to the other 240 degrees. By flying in Card formation at 2000 yards, each aircraft was able to cover a further 2000 yards beyond its wingman and, as a whole, protect the bubble from aggressive attack. When a SAM locked up the formation, he who was locked called a 30 degree turn away from the threat, and the formation took the evasive action, jamming and maintaining height and speed (100/500). The base principle to ensure maximum effect on the target (max. bombs on Desired Mean Point of Impact (DMPI)) was to maintain formation integrity at all costs. However, if a fighter was identified, either visually or electronically, evasive manoeuvres were carried out to offset any possible attack, by taking the formation away from the threat. If a fighter was lucky enough to see an aircraft against the desert floor (we had adopted a sand colour scheme only to discover that the fighters looked for shadows which we could not disguise!), and get into a killing position, the formation would break, the aircraft tracked would attempt to out-fly by evasive manoeuvre, chaff, BIF, height and speed whilst, at the same time, drawing the fighter away from the rest of the formation. Of course, Fighter

---

[7] Card – A formation of pairs of aircraft in trail, each pair in wide line abreast, designed to give maximum mutual support.

Escort and Sweep were often built into the Blue Package, and so it was our earnest hope that the fighters would be dealt with, and most often were, before we became vulnerable. Unfortunately, however, there was a culture amongst the fighter force that there was some mighty kudos to be had for anyone who could claim a Bucc at the debrief (and these were the days before electronic debrief facility and live fight monitoring was available). So, as a result, we were often deliberately targeted by the fighters, to gain their 'Bucc-killer' reputation, rather than they engage in traditional fighter 1v1 as per the Red Flag script. However, our tactics were successful in the main and we almost invariably outran our opponents and got our bombs through to target with safe RTBs[8]. I am aware of many apocryphal tales of Buccs turning F-5 aggressors on their backs because of jet-wash etc, but have no personal experience to back them up.

By the time I took part in RF 82-1 in November 1981, the Buccs were equipped with one AIM-9G Sidewinder on the outboard starboard pylon, which was more of a threat to the crews than the enemy! The thought of a Buccaneer looking for a fight with a one-shot, limited performance, Sidewinder against an aggressor, or worse an agile F-16 or F-15, made my blood curdle! Nevertheless, the missile did act as a deterrent, and any unwary fighter pilot who dropped mistakenly into the middle of the Card, thinking he was behind the last man, often met an untimely 'death' from the back marker, who was dealt the ace of the day and presented with a juicy target, ripe for the taking! Not an uncommon happening, if my memory serves me well. Weapon loads and targets for the Buccs on RF were almost invariably 1000 lb Freefall or High Drag (Retard in UK parlance), real or simulated, against the airfields at Tolicha, Kawich or Mt Helen. Freefall bombs were delivered in a 'Medium Toss' manoeuvre. Running into the target at 500 knots, minimum of 100 feet, the freefall weapons were tossed over the shoulder during a 3G pull, and released automatically by the aircraft's Control & Release Computer, which would determine the required release point from the pilot's inputs (height, speed and pull) during the manoeuvre. The weapon usually released at about 1500 feet, and the pilot recovered the aircraft back to low level in an aggressive high G wing-over escape manoeuvre onto a reverse track. High Drag weapons were released from low-level at 500

---

[8] RTB – Return To Base

knots, either in a level 100 feet "laydown" or bunted 5 degree dive attack, known as Bunt Retard.

My last sortie on Red Flag in the Buccaneer took place on November 6th 1982, when I was privileged, as a Royal Air Force navigator, to be appointed Mission Commander for the Blue Forces, tasked with leading a 36-Ship Gorilla as the leader of an 8-ship of Buccaneers! I was also lucky enough to participate in Maple Flag, also with the Bucc, and to return to Nellis twice in my Tornado career to sample Red Flag in a modern fly-by-wire aircraft, with all the avionics that modern technology could provide. But the Tornado never beat the Buccaneer for its enduring performance, comfort at low level and sheer manhood!

When Enough Is Not Enough

It was in the early 60s, and I was based in Bahrain, flying Argosy aircraft; we were on detachment for three months at a time. I was a newly-made- up 22 year old captain, with a crew each one of whom was old enough to be my father, and we were there to defend the Empire (most of the map was still pink), and to provide support if required for the Sultan of Oman, who had a rather nasty little war going on in the south of the country, as rebels from Yemen attempted to gain a foothold and overthrow him.

We spent time on QRA (Quick Reaction Alert) for this very purpose and, in the wee small hours of one such standby, we were called out. A rush down to Operations revealed a scene of frenetic activity. The southern Omani airfield of Salalah was under attack from the rebels, and our role was to rush certain army forces and their equipment there asap. There was no detailed scenario as yet, and the first aircraft had just got airborne as I and my crew arrived.

'Get into the air now' was the order from Operations; however, when I asked how much fuel I had on board, the response was 'enough'. Conscious of the fact that I bore the ultimate responsibility for the safety of the aircraft, I asked my Nav to do a quick fuel calculation; we didn't have enough, and I declined to move until I had sufficient, since the sole objective was to get 'the boys' where they needed to be and not to divert due to lack of fuel/weather. It was the monsoon season at Salalah.

After a small delay and much muttering from Ops, we departed. There was now time to discuss expected arrival events with the chaps we were taking, and what they required. There was no information, apart from the fact that the base was under mortar and machine-gun fire. Tactical landing? Short turn off? Unload during taxi? Shut down? Rapid departure. What to do if hit? The options were endless, and the crew didn't have a single gun between them.

This was now developing into your real Boys Own adventure, as the 'boys down the back' issued us with pistols and Stens from their armoury, and showed us how to strip and clear blockages. Job done; at least we could now shoot back if required. We landed, disgorged our troops and kit on the roll, and made a hasty tactical departure. As for the first Argosy, which departed before us? They diverted, due to poor weather at Salalah and insufficient fuel!

The moral of the story is to stick to your guns and not to be rushed into hasty action by authority when the responsibility is yours, not theirs. The saga of trying to hand in our 'unauthorised' arms on arrival back at Bahrain was pure Monty Python, and worthy of a story for another day.

Dinghy Drills

In the autumn of 1961, and newly married, I joined my first squadron - No. 47 Squadron, at RAF Abingdon - as a brand new Sergeant Signaller on the Blackburn Beverley. Being very green and inexperienced, the Signals Leader placed me under the guidance of a very senior Master Signaller. He was a tall, well built, authoritative man, with reddish hair and a large handlebar moustache, and sporting WWII medal ribbons. He was to me, at first, a rather intimidating character.

One of the first things I had to do on the Squadron was to attend the sea survival course at RAF Mountbatten, near Plymouth. Early one morning in late October 1961, within days of my marriage, my Master Signaller overseer (whom I shall call Ron) and his car were at the roadside door of my crummy, rented, Victorian, terrace house in Cowley, Oxford; as newlyweds, we were not too bothered about the house, and it was all we could find at the time. Ron was also due to do the course again, and so drove me down to Mountbatten. I had no real idea what to expect, but Ron certainly did. The course followed the pattern with which I became familiar in later years – ground school, some practical, then into the launch to jump into the sea, and go through the procedures of righting the multi-seat dinghy (MS9 or 11, I believe), then bailing it out, closing it off and 'working up a fug' - I believe that was the term the instructors used.

The winter of 1961/62 was particularly cold, and the period of our Mountbatten stay was no different. Came the day for the jump in the sea, it was very cold; we were wearing only old flying suits or overalls, with swimming trunks underneath; this was before a tragic accident, which led to personnel on these drills wearing immersion suits below a certain water temperature. With our Mae Wests inflated, we all performed the 'water walking' act, jumping off the back of the RAF launch, then righting and getting into the dinghy as quickly as possible. Soon we were all inside, more or less bailed out with the entrance openings closed, and working up the so-called 'fug'. And it was then that Ron's considerable experience of this adventure came to the fore.

As we all sat there, huddled against the sides of the dinghy with the floor almost dry, Ron produced from his pockets two screw-top waterproof jars: one containing a dry pair of socks, the other a number of cigarettes and a box of matches. After putting on his dry socks, and with a bit of a superior looking smile, Ron said that he was going to have a smoke. He undid the entrance-cover fastenings at one end of the dinghy, and knelt in the fresh air at the opening; soon he was puffing away. But shortly thereafter, we heard the sound of the launch as it approached on one of its periodic runs, making a swerving turn past the dinghy to create waves and giving those inside a bouncing around - an attempt to replicate the conditions of a rough sea, I guess.

However, as the launch swept past, we heard a yell from Ron, and shortly afterwards he re-appeared, ducking into the dinghy. The sight before us made it very difficult to keep a straight face – you can guess what had happened. Ron's hair was plastered down over his face, his resplendent moustache was similarly plastered across his cheeks, and his now soaking wet cigarette was dangling from his lips, broken and snuffed out. After a few moments, even Ron's indignation gave way to a rueful smile.

Many years later, when I was an Air Electronics Officer on the Handley Page Victor, I attended the Mountbatten sea survival course yet again, and once more it was in the winter (I never did attend the course in the summer). It followed roughly the same pattern as before, but this time the training centred on the single seat dinghy, and we got to wear the immersion suits that were intended to keep us dry. The older two-part type, with the roll-up rubber sleeves around the waist giving the feeling of wearing a rubber tyre, had been replaced with a much more comfortable single garment. This resembled an overall with feet, but with rubber wrist seals at the end of the arms, and similar around the neck. Donning of the suit was facilitated by a large zipped diagonal opening across the front, from left shoulder to right thigh. These suits worked pretty well, but the problem at Mountbatten was that they were used time and time again. Also, for one's own personal suit, the wrist and neck seals were cut to fit the individual. Thus, the major problem with the Mountbatten suits was that the seals tended to seriously leak.

On my course was a brand new aircraft captain (who shall be nameless). He, having completed a tour as a co-pilot on the aircraft, already had his cut-to-size personal immersion suit, whereas the rest of us were converting on to the aircraft and had not yet been kitted out. As we donned our well-used immersion suits, nice chap that he was, he had an itsy- bitsy look of superiority on his face.

The sea drill was by now quite different. Not only were we in the single seat dinghies but, rather than just jumping off the launch, we had to get into a pseudo parachute harness as well as the Mae West. The configuration was designed to simulate jumping out of the aircraft over the sea. To make it even more realistic, we had to leap off the back of the launch and be towed through the water as we have might been by the parachute, until we released ourselves from it. Thus, a part of the drill was to practice this release under realistic conditions.

First you had to inflate the Mae West, usually from a compressed air bottle but, if that did not work, then manually through a self-sealing tube. Then you jumped into the sea from the stern of the launch; the dinghy, in its pack-up connected by a clip-on lanyard to the Mae West, was thrown into the water as you jumped (under real circumstances the normal sit-on dinghy would have been manually released from the parachute harness in the descent – another thing to remember - and it would dangle from the Mae West lanyard). But now it was essential to get onto your back as quickly as possible; then, before your hands got too cold, first turn the parachute release mechanism, and then release the parachute harness by giving the mechanism a hefty whack. Now released and floating in the sea, courtesy of the Mae West, you had to haul in the dinghy, using the long lanyard attached to the Mae West, then find the inflation cord attached to the compressed air bottle (no easy task in itself), and inflate the dinghy; invariably it inflated the wrong way up, so first it had to be righted before you could climb in. Once aboard, it was essential to quickly get inside the protective upper part of the dinghy out of the wind and seal it closed. You then bailed and dried out the dinghy as much as possible (working up the proverbial 'fug'), before manually inflating the two-ply floor and upper canopy of the dinghy, which also covered the head. This provided reasonable insulation and protection from the elements, and it was possible to get quite comfortable and dry, bouncing around on the waves (or launch-generated pseudo- waves if it was calm), sometimes for over an hour, before being hoisted out on a helicopter sling - this usually involved being dumped into the water again (practice for them, but they were real sadists these helicopter crews) - and then deposited back on the launch or dry land.

Now, for nearly everyone who wore the immersion suit, it was customary to leave the zip undone, or at least partially undone, at the bottom, to let in a bit of air before and after getting airborne; however, this required remembering to complete the fastening before any wet activities. Not only had our new captain brought his own immersion suit, but he had also brought the fancy waterproof gloves that went with it (although in practice they were seldom used). So I was a bit surprised, when we were returning to disrobe from our activities, to see our man walking as if he had had a serious accident in his pants. He looked a bit disgruntled as we asked what the problem was - as nicely as possible of course. It turned out that he had forgotten to fully close the zip of his immersion suit and, as he entered the sea, the legs had filled up with water! He ended up being much wetter than we were. We resisted too much laughter, but guess who bought the beer that night!

50,000 Feet Or Bust

This is a tale of over-exuberance, or crew self-induced hypoxia. Shortly after the space shuttle Challenger disaster of 1986, when the Phantom F4J was a new aircraft to the RAF, a somewhat adventurous crew were determined to test the altitude limits of the aircraft's flight envelope. Perhaps this was rather unwise, as the US Navy oxygen regulators fitted to the aircraft were not capable of providing pressure breathing (needed at very high level to maintain the required oxygen flow to the crew).

On a bright sunny day, the pilot pointed the nose up, engaged reheat, and had managed to reach an altitude greater than 65,000 feet when the cabin pressurisation failed. The pilot, remembering his hypoxia[1] training, thought, "I've only got about 12 seconds to do something", so he pointed the nose down. Remembering that his own personal hypoxia symptom was tunnel vision, and in order to maintain situational awareness, he then concentrated on the Attitude Indicator "so that I could see it for as long as possible", while he and his navigator were heading downwards. He knew that he was going to lose consciousness, and duly did as, presumably, did the navigator. The pilot recovered consciousness at 23,000 feet. Both engines were in reheat, the aircraft was more than 60 degrees nose-down, and the speed was passing Mach 1.3. He recalls that he did a quick calculation regarding time to impact, moved the throttles to idle and, after passing the transonic region, deployed the speed brakes. He made another quick calculation regarding the aircraft's 'G' capabilities, at about the time the Nav regained consciousness. The Nav was then given a second opportunity to experience the effects of inadequate oxygen supply to the brain, when the pilot pulled 7+G to recover from the dive, and the Nav lost consciousness again (G-LOCed). Once he had come round, this rather interesting exercise was followed by an uneventful return to Base.

---

[1] Hypoxia - a pathological condition when the body is deprived of adequate oxygen supply.

There's One On Every Squadron

Do I remember the sturdy Swift fighter? I certainly do! In telling my Swift story, I am going to assume that not all readers, even those ex-Service people of my era (1954 – 88), are or were familiar with the Fighter Reconnaissance (FR) Swift sub-culture then extant in the Royal Air Force. Not an unreasonable assumption, because the Swift world itself was small. Although only a small part of the Service at large, we considered ourselves the most elite element of the fighter culture, the whole of which, in the late 50s and early 60s, was infused with 'pressing on regardless'. Achieving one's goal, at whatever the cost, was the 'sine qua non' of the fighter pilot and, for the FR pilots, it was all that mattered. The cost in my case was that I very nearly became overdrawn on my 'life' account, and came within a gnat's clock of meeting 'the big FR pilot in the sky'.

I will now set the scene. The Swift FR world comprised two squadrons, No 79 and another one whose number presently escapes me, and competition within this small world was thus very focused and fierce. The coalescence of the 'press on' culture, and its concomitant competitiveness, I found most exciting. It influenced me in nearly all I did, and only with hindsight have I realised that this, allied to other factors, was the trigger that led to my accident. Looking back at myself, with the 20/20 vision of fifty plus years of hindsight and mainly fighter flying, and having finished my time in the Service in the late eighties as the then Inspector of Flight Safety, I saw I was an accident waiting to happen. With my attitude to life and to flying at the time, I did not have too long to wait.

Let me also explain in more detail some of the other contributing factors. I will try to do so in a way I hope anyone reading about my 'fall from grace' will understand, even if he or she were never in the Service or never flew at all in any aircrew capacity, military or civilian. For those who were in the Service, especially fighter pilots of the 60s era, please be patient with my attempts to explain in some detail the background to the saga, for the benefit of those who were not as fortunate as we were, to enjoy the golden years of jet fighter flying. My hope in doing so is that those readers not of our ilk or era will understand and appreciate why and how I erred; and also to acknowledge (too late) that the essential positive 'can do' ethos of military aviation needs to be intelligently interpreted - clearly something I did not do.

I was 26 years old at the time, had done a tour on day fighters at RAF Jever in Germany, and was now on my second tour as a low level fighter recce pilot, also in Germany at RAF Gutersloh, so I had some fighter hours under my belt. My accident was, as I believe pavement artists are wont to say, 'all my own work.' Although I make light of it in this story, at the time it was very embarrassing, and also very worrying for me, because I was sure that I was in danger of being kicked out of the Service. Please, you younger aviators and you 100 hour older 'aces', just remember (if you read on) that it was my 'succeed at all costs' attitude to life in general, and to flying in particular, that got me into trouble. Do enjoy the sheer exhilaration of flying; however, don't ever get on such a high that you believe you are immortal. Remember as you fly, the Grim Reaper is always at a high alert state for guys and girls who believe they are immortal and get carried away, which is what they literally will be if they don't keep a grip on themselves.

I view this episode in my life as a good safety lesson for all who fly, both military and civilian, but especially for young, press on 'smarties' of either sex who think they can't go wrong. And it's not just younger pilots who are at risk, but also the older ones, with newish Private Pilot's Licences and all of 100 or so hours behind them, who think they are the 'bees' knees'. Confidence is vital to handling emergencies well; overconfidence can induce them! Be attitude and situationally aware, and live to collect your bus pass! What saved me was the way that Supermarine had built the Swift. It was an exceptionally sturdy aircraft, with a robust, if unexciting, handling performance; somewhat of a charging rhinoceros, and able to withstand considerable impact.

My little incident came about as a result of the weekly competitive exercise, referred to as 'Exercise Poker'. You will need to understand the main rules of 'Exercise Poker' to appreciate how such intangibles can contribute powerfully to the chain of events endemic in every accident. If you ally the rules of the exercise with the overall cultural scene I've noted and, in particular, my attitude at the time, you may be able to regress mentally to my state of mind on the day. If you do regress, then you will be able to 'follow me through', and so understand better the events leading to the accident, the accident itself, its airborne aftermath and, worst of all for me, the post accident fallout.

The essence of the competition was that you flew against the clock. Normally, there were 3 or 4 different types of targets, and you were marked on various aspects of the sortie. Some examples were: how well you photographed the targets (whether you had the target in the part of the frame that the photographic interpreters could analyse relatively easily); and how accurate your inflight debrief was (this debrief being given in flight, either to a Ground Liaison Officer or, if the Army had run out of them, to Air Traffic Control, as you approached base). As an added inducement to make training as realistic as possible, points were also deducted if certain parameters were 'blown' or were not met. The potential effects of these rules should become evident, as I walk you through my problem sortie.

We began with morning briefing, at 0800 in Station Operations Briefing. It was the usual tale from the met man of 'maybe there will or maybe there won't' be fog, low cloud, scattered showers of rain et al, followed by operational aspects. Then down to the Squadron, to check the programme and plan the morning. I saw I was the third off on 'Exercise Poker'; that is, third sortie taking off at a specified interval after the preceding aircraft, to prevent you following him, and to deconflict you both in the target area. I changed into my flying kit, and waited to be called for my briefing. Because 'Pokers' were competitive sorties, all details were hugged to the bosom of the squadron 'wheel', who ran that day's flying, to ensure you could not find out in advance what the targets were, and so start some illegal pre-briefing preparation.

When the pilot ahead of you on the programme left the briefing room, you entered, and were handed a sealed envelope, with the same target data and target area maps, normally 1: 100,000 scale. The envelope was to simulate a war role briefing and, apart from any special instructions, the envelope covered among other things: latitude and longitude; target description (in other words what type of target it was), perhaps armour, a strategic bridge or, a favourite with some supervisors, a small electrical junction box in a remote rural area. Often very difficult to see, and so considered good training.

The pressure then started. You were on your own, and had 15 minutes to sort it all out; plotting the exact target location, deciding the best run-in to it, adding minimum fuel states along the route to complete the sortie and many other points. You often had to glue together 2 or more target area maps (scale 1:000,000) for each target, and that took time and added pressure. You also had to select what was called an Initial Point (IP) for each target, and it was very important to select a good one that was easy to locate, preferably with some vertical extent so that, at 250 feet Above Ground Level (AGL), you could see it well before the actual IP. More about IPs later, because my first one on that sortie, and what I did not do at it, were significant factors in the accident.

Although on your own in terms of planning, you nearly always had someone else in the room, to ensure that you had not worked out any ploys to overcome the deviousness of the 'Exercise Poker' supervisor. With all that competitiveness surging around, any head start you could get at the planning stage could prove invaluable because, if the planning went well, it took some pressure off the sortie. I am not saying that anyone actually cheated; however, we all tried exceedingly hard. I don't really mean cheating, more, perhaps, just using our initiative, by taking full advantage of any information or action that would enhance one's personal performance. After all, this was training for war, and in war you are hardly likely to say, "Sorry, I really do not want to give myself unfair advantage because it's against the rules and is not 'cricket'". We might not have been gentlemen, in the Victorian sense, but we were practical and operationally focused officers.

As just noted, the IP was important in planning, because you were looking for a precise location you could positively identify with relative ease and, after you had re-started the stop watch, from where you would head directly to the target. Normally you would plan the IP and the target to be within 2 minutes of each other. The short duration minimises the chances of navigational error, because the longer you fly from a known point, the more likely it is that your navigational accuracy will decrease. In which case, if you are looking for a small target, like an electricity junction box, you will most probably not see it. Therefore, by keeping the time between the IP and the target to a minimum, and maintaining an accurate heading and speed, you increase your chance of being in the right position to both see and photograph the target. It might just be worth adding that all this high speed low-level navigation was achieved using a 1:500,000 topographical map en route, a 1:100,000 from IP to target, a stopwatch, and cunning and experience. Unfortunately there were no inertial navigation systems available in those days. If there had been, I might have avoided my accident.

Anyway, back to the competition. You were obviously penalised if you missed the target but, if you didn't see it, you could reduce the points-loss to some extent if you managed to photograph it by pressing the camera button for a few seconds - based upon your stopwatch timing that you had restarted from zero at the IP. For example, if you had flown for 40 seconds and knew the target was due in 10 seconds time, but you could not see it (some targets were very small or well camouflaged), you would press the camera button to bracket 50 seconds, and pray that you had covered it. However, if you had not seen the target, you could not send the in-flight debrief, so you were penalised for that failure. The same rules applied to each target.

Planning the sortie had to be completed within the allotted 15 minutes, or the supervising officer would either stop the timing or point out that you were over time, and immediately start deducting points until you left the room. You would then sign for the aircraft, fire it up and taxi to the take-off point. You were not timed from the end of planning until wheels rolling for take-off, to reduce the chances of pilots rushing, and possibly having taxying accidents. Personally, as things turned out on that day, I would have settled for a taxying accident!

Before 'we' take-off, I will comment a little more on the issue of timing. Reconnaissance intelligence gathering, and the timeliness of the information, is important and, therefore, to add operational realism, as much as could sensibly be timed was timed. There was, however, given the competitive culture, an even more cogent reason for timing everyone during these exercises: to minimise the opportunity for anyone to use their initiative/cheat. As noted earlier, in a different form of words, all is fair 'in love and war', and we all loved to win, so all of us tried every subterfuge to gain any competitive edge. It was never formally acknowledged, but was accepted in the culture, that if your supervisors (normally Flight Commanders and senior pilots) were not sharp enough to stop you using 'all possible initiative', you should use it. By the way, our supervisors were also 'at it', if they thought they could get away with it and, of course, there was always a very good reason for their non-conformity if they were caught.

How did timing stop someone cheating? The short answer is that it did not entirely, but what it did do beyond doubt was to make it extremely difficult to use excessive initiative. It also added notable additional pressure, because timing infringements were very heavily penalised. You were timed by Air Traffic Control from release of brakes until you broke (normally going like smoke out of a goose) into the circuit for landing. You were not timed until you landed, because you might be forced to overshoot by Air Traffic and that would be an unfair penalty. All timing was based on an average speed of 420 knots; therefore, every moment you were below that speed would cost points, and you were clearly well below that speed as you released the brakes on take-off! The overall sortie time allowed was based on straight lines from base to first target, between additional targets, and back to base. No allowance was made for the additional track miles covered during turns which, at those sorts of speeds, could mean quite a significant number of additional miles, as 'g' forces compelled you to fly wider or outside the direct, point-to-point, track. You therefore had to fly faster than 420 knots to offset this. In addition, most pilots tended to fly the IP to target run somewhat slower. Speed would be reduced to, say, 360 knots, so you had longer to see the target and therefore increase your chances of getting a better inflight report, photograph, and information for your post-flight target reports. As already noted, all three aspects were scored for each target.

To keep ahead of the 420 knots average minimum speed required to avoid penalty points, most of us flew at 480, or possibly faster, for certain parts of the sortie, for example from after the target to the next IP. What tight timing rules did was effectively prevent you from orbiting a target, or flying past it twice, to get a better photograph or description. At 420 (or even 360 knots), an orbit would cost you dearly, and you would often need to return to the IP, involving even more distance and associated time penalties. Also, to discourage the use of excessive initiative, the supervisors would sometimes ask Army units to position themselves at targets, and report the time of anyone orbiting. This made you readily identifiable, so normally it just wasn't worth it. In addition, no excuse whatsoever was accepted for exceeding the total direct point-to-point flight time; so if you had to fly around any bad weather and thus incur extra time, well too bad.

If the weather forecast was bad, it sometimes paid to try and get your sortie delayed, in the hope of flying in better weather or, conversely, finagle to bring it forward for the same reason. This ploy was something of a double-edged sword because, as I inferred earlier, in those days a good met forecaster probably got it right half the time. So, by changing your sortie slot time, you risked going from the met frying pan into the bad weather fire. It was always best to base that decision on personal experience. Alternatively, have a quick chat with a mate on one of the Hunter day-fighter squadrons on the station, if he had flown in the period before your planned time slot, and therefore knew what the actual weather was.

On with the sortie! Shortly after getting airborne, and changing radio frequency to Gutersloh Approach, I heard the Squadron Boss (an ancient man in his mid thirties), who was flying in the slot ahead of me, say that the first target was obscured by bad weather, and that he was going on to the second one. I thought to myself, that the poor old chap couldn't hack it, and here was a chance for me to get ahead on points, so I pressed on. Some 15 or so miles from the IP, I could see that the weather was deteriorating sooner than expected, so I increased speed, because I knew would have to slow down when I encountered the rain and low cloud. Soon I was flying very low, to stay under the cloud base, had slowed to 360 knots, and dropped half flap to increase manoeuvrability. I concentrated on keeping a sharp eye open for electrical pylons, and also looking hard at the weather over any woods. As air becomes moister, it condenses into cloud and eventually causes rain. The air over wet woodland tends to be moister, and so visibility is often reduced in forested areas. I steered my heading for the IP (which I saw slightly off to my left) but, in my preoccupation with the weather, I failed to reset the stop watch to time my flight from the IP to the target.

The target was one of the electrical junction boxes (about the size of a telephone kiosk, and normally painted grey). It was located near a small crossroads, to the west of a ridge of hills that ran North to South. My plan was to fly on a southerly heading, with the target coming up on my port side, and to photograph it with the port-facing camera, at the same time looking at anything else nearby – sometimes there might be two of them, or adjacent military activity. By flying my IP to target run on a southerly heading, I could then turn port onto an easterly heading toward the next target - that was what I had planned in the navigation room.

The weather was, by now, extremely poor, with lowering cloud and rapidly deteriorating visibility. I was also very, very nervous, but determined to press on. I knew that I was well and truly busting the minimum criteria for low flying in bad weather, and my common sense and sense of self- preservation were hammering away in my head! Even so, in my misplaced determination, I overrode them and pressed on.

Out of the corner of my eye, I saw a railway line cross my track at right angles. The significance of this was that there were two lines at right angles to my track, about 6 miles (or 1 minute in time) apart, and the terrain between them was flat, with the ridge of hills I previously mentioned only beginning after crossing the second railway line. At that point, the weather was so bad I decided to abort. Believing, wrongly, I had seen the first railway line to the north of the ridge of hills, I remained at low level, selected full throttle, simultaneously turned very hard to port on to an easterly heading, and flew toward the second target. All the time, I was thinking that the terrain ahead was flat.

Although the weather was atrocious, I did not pull up steeply for a bad weather abort (as per the Standard Operating Procedures), because I did not want to enter the main cloud base, get enmeshed with air traffic chatter, and then have problems getting back below the cloud en route to the second target. I assumed that this was a local deterioration in the weather, and that a gentle climb through the lower cloud would get me out of it. This would also allow me to continue, untrammelled by air traffic considerations, and avoid infringing lower civil airways.

I had been flying on instruments, I believe, for around 10 – 30 seconds, and climbing gently away when, to my total amazement (not horror, I did not have time for that!), I saw the tops of pine trees coming rapidly towards me. It's peculiar how you can sometimes think and do several things simultaneously. I remembered, in a nanosecond, the advice of my Flight Commander, Flight Lieutenant, as he then was, Bunny Warren. He had supervised my conversion onto the Swift but, since there were no dual-control Swifts, the conversion had been mainly 'chalk and talk'. Bunny stressed that the Swift was a heavy aircraft, and so relatively prone to 'high speed stall', if you overrotated it (pulled back too hard and too quickly on the pole). This would stall the aircraft well above the conventional stalling speed, whereupon it was more likely to continue on its current flight path than adopt the one you had selected or, in my case, desperately needed!

Notwithstanding Bunny's sage advice (he was an A1 QFI[1] from his previous

---

[1] A1 QFI – A Qualified Flying Instructor who has achieved the highest grade of proficiency (A1).

flying), I gave a fairly brisk and hefty, rearward heave-ho on the pole, which fortunately did not induce a high-speed stall. At almost the same instant, there was a horrific hammering and rending noise, not unlike a pop drummer going absolutely berserk, but amplified many times more. Simultaneously I saw the ventral (belly) tank 'dolls eye' go white (indicating rapid loss of fuel), and knew that I had incurred more than a scratch. Shortly afterwards, I felt a decrease in thrust, and saw the engine RPM start to go down and the Jet Pipe Temperature (JPT) start to go up. I had by then ricochet'd back into the cloud. The engine stabilised at an RPM I cannot now remember, but it was high enough to keep me going up. The JPT did not increase much, and then it too stabilised. As things seemed to be in a working order of sorts, I decided not to touch the throttle because, although more power would have been most welcome, I did not know the extent of the damage – if it's working, leave well alone! I changed hands to fly with my left hand, and raised my right hand above my head to grip the ejection seat handle – in those days there was no bottom handle as well. If anything changed much, I was as ready as I could be to punch out. I also checked, and was relieved to see, that the ejection seat pins had been removed (many people have, at some time, missed removing them during checks), and the seat was therefore armed.

I continued the climb, although now more steeply, came out on top of the cloud at about 5000 feet, and turned onto an approximate heading for Gutersloh. As all still seemed to be working, I did not interfere with the aircraft, but kept a couple of very beady eyes on the engine instruments, fuel gauges, fire warning light and hydraulic pressure. Meanwhile, I devoted some thought to how I might explain away my difficulties. It did not take me long to work out that, however good my story was, I was unlikely to talk my way into the award of an Air Force Cross. Indeed, it looked as though my flying, rugby playing and great bantering camaraderie days in the Service might well be over, with a forced entry into civvy street. Perhaps I should have been carefully analysing the airborne situation (in Biggles mode), but I could only think of the reaction when I landed.

I tried to put out a PAN[2] Call, but got no reply; anyway, Gutersloh was the

---

[2] PAN - A state of urgency exists although there is no imminent danger to life or the continued viability of the aircraft.

nearest airfield, so I would not be diverting. I called base on the approach frequency, again receiving no reply, but did not appreciate at the time that all the underside radio aerials were in a pine wood (if you ever look at the photographs published in Flight Comment, the Royal Air Force Germany Flight Safety Magazine, you will get a clear idea why I could not raise anyone on the radio at that stage). However, as I got close to base, I managed to contact Air Traffic Control about strength 2 (weakly).

The weather overhead base was clear, so I remained at 5000 feet. I said to Air Traffic, "I believe (?) I may have hit some trees'", and asked for an airborne inspection. It so happened that a friend of mine (Jock McVie), on a Hunter day-fighter squadron, was re-joining the circuit pattern, and offered to give me a quick 'shufti'. He flew alongside my starboard wing, swooped quickly underneath, and reappeared on my port wing. At the time, I had the nickname 'Lumpy'; quite unfair really, as I was fit, being into jock strapping, however I did carry some extra pounds storing Herforder Pils. Very succinctly, Jock said, "Lumpy, you are in it mate". I understood completely what the 'it' was. Confirmation of my worst fears of the possible outcome for me was not at that moment particularly good for my morale. We exchanged very brief pleasantries, after which I asked him to give me more details of the damage, to determine my possible courses of action. He did, and I was not encouraged. I then continued with a descending spiral approach, in case the engine quit, and I had to fly a flame out landing. During the course of my descent, I also carried out a low speed handling check, to ensure, as far as possible, that the aircraft would remain controllable during an approach and landing. In fact I landed uneventfully, if well down the runway.

On the roll out, toward the end of the runway, I looked to my left and saw, parked on the hard-standing, all the people I wished to see least. The Station Commander, Wing Commander Operations, my Squadron Boss, and a few of the pilots who waved encouragingly with their fingers!

When I had signed the aircraft back in, I was duly summoned by the Squadron brass, and asked what on earth I had done - or words to that effect. I decided that I should tell it like it was and said, "I mucked up, Sir", or something very similar.

The Board of Enquiry started next day, and Squadron Leader Edmonds, the

Boss of one of the Hunter squadrons, was President. I duly confessed my mistakes and indiscipline to the Board. The President was very understanding and, in private, gave me some sage off-the-record advice. He made it clear that things did not look too good for me, but that I was not the first pilot in the Service to have made a 'dumkopf' of himself, and probably not the last. He then said that there were some factors that he felt might help me, but did not elaborate on them, apart from telling me, for my own good, to say absolutely nothing to anyone other than the Board.

Those mitigating factors became obvious to me over the following few days. In essence, I was relatively inexperienced, and had only been doing what the other, more experienced and senior pilots (on both our squadron and our sister Swift squadron) had been doing. They too pressed on from time to time in bad weather, and they too had busted the rules. It was an unspoken understanding. They, however, had done it more intelligently than I had. Additionally, we all flew low outside the authorised low flying areas, because the areas were so small that we knew them well. Consequently, they did not provide realistic low-level navigation training, and we were very keen to be as operationally proficient as possible. This was tacitly understood, but not readily acknowledged, either in the upper echelons of the station or, it is reasonable to assume, by some of the Air Staff at Headquarters, Royal Air Force Germany. Clearly then, mine might not be the only head that would roll. I drew some comfort from this because I surmised that ,if I took it all on the chin, and did not try to drag others down with me, there would be some pretty hard 'string pulling' on my behalf. One in 'it', all in 'it', as it were.

It was not all that amusing, at the time, when I heard vague murmurs about a Summary of Evidence, the precursor to a Court Martial. Two good friends on the squadron told me if it came to that, they would stand by me and give evidence that I was only doing what others did. That would, of course, have had major career implications for them, and those two or three levels above us. Thankfully, those murmurs gently subsided. Also, there are two things I have not yet mentioned. Firstly, the trees I hit were well and truly outside a low flying area, which added some notable complication to the whole fallout. Secondly, the aircraft and engine were categorised as Cat 5 – in Service parlance, totally written off. Neither of these helped my case!

At the Queen's expense, I had a trip to the Command Headquarters, and some prime time on the Air Officer Commanding's one-way chat show. I had previously met him very briefly after rugby matches, when I was playing for the RAF in Germany. He was a very genial Irishman, who had been a wartime fighter pilot, but he did not come across as particularly genial as I entered and saluted. After my formal rollocking (or career advice, as I prefer to call it), he told me to sit down. He said he had had a similar accident shortly after the 1939-45 war, but that aircraft were now more expensive and that I really had been stupid. He said that I was fortunate not to have been made an example for others. He then indicated I should leave. I stood up, thanked him and apologised for my poor performance. As I saluted and left, he looked at me with just the slightest hint of a smile on his face.

Well, I certainly recall the sturdy Swift, its robustness saved my life. If I had been in any other fighter aircraft of the time, I am quite certain that I would, on that day, have made a contribution, albeit minor, to organic pine tree growing in the Federal Republic of Germany. I have never had any complaints about how I was dealt with, as I had been unwise, to say the least. My greatest joy was that I was not booted out the Service, although I did receive a punishment posting some two years later. The Swift and November 17th 1960? I remember them both well.

So watch your Attitude to Flying and, as I've already stated, you will live to get a Bus Pass! Oh yes, I've just remembered, the second best Swift outfit was No 2 Squadron.

How To Stretch Your Glide

In 1964 I was a student at The Empire Test Pilots School (ETPS), which was then based at Farnborough. My relief at having escaped from five years as a Victor co-pilot and captain had been replaced by supreme self-confidence at having been selected for this prestigious year long course, and the knowledge that I was now being let loose on a bewildering array of new heavy metal and fast jet types. The course was designed to ensure that we students were introduced to the "complete aviation experience", and therefore included such events as parachute jumps, hovercraft handling and gliding.

Following this principle, I found myself on the airfield on one warm Sunday afternoon in midsummer, providing aero tows in a Chipmunk for colleagues in a variety of gliders, which included the venerable T21 Sedbergh. A competition soon developed to see who could make the best height gain and/or remain airborne the longest, and the presence of rapidly developing cumulo-nimbus cloud, with its strong up-currents, only added to the interest.

Soon it was my turn and, as an embryo test pilot with previous experience of gliding and the T21, both as a CCF Cadet and Cranwell Cadet (with the Licenses to prove it), there was no doubt who was going to win the competition. I think the Chipmunk pilot became a little concerned when it became clear to him that he could not get rid of his glider, whose pilot seemed determined to remain attached to the tow line until the 'tug' ran out of fuel. Steep turns and a roller coaster ride failed to deter me, as I hung on until I was obviously not being offered any height increase, but was at least being taken under the biggest and best cu-nim of the afternoon.

I duly released the cable and, as anticipated, found the strongest patch of lift that I had ever experienced, followed shortly by a more personal acquaintance with the inside of one of these clouds than I expected. The turbulence was something else, and IMC[1] at terminal velocity with the airbrakes fully out seemed to be making little impression on my vertical ascent. To add to my woes, the hail made it extremely difficult to see the instruments, such as they were, and resulted in my having to bend forwards and duck my head down until my nose was

---

[1] IMC – Instrument Meteorological Conditions

approximately six inches from the Turn and Slip indicator. I then indulged in a game of moving the stick to full deflection in one direction, as the needle on the T&S proceeded to full deflection in the other direction. At the same time, I was conscious that a relatively strong wind would be carrying me to the south-west of Farnborough, and I needed to ensure that I could regain the airfield when, and if, I ever regained visual contact with the ground.

Eventually, and fortunately before oxygen became a necessity, I was spat out of the cloud, but short term relief was quickly replaced by anxiety as it became evident that, despite my efforts, I was downwind to the south-west of Farnborough, and it was by no means certain that I could regain the airfield. To complicate matters further, the intervening ground was forested, which meant that, once committed, if it became obvious that I was not going to make it, the outcome was likely to be a nasty crash landing.

However, self- confidence was returning, and a cunning plan was soon hatched. A small patch of green in the middle of the forested area offered a bolt-hole, if it became clear that the T21 was incapable of a glide angle which would save my bacon. Furthermore, if I did land there, it was quite close to a road and the airfield, and I would not be quite so unpopular, bearing in mind the need to disassemble the glider and return it by road to the ETPS hangar. Superior flying skill would ensure a satisfactory outcome, wherever it became necessary to land!

It soon became clear that the answer was the patch of green, which began to reveal itself as playing fields, with a sports pavilion in the centre. It also became clear that superior flying skills were becoming compromised by my poor posi-tioning on the approach, large trees and a security fence, such that the thresh-old speed was a little high; in fact, probably high enough to carry out several aerobatic manoeuvres before touchdown! As the glider swept across the field a foot or so above terra firma, we passed between the stumps of the cricket match, whose players were lined up in the pavilion applauding, having been rained off by one of the nasty cu-nims that had caused all the problems in the first place. Eventually, glider and earth regained contact and the machine began to slow down - a little - before dropping into the slightly sunken bowling-green area, whereupon the skid really began to dig in, leaving a neat groove of ploughed turf behind it. The excitement was not yet over. Ahead was the five- metre wire mesh fence surrounding the tennis courts, whose players had, fortunately, also been rained off. At this point, since there seemed little else to do, it flashed through my mind that this must be a good simulation of taking the barrier on an aircraft carrier, before the advent of the angled deck. Fortunately, the impact was slight, and calm and silence descended, until the cricketers arrived to rescue the brave pilot.

Fortunately also, the T21 was not badly damaged, or certainly less so than the pilot's pride. However, I did have to write to the Director of the National Gas Turbine Establishment at Pyestock, apologizing for having ruined his competition standard bowling green and promising not to do it again. My test pilot tutor's remarks will go unrecorded, and I was grateful eventually to graduate with some of the silverware, so the incident did not seem to be held against me – BUT I certainly learnt about gliding from that!

You Have Control!

As we were not allowed to fly wives in Her Majesty's ejection seat aircraft, it was decided that the squadron would have an evening BBQ, and fly them in a selection of invited, privately owned, Tiger Moths, operating from the grass strip. All went well until the last flight when, since everyone else had enjoyed a trip, the owner asked if I would like to fly. The simple brief was that, once we were airborne, he would give me control and, after strapping me into the front seat, he passed comment that this Moth was the upgraded version with the intercom. Unfortunately, though, it only worked on the ground when the engine wasn't running!

At a couple of hundred feet, I could hear shouting from the rear and the stick shook forward and aft, a standard procedure to indicate that the occupant of the front seat should take control. I duly shook the stick and took control. Climbing slowly, and by this time over the nearby ridge, I decided to see just how tight a turn the aircraft could do. Having completed the turn, the stick shook violently left/right (a standard signal for the rear seat to take control), which I acknowledged immediately by shaking it left and right and letting go, to ponder on what we might do next.

We immediately rolled left and descended, prior to pulling up into a wing over, and then did a much steeper climb into the vertical. The engine stopped and it all went quiet! This was followed by an impressive, perfect stall turn without rudder to the left, and back into the vertical going down. Through the stopped prop, I could see a man waving furiously in the church grounds directly in front of me and alarmingly close! The prop turned, the engine banged back into life and the trusted Tiger then eased out of the dive. As the nose climbed through the horizon level with the ridge, I thought I should just see if there was any resistance to me flying the thing again. None! I duly headed back towards the grass strip, gently climbing to a respectable height above the ridge, and, at about 500 feet, flung my arms out sideways to make it quite clear that I was no longer in control. The subsequent landing was uneventful.

As we climbed out of the cockpit, there was a huge grin on the owner's face as he praised my outstanding stall turn, and calm way in which I instinctively knew to hold it in the vertical until the engine restarted. All this, considering that I had never flown a piston aircraft before. About 10 minutes later, when I could get a discreet word in, I thought it wise to explain the standard handover of control procedures for a non-intercom aircraft!

Tiger Moth

De Havilland Hornet

The following story is taken from SILVERED WINGS, by kind permission of the author, Sir John Severne.

In 1946 my squadron, No 264 (Night Fighter Mosquitoes), moved from Church Fenton to Linton-on- Ouse. Already at Linton were two other squadrons, Nos. 64 and 65, equipped with single-seat Hornet day fighters. These were splendid aircraft which, to me, were rather like sports car versions of their older big brother, the Mosquito. They were said to be the fastest piston-engined aircraft in service anywhere in the world. They had 'handed' propellers going round in opposite directions to each other, so that there was no tendency to swing on take-off. There were serviceability problems with this new aircraft, and the hours the squadron pilots were allowed to fly each month were severely restricted. Consequently, outsiders were not allowed to fly them.

I was still making model aircraft at that time, and decided to make for myself a 1/72 scale model of a Hornet. I was keen to make the cockpit details as accurate as possible, so I went across to 64 Squadron's hangar, climbed in to one of their aircraft, and started sketching the cockpit. I should, of course, have asked permission; furthermore, I failed to notice a Squadron Leader's flag painted on the side of the fuselage. No wonder, therefore, that a few moments later a very angry squadron commander arrived, and shouted up to me in the cockpit, 'What the hell are you doing in my aircraft?' When I explained what I was up to, his whole attitude turned through 180 degrees, and he said, 'It's a funny thing. I've been trying to persuade De Havillands to give me a model Hornet, but to no avail.' I cheekily replied, 'Well sir, if you let me fly one of your aircraft you can have my model.' We both kept to the deal and, shortly afterwards, I flew a Hornet, three years to the day after joining the RAF. I believe I was the only outsider on the station who managed to fly one of those wonderful aircraft during that period. It was my first experience in a single-seat aircraft, and was very memorable.

The Hornet was a joy to fly; its performance on one engine was far superior to that of the non-aerobatic Mosquito, and I therefore amused myself by doing some rolls on one engine before I landed back. No wonder I have heard it referred to as a 'Hot-Rod Mini-Mossie'. Sadly, no example of this magnificent aircraft exists today. Someone, somewhere, must have destroyed the last Hornet without realising what he was doing.

De Havilland Hornet

Mum's The Word

We were getting towards the end of the night flying phase of the multi-engine, advanced flying training course, and it was time for mutual solos, where everyone got to fly with a fellow student acting as co-pilot. The venerable old Varsity was great fun to fly with its large radial engines, antiquated cockpit and leather seats; and bumbling across Cambridgeshire on a clear, autumnal evening, we could almost imagine ourselves back in the early 1940s.

We were nearing the end of our cross-country, and inbound to Oakington, when we heard a familiar voice on the R/T. The unmistakeable sound of our squadron commander filled the airwaves, as he requested clearance to taxi. He and another instructor who, for the sake of it, I shall call Pete, were about to get airborne to check on the local weather for the second phase of the flying programme. Air traffic cleared the Boss to taxi but, when he acknowledged this, his radio transmit button stuck on. This meant that we could now hear everything that was being said in the aircraft, but they (the Boss and Pete) couldn't receive or make any radio calls. Air traffic quickly realised what had happened, and ordered us to orbit at 2000 feet above the airfield while they sorted the Boss out. What happened next is recorded below.

OK Pete, clear my side, check yours?

Clear my side boss.

Right...we're moving, brakes are fine and pressures are good. Check yours please. You have control.

I have control, my brakes are OK and pressures are good. You have control.

I have control. OK turning right, needle right, ball left, compass increasing, horizon steady... turning left, needle left, ball right, compass decreasing and horizon steady.

My instruments are ok too.

Having left dispersal, they set off around the perimeter track towards the end of the runway.

Right Pete, I'll do the take-off, then we'll depart to the North and bimble around for a bit at medium level. Then you can take over, have a look at the weather to the East, and recover us back to the circuit.

OK, Boss. It's a bit quiet tonight though, isn't it? I can see at least one aircraft in the circuit, but I haven't heard a radio call since we left dispersal.

Hmm. Let's give 'em a shout. "Oakington Tower, this is Delta 99... radio check (pause) Oakington Tower, this is Delta 99, do you read?" Pete, try your side.

OK. "Oakington Tower, this is Delta 99, do you read?" Looks like we've got a radio failure Boss.

OK. Just to be safe, can you get out the night emergencies sheet, please Pete?

Where have you stowed it, Boss?

I didn't bring it.

Neither did I.

At this point, it's relevant to point out that the Varsity was so old that it carried a Very Pistol[1], a set of coloured cartridges and a port in the fuselage through which to fire it.

Right, let's get out the pistol and poop off a red or something, shall we?

Hang on Boss. The caravan[2] has seen us, he's flashing a green.

Ah yes, so he is. The approach looks clear, so we'll just taxi down the runway then, and make our way back to dispersal.

 Pregnant pause

Bit of a cock-up this, Pete.

Yes, Boss.

Even longer pregnant pause

I don't really want this getting out, because I'll look a bit of a prat, what with forgetting the night emergencies sheet and everything. You catch my drift?

Don't worry Boss, mum's the word.

---

[1] The Very Pistol was named after Edward Wilson Very (1847–1910), an American naval officer who developed and popularized a single-shot breech-loading snub-nosed pistol that fired flares.

[2] The caravan refers to the runway controller, who sat in a small caravan adjacent to the runway threshold and monitored aircraft about to take-off or land. The controller used an Aldis lamp to communicate with aircraft, and by flashing a green he indicated that it was clear to proceed.

It Went Straight Down The Middle

My first squadron posting was as a co-pilot on the Victor SR2 which, at the time, fell somewhat short of my personal ambition as far as aviation was concerned, although not necessarily my capability. In the event, I quickly learned that the aeroplane was challenging to fly accurately, and capable of quite extraordinary performance at light weight. Equally importantly, it promised to regularly take me to interesting and faraway places! So, I soon settled into the multi-engine environment, and learned to appreciate the importance of teamwork and the roles that the other crew members played.

Fast forward a year, and I was anticipating the Intermediate Co-pilot's Course, which would allow me to fly in the left-hand seat and effectively run the sortie, although I would always have the guiding hand of an experienced captain available in the other seat. Just before my course started, I had the prospect of a 'Far-East Ranger' to look forward to, eastbound to Hong Kong and returning westbound. Everything went smoothly on the way out, as we staged through Cyprus, Masirah (in the Arabian Gulf), Gan (a small island base in the middle of the Indian Ocean) and Changi (Singapore), before finally reaching Hong Kong. A Ranger exercise was all about achieving rapid, unsupported deployment to anywhere in the World, so what might appear to be a bit of a 'jolly' was, in fact, quite hard work. We only had room for one technician flying with us (on the optional sixth seat in the cabin), so most of the support work, such as re-fuelling and post/pre-flight servicing, was carried out by the aircrew. Adding this requirement onto two hours planning, and five or six hours of flying, made for very long days, so we welcomed the opportunity to relax for a while before starting back home.

Five days later, and with personal batteries recharged, we set off westwards, and all went fine until we were at top of climb out of Gan, when the Air Electronics Operator (AEO) told us that a hydraulic system failure light had just illuminated on his panel. The Victor had two, entirely independent, hydraulic systems, so 'no sweat' really, other than the inconvenience of having to return to Gan and get it fixed. We advised Gan that we were returning for a precautionary landing, and had just settled down on our new heading when the AEO came on the intercom again, and said that the other hydraulic failure light was now on too. This was serious and, as far as the experienced members of the crew knew, a first-ever for the Victor. We ran through the emergency drills twice for good measure, and then made a 'Mayday' (aircraft in distress) call to Gan. A double hydraulic failure required us to land as soon as possible, as there was an increased danger of fire and ultimately the possibility of losing control of the aircraft. However, when you're at 40,000 feet over the middle of the Indian Ocean, you are not exactly flush for options; it had to be Gan.

On a personal level, I was quite comfortable with the situation, as I knew that Gan had a long runway, albeit with the sea at either end, and the emergency services would have plenty of time to prepare for our arrival. I was somewhat less comfortable when we got the Gan weather: frequent tropical squalls with heavy rain, and a crosswind that was on the limit for the Victor. It's now appropriate to explain that the Victor had a 30 foot diameter braking parachute, that was deployed on landing as the primary means of slowing down, but it caused the aircraft to act like a wind vane in a crosswind, and you needed to use nose-wheel steering, rudder and sometimes differential brake to keep it pointing along the runway. With a double hydraulic failure, we had no nose-wheel steering, and only around 8 applications of brake in total. With nowhere else to go, we started our descent, and commenced jettisoning fuel to make the aircraft lighter, and therefore easier to handle and stop. On the way down, we got a weather update; the runway was flooding, and needed around 15 minutes to drain between squalls, which were arriving every half hour or so. I should add that, although the runway had been constructed to deal with this sort of eventuality, it tended to clear the middle portion fairly quickly, but take some time to drain the edges.

We set off down our final approach, with one squall to the left and another to the right, and only the centre section of the runway clear. As the non-flying pilot, my role was to manage the throttle settings and flap selection but, in addition on this occasion, I had been briefed to monitor the captain's actions, keep my eyes glued to the speed, and start turning off anything we didn't need as soon as we were on the runway.

In spite of the difficult crosswind, we made a firm landing (which is what you want on a wet runway), on the centreline as near as damn it, and the captain deployed the parachute. Almost immediately, the aircraft turned left as the crosswind took effect and, in spite of full right rudder being applied, it seemed to take an age to start straightening up. No sooner had it done so than it snapped left again, at which point we jettisoned the parachute, having already lost some 50 knots of speed. However, the left undercarriage was now entering the water that had yet to clear from the runway edge so, without steering or effective brakes, we simply continued turning left and departed the runway.

As we left the runway, I started turning off fuel pumps and anything else that could compound our situation, but effectively we were passengers as the Victor rumbled down Gan's golf course (only recently refurbished as we were later to discover), before coming to a halt pointing at the palm trees that fringed the beach. We rapidly completed our shutdown drills, and evacuated the aircraft just as the fire crew arrived. From the outside, the Victor looked a sad sight, up to its ankles in muddy water and with a series of furrows behind it leading back to the runway. However, we were unhurt, the aircraft was structurally undamaged, and far enough off the runway for the airfield to stay open, at least for the time being.

I was reflecting on the truism that such events unfold in slow motion, when my reverie was broken by the roar of a VC10 transport aircraft departing, the story of which is a fitting conclusion. The VC10 was waiting to take off as we stumbled down finals, so the crew had a grandstand seat as events unfolded. Once the panic had subsided, air traffic told the VC10 captain he was clear to take off at his discretion, or return to the terminal. Apparently he replied that he would like to take off as soon as possible, "Before the passengers on the right have explained to those on the left what they've just seen happen and we have a mutiny on board, because they've lost any enthusiasm for flying."

Post Script

The double hydraulic failure was two separate problems and, therefore, a one in an umpteen million chance of happening. The aircraft was dragged out of the mud, restored to full flying condition in less than a week, and we returned home without further mishap.

Over thirty years later, I was sitting in a pub in Liverpool, having a drink with the other members of an inspection team. It was a good opportunity to get to know each other, ahead of the following day's airport visit, as some of us had not met before, and talk got around to our individual backgrounds. I fell into conversation with Denis who, it transpired, was also ex-RAF so I asked him where he had served. He reeled off a list of locations, including Gan at which I smiled wryly. "Yes, I know Gan", I said. "I had an interesting experience there in a Victor". Denis's jaw dropped. "I saw it!" he exclaimed in disbelief. "I was in the ground radio workshop at the base of the air traffic tower and, when I heard the tannoy about a Victor inbound with an emergency, I rushed upstairs to watch. It was a spectacular sight, although I was rather taken aback by the ripe language of the air traffic controller. I thought it was very unprofessional, until someone told me that he was captain of the Gan golf club".

Victor SR2 (Credit: Author)